Transformative Lutheran Theologies

Transformative Lutheran Theologies

Feminist, Womanist, and Mujerista Perspectives

Edited by Mary J. Streufert

Fortress Press

Minneapolis

TRANSFORMATIVE LUTHERAN THEOLOGIES
Feminist, Womanist, and Mujerista Perspectives

Additional resources for instructors and students are available at fortresspress.com/streufert.

Cover image: Clarke, Brian (b. 1953) / Private Collection / © DACS / The Bridgeman Art Library International. All rights reserved.
Cover design: Joe Vaughan
Book design: PerfecType, Nashville, TN

Library of Congress Cataloging-in-Publication Data
Transformative Lutheran theologies : feminist, womanist, and mujerista perspectives / edited by Mary J. Streufert.
     p. cm.
  Based on a conference held in Jan. 2009 in Chicago, Ill.
  Includes bibliographical references (p. 237) and index.
  ISBN 978-0-8006-6377-3 (pbk. : alk. paper) 1. Lutheran Church--Doctrines. 2. Feminism--Religious aspects--Lutheran Church. 3. Feminist theology. 4. Womanist theology. 5. Mujerista theology. I. Streufert, Mary J., 1966-

  BX8065.3.T68 2010
  230'.41082--dc22
                              2010018981

Contents

Contributors

Krista E. Hughes is Assistant Professor of Theological Studies at Hanover College, Hanover, Indiana. A constructive theologian, she works at the intersection of feminist and process theologies, history of doctrine, and continental philosophy. The author of several essays and book reviews, she is currently working on a manuscript tentatively entitled *Dance of Grace: A Feminist Theology of the Gift*, which explores questions of agency, gift, corporeality, and aesthetics in the movement of grace.

Kathryn A. Kleinhans is Professor of Religion at Wartburg College, Waverly, Iowa, where she has taught since 1993. An ordained pastor of the Evangelical Lutheran Church in America, her scholarship focuses on the contemporary relevance of Martin Luther and Lutheran confessional theology. In addition to scholarly articles, she writes frequently for lay audiences. Her "Lutheranism 101" remains the most frequently requested reprint in the history of *The Lutheran* magazine.

Kristen E. Kvam, a lay member of the Evangelical Lutheran Church in America, is a native of Litchfield, Minnesota. Scriptural interpretation, Luther studies, and the doctrines of anthropology and ecclesiology form primary concerns for her scholarship. The author of many articles, Kvam co-edited *Eve and Adam: An Anthology of Jewish, Christian, and Muslim Readings on Genesis and Gender.* Kvam is Associate Professor of Theology at Saint Paul School of Theology in Kansas City, Missouri.

L. DeAne Lagerquist, Professor of Religion at St. Olaf College, is a historian of Christianity. Much of her research focuses on Lutherans in the United States, often with particular attention to women or higher education. Her publications include *From Our Mothers' Arms: A History of Women in the American Lutheran Church* and *The Lutherans.* Currently she is learning about Christianity in India and religious pluralism in the United States.

Mary E. Lowe is Assistant Professor of Religion at Augsburg College. Born and raised in Alaska, her teaching and research focuses on contemporary theology, particularly theological anthropology with special attention to new understandings of the human person, the doctrine of sin, and human sexuality. Mary speaks in congregations on topics ranging from the theology of Martin Luther to feminist views of God. She holds a Ph.D. from the Graduate Theological Union.

Lois Malcolm is Associate Professor of Systematic Theology at Luther Seminary, St. Paul, Minnesota, where she has been teaching since 1994. She received her Ph.D. from the University of Chicago (1998). In addition to authoring numerous articles, Malcolm has published *Holy Spirit: Creative Power in Our Lives* and is completing *Curse for Us: A Trinitarian Theology of the Cross*, among other book projects.

Anna Mercedes is Assistant Professor of Theology at the College of Saint Benedict/Saint John's University, where she also teaches for the Gender and Women's Studies Program. A candidate for ordination in the Evangelical Lutheran Church in America, she is currently working on her first book, *Power For: Feminism and Christ's Self-Emptying*.

Cynthia Moe-Lobeda lectures and consults globally in theology and ethics. Author of *Healing a Broken World: Globalization and God; Public Church: For the Life of the World;* and many articles and chapters, she also co-authored *Saint Francis and the Foolishness of God* and *Say to This Mountain: Mark's Story of Discipleship*. Moe-Lobeda is on the faculty of Seattle University's Department of Theology and Religious Studies, Environmental Studies Program, and graduate School of Theology and Ministry.

Cheryl M. Peterson is Associate Professor of Systematic Theology, Trinity Lutheran Seminary, Columbus, Ohio. An ordained pastor in the Evangelical Lutheran Church in America, she has written several articles on ecclesiology and pneumatology, most recently "The One, Holy, Catholic, and Apostolic Church in the Context of North America," in *One, Holy, Catholic, and Apostolic Church: Some Lutheran and Ecumenical Perspectives*, ed. Hans-Peter Grosshans. Her current work is a book on ecclesiology.

Mary (Joy) Philip holds a Ph.D. in theology from the Lutheran School of Theology at Chicago, where she studied with Vítor Westhelle. Her dissertation is titled, "Can Humanization Be Salvation: A Journey with the Musings of Madathiparambil Mammen Thomas, Juan Luis Segundo and Arundhati Roy." Prior to her journey into theology in the United States, Philip was a zoology professor in India for 12 years.

Caryn D. Riswold is Associate Professor of Religion and chair of Gender and Women's Studies at Illinois College in Jacksonville, Illinois. She is the author of three books, including *Feminism and Christianity: Questions and Answers in the Third Wave*, and *Two Reformers: Martin Luther and Mary Daly as Political Theologians*, in addition to articles on Lutheran and political theology and gender.

Mary J. Streufert directs the Justice for Women program in the Evangelical Lutheran Church in America in Chicago. She has published articles and chapters on christological method, christology, atonement theory, and a theology of power.. As an educator in various settings in the church and academy, Streufert offers the gift of deep theological thinking for everyday life. Christology and ecclesiology shape her current research and lecturing. She holds a Ph.D. from Claremont Graduate University.

Deanna A. Thompson is Professor of Religion at Hamline University, Saint Paul, Minnesota. Author of *Crossing the Divide: Luther, Feminism, and the Cross*, as well as numerous book chapters on topics ranging from Luther and Romans to feminism, friendship and empire, she enjoys speaking widely to lay and professional groups about intersections between Lutheran theology and feminist thought. Current research includes a commentary on Deuteronomy for a biblical commentary series by theologians with Westminster/John Knox.

Marit Trelstad is Associate Professor of Constructive and Lutheran Theology, Pacific Lutheran University, Tacoma, Washington. Her scholarly work combines feminist, process and Lutheran theologies and has focused on christology, the doctrine of God and theological anthropology. As contributor and editor, she published *Cross Examinations: Readings on the Meaning of the Cross Today* and has published articles on feminist christologies and pedagogy. She served as a theologian on the ELCA Task Force on Human Sexuality (2005-2009).

Alicia Vargas is Associate Professor of Multicultural and Contextual Studies at Pacific Lutheran Theological Seminary (PLTS), Berkeley, California. Vargas' publications include "The Construction of Latina Theology" in *Currents in Theology and Mission*, "Reading Ourselves into the Cross Story: Luther and United States Latinos" in *Cross Examinations: Readings on the Meaning of the Cross Today*, "Introduccion a La Disputacion de Leipzig" en *Lutero al habla*, and *Como estudiar la Biblia/How to Study the Bible*.

Beverly Wallace is the interim director of the Lutheran Theological Center in Atlanta and assistant to the bishop, Southeastern Synod of the ELCA. Ordained in 1999, Wallace served in congregations and hospital and university chaplaincies at Emory and Hamline. She earned her Ph.D. in Family Social Science at the University of Minnesota. Wallace has co-authored articles on African American religious resources for end-of-life care and substance abuse and is the co-author of *African American Grief*.

Introduction

Mary J. Streufert

THE WITNESS OF THE women at the tomb in Luke was first heard as "an idle tale," so unbelievable that it could surely only be the drama of gossip. Yet as follow- ers of Jesus came to realize the radical message that Jesus Christ was raised, the witness of the women came to stand as one of the central features of Christian evangelism throughout history. As feminist biblical scholars have long pointed out, despite the marginalization of women from the ongoing formation of the theological tradition, women have always had a role in the lifeblood of Christi- anity. Women today have no less a role in contributing to the ongoing transfor- mation of the Christian tradition.

Beginnings: No Idle Talk

The contributors of this volume of feminist, womanist, and mujerista Lutheran theologies are witnesses, too. We offer "no idle talk"[1] for the transformation of the church and the field of academic theology. In this book is some of the most exciting work across various loci of systematic theology from Lutheran perspec- tives. Each section of the book is organized under a major locus of systematic theology, such as the doctrine of God, christology, or eschatology. We seek to be faithful to the witness of the Christian tradition and the central wager of the Protestant Reformation—justification by grace through faith—while at the same time raising the critical and constructive wager that all humans, no matter our class, skin color, biology, ability, or sexuality, are equally created, broken, and redeemed. Taking this equality fully to heart changes how theology is done and what theology says.

1

Although many people have long desired a volume of Lutheran feminist theology, this book finally arose from a conference sponsored by the Justice for Women program of the Evangelical Lutheran Church in America (ELCA) in Chicago in January, 2009. Six months after the conference, fifteen of us gathered in a large, sunny room usually occupied by radical Roman Catholic nuns to discuss our ideas and challenge each other on identities, theological authority, method, and methodology. Weeks after our summer meeting, we continued our theological discussion online. Part of our online discussion is now available at www.elca.org/justiceforwomen in the form of "table talks" on various subjects. This volume is truly a communal and collaborative work. What we seek is a reformation of the church and the world, not by nailing theses to a cathedral door, but by giving voice to new perspectives in theology that continue to transform the church and the world.

Our beginning, however, was not in our ideas but in the Eucharist, one of the two sacraments Lutherans profess are God's acts that bind us together in Christ, no matter our differences. Grounded in the sacrament of the Eucharist, we turned to the work of this volume, to offer new theology that is engaging systematic theology from feminist, womanist, mujerista, Asian, and queer Lutheran perspectives. We are a small community of Lutheran women that embraces the Lutheran theological tradition in diverse ways, yet we began in a common place in the sacrament of the Eucharist.

Many of us grew up in the Lutheran tradition, some of us connected to family trees with multiple theologians, pastors, and other church workers. Others of us came to the Lutheran tradition as adults. What we find interesting is that our questions about our places in the Lutheran faith as theologians are two sides of a coin. On the one hand, those of us who grew up Lutheran often ask ourselves, "What keeps me here?" Those of us who became Lutherans as adults often ask ourselves, "Do I belong?" What we so clearly see from the results of this collaborative project is that we all have reason to be here because the Lutheran tradition in the twenty-first century is vibrant and multifaceted.

Transformation through Paradigm Shifts: No Idol Talk

When Martin Luther argued with church leaders and theologians about the central biblical promise of justification by grace and the primary theological and ecclesiological place it must hold, he assisted in forming a movement that transformed the church and the world. The transformation that the Protestant Reformation wrought was a "paradigm shift"[2] in theology and thus in the church and the world.

During the Reformation, a number of shifts contributed to many people participating in the transformation of the way God and the world were understood. From a Lutheran historical perspective, there are a number of notable challenges and changes that contributed to a major alteration in theology. Here are a few examples: Martin Luther participated in a formal Augustinian disputation in 1518 and confessed his understanding of a theology of the cross that emphasized grace over works; ordinary people started to read Luther's tracts, which were small theological teaching tools; Luther protested that the church was not the intercessor between believers in Christ and God; reformers challenged the authority of the pope as the correct interpreter of scripture, often using vitriolic and debasing cartoons of the pope to emphasize their distrust and despise.

Such sweeping theological changes were in large part wrought by Luther's call for more Christians to have access to scripture. The shift of focus from church tradition to scripture and from works to grace allowed paradigm shifts in practice as well, such as the moves from priests reading scripture in Latin to citizens reading scripture in German and from Latin liturgy to German hymns set to beer hall tunes. Christian theology has not been the same since the Protestant Reformation and its herald calls to shift church authority, the understanding of grace in salvation, and theological engagement that included more and more Christians.

Christian theology continues to be transformed.[3] Recently, a shift in theological paradigm has occurred through the growth of liberation theologies. This paradigm shift in theology that all liberation theologies have wrought characterizes the lifeblood of change in theology. Feminist, womanist, mujerista, Latina, Asian, Native American and queer theologies are all forms of liberation theology, among which we also find Latin American and black liberation theologies. Although every form of liberation theology is different in its specific characteristics, a central feature of each is its press for liberation from all forms of oppression, given the grace-filled message of the gospel.

Like the Reformation, another recognizable paradigm shift in Christian theology began when women gained greater access to theological education in the twentieth century.[4] Although the nascence of feminist theology in the United States can arguably be located in the religious questions with which such notable feminist figures as Elizabeth Cady Stanton, Susan B. Anthony, and Anna Howard Shaw wrestled,[5] it was not until scores of women attained formal theological training beginning in the 1970s that the discipline of theology itself began to reveal a fuller vision of God, self, creation, and God's relationship with creation. In other words, more of humanity was involved in theological speaking. Indeed, this was a paradigm shift. Such a paradigm shift has also been the case in the Lutheran tradition; women who served as teachers and deaconesses began feminist theological reflection in the Lutheran tradition, and as Lutheran women began not only to be ordained, but also to earn advanced degrees in biblical studies, theology, and ethics, the nature and scope of Lutheran theology itself experienced a paradigm shift.

In this paradigm shift, it is not only who is speaking that is expanded, but also what is being asked and what the answers look like. Just as "the priesthood of all believers" in the Protestant Reformation began to read scripture for themselves and to think theologically, women started to read for themselves and to think theologically. As a theologian, Luther began to ask questions through the radical wager of justification by grace through faith. In a similar fashion, feminist, womanist, and mujerista theologians ask questions through the radical wager that women and girls in all their multiplicity are fully human—equally created, equally sinful, and equally redeemed.

As theologians and ethicists, we see ourselves connected to the Lutheran tradition and the discipline of Christian theology that always presses to express God's grace in new contexts. And as women with particular experiences, we are searching for more from the Lutheran theological tradition. We all feel urgency for new models because some of the old ones have broken down. What each of us offers is easily characterized by Swiss theologian Hans Küng's description of theological paradigm changes: all changes include "a fundamental reorganization" of and "a fundamental continuity" with Christian theology up to that point.[6] In other words, there is both connection and transformation in the theology we offer. From various places in the Lutheran family, we challenge selected nodes in the normative Lutheran theological tradition and in the greater feminist theological discourse in order to reconstruct and refine central theological claims—seeking to remain faithful to the reality of God's grace and the flourishing of all creation.

As with all shifts in theological paradigms, new ideas evoke different responses, sometimes fear and doubt, and sometimes joy and relief. For example, in the last century, Nelson Mandela was imprisoned for twenty-seven years by political opponents to black liberation for his theology that black people are created equally to white people and therefore have political and social rights in South Africa. At the same time, however, Mandela's liberating theology meant joy and relief to scores of people worldwide who struggled to overcome a colonial theology of white superiority.

Difference and Unity

As the subtitle of this volume makes clear, we speak as women with various theological identities: mujerista, womanist, and feminist—but also Asian, Latina, queer, African American, and Euro-American. We are different. As several contributors readily note in their chapters, feminist theology itself has been challenged to be plural, to avoid universalizing definitions of being a woman or of women's experiences.[7] In fact, notes British feminist theologian Ursula King, theology that arises from reflection on women's lives and experiences by "particular women in particular communities and churches means that [feminist theology] can only occur in contexts of radical plurality. There is no one single, universal feminist theology; there are only feminist theologies in the plural. Their plurality represents a celebration of diversity and differences."[8] Neither is this volume a univocal treatise. Some of us disagree with each other. Some of our ideas are in creative tension with each other. Such are the signs of the multivocality that stretches theological imagination into meaningful new paradigms.

Our theological differences surface in a variety of places, but perhaps never so clearly as in our self-identities and in the ways we understand ourselves as unified. Historical review shows the slow and sometimes halting way in which Lutheran women have been active in shaping theology, leadership, and polity. That so many Lutheran women are now pastors and theologians is cause for celebration because we are veritably in the midst of living the vision that Luther's theology held fast to but could seldom find expression in life. Women are also shaping the life and thought of the church in the world. After centuries of the radical realization of the Reformation, who we are as the body of Christ has finally begun to shift significantly. However, the struggle to listen to and be changed by diverse voices and bodies remains. Of particular challenge for this book are numbers and words.

There is the ever-present challenge that there is a white, Euro-American feminist majority of writers in this book. Such a majority can influence group identity in dangerous ways, for a majority can unintentionally and intentionally universalize the group's identity. Given the reality of the number of Lutheran women theologians from multiple ethnic communities, we have labored, sometimes at odds, to resolve how we could even begin to name ourselves as a group. Do we risk this volume being "just feminist" with a few "guests"? Does a majority totalize our identity as a group? In actuality, because not all of us identify ourselves as feminist, this book is not "just feminist." In one sense, every writer in this book is convinced that the minds, bodies, and lives of women and girls are no less valuable than those of men and boys. At root, the word *feminist* can refer to this commitment, yet because the word *feminist* has been used to colonize the perspectives of *all* women, we continue to have a challenge of language and meaning always with us. Neither Beverly Wallace nor Alicia Vargas identifies herself as feminist; hence, the title of the book includes their self-identifications as womanist and mujerista theologians.[9] However, Mary (Joy) Philip claims no exclusively woman-identified moniker, nor does Mary Lowe centrally claim a feminist identity, preferring, rather, to be identified as a queer theologian. Problematically, their particular self-identities do not show up in the title of this book, which itself decrees a kind of group identity. The tension has not been resolved.

As theologians, we invite readers into these tensions, into the places from which the texts speak and the spaces in between the texts that have yet to be formed by language. Mary (Joy) Philip offers a strong challenge to voice, marginality, and individual and church identities through the metaphors of hybrids and estuaries. Asian feminist theologian Kwok Pui-Lan describes the social and theological location of many Asian theologians in North America as an "in-between" place, truly a place of hybrid identities, whose gift is to "disrupt homogeneous national tales."[10] In other words, Kwok describes the place that Asians in North America occupy as hybrid places, which, due to their in-between status between cultures, are able to wake up the predominant cultural understandings from its singular identity slumber. Several chapters in this volume claim a similar place, not only for Lutheran theology in general, but also for this volume itself. Many voices are under the broad Lutheran theological canopy, a chorus that this volume demonstrates is at times dissonant. Such difference is vital.

Perhaps there is another way to think about unity and identity in the midst of difference. To be in one volume, to be in theological dialogue with each other, and to be Lutheran together—to be in unity—requires neither flattening our differences and universalizing our ideas, nor homogenizing our individual identities. Rather, being clothed with Christ, as Paul described in Galatians, is our unity. As biblical scholar Brigitte Kahl notes, the unity in difference of which the entire Galatians text speaks is quite instructive, not only when considering the wealth of distinctly different womanist, mujerista, queer, Asian, and feminist theologians, but also when thinking about the unity in difference within the entire realm of Christian theology, including the tension between what is perceived to be "traditional" Lutheran theology and the theologies of this volume.

In an astute interpretation of the way in which Paul treated difference in Galatians, Kahl leads us to see that what the apostle urged upon new converts was central to being clothed with Christ. First, being clothed with Christ means *difference is not privileged*. One identity is not better than the other.[11] Second, being unified in the body of Christ means "a new way of co-existence, mutuality and community that *both changes and preserves* the old identities and distinctions."[12] Being unified means that one identity does not erase the other; rather, there is a new identity, a third way, when the differences are held collectively and allowed to exist together.

Methodology and Method

Our differences mean that in this volume we have used various methods that stand within a larger framework of feminist theological methodology, generally described as critique, retrieval, and construction. The chapters in this book weave among these three movements. Feminist theologian Anne E. Carr aptly describes the work of feminist theology to "protest and critique" the theological tradition as a naturally occurring practice of theology. What makes feminist theology distinctive from other shifts in theology is the focus on the effects of patriarchy and sexism in the Christian tradition, thus the *critique* and protest. What feminists *retrieve* not only are women's voices, presence, and silent spaces, but also the treasures of the tradition hitherto forgotten, disregarded, or simply ignored.

Over the last forty years, a preponderance of feminist theological writing has centered in critique and revision. This has been important and necessary work.[13] Feminist theological *construction*, present from the beginning of such work, only recently has become more comprehensively constructive and turned more consistently to an engagement with systematic theological loci. As a descendant of liberal theology, in many avenues feminist theology developed in such a critical fashion that systematic categories were dismissed along with creeds. However, many feminist, womanist, and mujerista theologians have been hard-pressed to leave their faith traditions.

Over the past two decades, increasing numbers of women theologians, Roman Catholic and Protestant alike, have constructively engaged traditional theological themes. As feminist theologian Joy Ann McDougall notes, "Like Jacob wrestling with the angel, many feminist theologians are 'taking back' their confessional traditions, refusing to let them go until they wrestle a feminist blessing from them."[14] Throughout this volume you will find a number of central Lutheran theological bases for empowering a critique, retrieval, and reconstruction of this tradition. From the outset the argument is that contemporary Lutheran theology finds a rich partner with the intersectional methodology of third-wave feminism. This means that analyses of racism, classism, and heterosexism clearly intersect with the womanist, mujerista, and feminist commitments of the authors through the theology we offer. Positively, our differences and our attempts to be faithful to analyses of systems of oppression lead to a kaleidoscopic view of theological method.[15] To write without such a multifaceted methodology would be an ecclesiological problem, for we would not hear and see the constellation that the body of Christ truly is.[16] As feminist theologian Rosemary Radford Ruether points out, reconstruction means changes in the symbolic system.[17] What we hope is that our initial work in this volume provides even more space for Lutheran theological reconstruction, something for which many marginalized voices have argued for many years.[18]

For the last several hundred years, since roughly the 1700s, theologians have argued over the most appropriate method for theology but generally agree upon four sources in method: (1) scripture, (2) tradition, (3) reason, and (4) experience.

Generally speaking, Lutheran theologians begin with *scripture*. In the contemporary culture in the United States, there is a tendency to view Christian scripture as a corpus of writing that can be taken at face value; that is, we have a cultural proclivity to take the Bible literally. In the stretch of the Christian tradition, this has not always been so; one could, in fact, make the statement that to understand the Bible literally is not traditional.[19] Although Luther is often quoted for the saying *sola scriptura*, meaning "scripture alone," like Augustine before him, Luther thought that scripture needs careful and thoughtful attention because some of it speaks more clearly the promise of Christ for us. Luther's call to "return" to scripture in part meant that he wanted to see Christians and Christian theology to be guided primarily by the proclamation of God's grace for us through Jesus Christ that scripture holds. Although many of us quote scripture directly, what is more important for theological method from a Lutheran perspective is that it is clear that the promise of God's grace is central to our collective theological works.

Tradition refers to the theological history of the Christian church. The church's teachings began to develop early in Christian history as the first generations of Christians worked to explain themselves to the cultures in which they lived and to explain to each other the best ways to understand God, the significance of Jesus Christ, the Holy Spirit, creation, and humanity. Some teachings in Christianity stand out more authoritatively than others. For example, the creeds that the Christian councils of bishops hammered out between 325 C.E. and 451 C.E. continue to serve as touchstones in a great deal of Christian theology, yet the entire scope of the theological tradition represents the ongoing conversation that the church has as it works to refine what it professes and teaches. Different communities take up different conversation partners, and the Lutheran tradition is no different, for Lutherans continue to see Luther's theology and the Augsburg Confession as sources.

To use *reason* as a theological source means to think carefully and critically about the ways in which what one is saying fits together and is not self-contradictory. Unlike the wave of rationalism that swept intellectual pursuits after the Enlightenment, the theology in this volume does not disregard what is not provable by human reason. Rather, we seek to be reasonable, insofar as humans can be reasonable about divine mystery.

Experience is perhaps the area in theological method that is the most ambiguous and misunderstood. An absolutely necessary corrective that feminists first brought to theology was the argument that women's experience matters in theological and biblical interpretation. The particular experiences upon which theologians draw as a source for theology are the religious and social experiences of females, individually and collectively. Making this claim highlighted the striking realization that scripture and theology were focused on the male experience as a universal norm. Theologians have become more articulate in the specificities of identities as related to experience.[20] For example, the three types of theologies named in the subtitle of this volume are each linked to specific experiences and identities. Mujerista theologians evoke central theological themes through thick, contextualized, and personal narratives, most often with little conceptual narrative; instead, the telling, the acts of breaking silence, are part of the theological content of mujerista theology. Likewise, womanist theologians begin and end with the livelihood of the community under God's care; African American women who identify themselves as womanists contribute critical and constructive voices to the white ideology of the United States and its churches. Euro-American feminist theologians often spend great effort to address the Christian tradition from within itself by writing conceptually; although as yet imperfect, we (I among them) are growing in our abilities and commitments to theologize in ways that do not speak for all women at every moment and may speak for all women some times.[21] Other means of addressing experience that theologians use, including in this volume, are post-structuralism, process metaphysics, and sociocultural studies. The latter includes what have been described as thick, local descriptions of experience and analysis of the interactive relationship between beliefs and practices.

Nevertheless, this does not mean that experience alone drives the cart of theology. Scripture, tradition, reason, and experience must come together in each age. This is the task of the community—to keep these together. Many years of theological development have brought contemporary Lutheran theologians to the point of stressing the interdependence of these sources.[22]

Luther and Lutheran Identity

Assuredly, the backbone of this volume's specifically *Lutheran* method and methodology is justification by grace through faith—the gospel, the central promise of scripture. We *are* speaking of God's grace for us through Christ.[23] This is the Lutheran core on which we stand. Because of and out of this assurance that we are redeemed for Christ's sake, we ask deeper questions about the means and nature of justification and what it means to live the radical freedom of the Christian to which justification leads. From anthropology to ethics to eschatology are constructively addressed here under this twofold condition—justified and free. Lutheran, yes.

As Lutheran systematic theologian Carl E. Braaten argues, both content (the gospel) and context are relevant to theological reflection.[24] According to Braaten, "Every generation of theologians is doing a new thing in conformity to criteria of adequacy and rationality. . . . Our aim is to make new theological statements that make sense under the modern conditions of experience and knowledge."[25] Our context, as Brazilian Lutheran feminist theologian Wanda Deifelt so readily points out, is that women have learned "how to read and write theology," an act that brings "a new dimension in research" because women are assigning theological meaning.[26] Although not every author in this volume directly addresses either scripture or the Augsburg Confession, every author does speak *to* the promise of the gospel, that for Christ's sake, we are redeemed. As Lutheran theologians across a wide spectrum make clear, the confessions point to scripture, which holds the gospel. The creeds point to scripture, which holds the gospel. The gospel is precisely the reason for practicing theology that places the equally redeemed full co-humanity of all front and center. In other words, these transformative perspectives in Lutheran theology *are* reformation theology, not simply for the sake of reformation, but because of the heart of Luther's theological rediscovery: we are made right with God for the sake of Christ by God's grace alone. Every argument we offer is implicitly linked to this central Lutheran claim.[27]

As we reflected together on our sense of belonging to the Lutheran theological tradition, one common task became amply evident: faithful criticism. Although we come from different perspectives within the Lutheran tradition, we share a common commitment to Lutheran theology as a continual process of reform. Sharing our stories surfaced a common value we hold in learning as a liberative process; in other words, education emboldens our commitments to the transformative work that faith *is* for the world. We see our critical faithfulness in this volume as one expression of the many theological works that seek to build up others in critical and constructive learning.

Central to our shared understanding of faithful criticism is what might be classified as our Lutheran identity. Our Lutheran identity does not come from using Luther as an authoritative source. Although Luther is directly engaged in many of the chapters that follow, his voice is not here because he settles a debate; rather, Luther is an ever-present conversation partner because of his theological insights and his commitment to faithful criticism, which we seek to continue. What makes this volume Lutheran is the focus on central themes he addressed, which are understood to represent the logic and dynamic of what makes something Lutheran.

Two important themes that serve as the axes of this volume, whether directly addressed or implicitly assumed, are justification by grace through faith and a theology of the cross. These are theological models that continue to prove rich resources, even in the midst of faithful criticism. Most of the chapters in this volume address God's radical grace through Jesus Christ. Additionally, some make further connections to the related themes of a Lutheran understanding of sin—that the human is simultaneously justified (or saved) and guilty—and the freedom all Christians share to serve each other because of Christ's love for us. This focus on justification by grace through faith is certainly our "confessional lens," meaning that this Lutheran wager grounds and guides our work; yet how this tenet is expressed is invariably differently, given the many different contexts in which even North American Lutheranism is vibrant.

A second central theme is Luther's theology of the cross. As numerous contributions to this book make clear, Luther's theology of the cross keeps cadence with the world across time, from the sixteenth century to the twenty-first century. As feminist Lutheran theologians Mary Solberg[28] and Deanna Thompson[29] point out, a theology of the cross means that the God hidden in our world not only disrupts the very expectations we humans have of God, but also changes the way we create and live theology. What we expected God to be is not how God shows up. Yet Luther's theology of the cross is also a source of hope in the midst of the difficulties of discipleship. A theology of the cross holds that God does work in and through the world, not above it. This means that God's solidarity with us is reason to hope. God does not negate the world, which is confirmed through the incarnation and the cross, but works to transform it. Thus there is reason to rejoice over the transformative nature of a theology of the cross! Here is the heart of what we see as the ecclesiological function of this volume. We offer it for the transformation of the church and academic theology.

A Third Way in the Third Wave

As British feminist theologian Linda Woodhead explains, moving more fully into conversation with the theological tradition and other disciplines depends upon the diversity of feminist theology itself.[30] It is the contention of the authors herein that as Lutheran theologians, we are meeting the challenge Woodhead addresses by offering a third way within the field of theology. Not a final say on any one theological locus, this volume represents many options for "a third way" in the third wave of feminism that takes analyses of systems of oppression seriously. Neither rejecting our tradition and its figures, nor refusing to sublimate our commitments to the flourishing of the female subject—real women and girls—we take up our paradoxical identities and intentionally address systematic theological loci to offer a third way to see.[31] As only sixteen of the many theologians committed both to their traditions and to the flourishing of all creation, we realize our small yet constructive roles in the ongoing quest for truth that all theology is.

My gratitude reaches to two communities of people who have made this book possible. I thank the women who have contributed to this work, whose kindness and scholarship inspire me, and I thank my spouse, Douglas Wold, whose humor and generosity keep me steady in the twin vocations of feminist theologian and feminist parenting to our three sons, Jules, Evan, and Mattias, who learn the meaning of grace together with us daily.

PART I

Legacies and Margins

PART 1 SITUATES LUTHERAN women's work in theology. In the first chapter, L. DeAne Lagerquist's historical narrative relates some of the memories of Lutheran women in the United States, unfolding a portrait of multiple, contextual, and often marginal theological and social locations in the Lutheran tradition. Caryn Riswold closes the chapter with a theological reflection that highlights the characteristically Lutheran and feminist theological themes that embolden and equip the Lutheran theological enterprise. In the second chapter, Mary (Joy) Philips explores the theological meaning of margins. Her methodological proposal identifies marginal social locations that produce a certain type of hybridity and access to particular memories. These locations and memories open up Christian understandings of identity and make demands on the church—and its theology—to be marginal.

Chapter 1

Historical and Theological Legacies of Feminism and Lutheranism

L. DeAne Lagerquist and Caryn D. Riswold

"For to remain a member of a historic Church is not to achieve finality.
A creed is not an imprisoning wall; it is a gate, opening on a limitless country
that cannot be entered in any other way."

—Vida Dutton Scudder, *On Journey*[1]

"I AM A STUDENT of theology. I am also a woman."[2] When feminist theologian Valerie Saiving (1921–1992) made these declarations in 1960 they pointed to the rarity of one person claiming both identities. Her essay "The Human Situation: A Feminine View" signaled the beginnings of theological engagement in the second wave of feminism in the United States. Since then an increasing number of women here and around the world has taken up the study of theology. Feminist theology is now a recognized field with its own distinctive themes, classic texts, and characteristic questions. Feminist theologians, like feminists more generally, recognize their commonalties as women and insist that women's experiences must be taken into account. They also recognize the profound reality that all women are not the same. Significant differences grounded in factors such as race, sexuality, class, nationality, or confession, as well as in the particularities of individual life experience, contribute to womanist, mujerista, queer, and other theological conversations.

15

The theologians in this book were young or not yet born in 1960. They join Vida Dutton Scudder (1861–1954), Valerie Saiving, Martin Luther, and a host of witnesses in exploring the country entered through the gospel gate. Their work enriches the traditions they draw upon and encourages expressions of Christian teaching that are Lutheran and feminist. It explores affinities and tensions between feminism and Lutheran theology as well as the ambivalence and generativity produced by the two together. Moreover, these women bring their varied talents and education, relationships and life experiences to the task of articulating the life-giving message of God's love for their own communities and in their own time and place. They add their voices to a song as rich, dynamic, and resonant as the harmonies of the traditional spiritual "Oh Mary, Don't You Weep" performed a cappella.

Echoing Saiving, the authors declare, "We are Lutherans; we are women; we are theologians." Simultaneously claiming multiple identities, they display a characteristically Lutheran insistence that one can be two (or more) things at once and suggest that their theology and their identities are intricately interwoven. Lutheran theology is thick with both/ands: the Christian is at the same time justified and still a sinner; God governs through both spiritual and temporal means; at the Lord's table we receive Jesus' body and blood truly present in bread and wine that remain bread and wine; a Christian's freedom in God's grace is as absolute as her obligation to her neighbor. The two-ness of being Lutheran and feminist (and other things as well) is more akin to living simultaneously in liturgical and academic time than it is to binary, contesting opposites. These authors also participate in the venerable Lutheran practice of publicly stating and defending one's belief. Such confession is the interpretive activity whereby divine love is spoken into new circumstances.

I am both a historian and a participant in these discussions and developments. I am a feminist because I am a Lutheran Christian; the way I am a Lutheran is shaped by my being baptized but not ordained, feminist, American, a monolingual native speaker of English, of pan-Scandinavian descent several generations removed from "the boat." My feminist and Lutheran identities are those of a woman of a particular age. I was five when Valarie Saiving wrote her landmark essay; the year I graduated from college about fifty American Lutheran pastors were women. My development as a historian of American Lutheranism coincided with the emergence of feminist theology. As I recount recent decades, my recollection of specific people and events is informed by my own experiences. What follows is more a first, personal effort to reflect on what has transpired than an exhaustive, authoritative account—yet it is one that serves the purpose of tracing some of the work of Lutheran women, on whose labor contemporary Lutheran feminist theology builds.

Luther and the Lutheran Heritage

Neither Martin Luther nor the movement he launched can be unambiguously described as feminist, still there are hints of affinities with contemporary feminist concerns. God's gracious love, the heart of Luther's theology, makes no distinction between women and men who are equal in their brokenness. Divine grace is poured out without regard for any human distinctions, accomplishments, or shortcomings. Everyone comes before God as a beggar needing to be made whole and is fed forgiveness in, with, and under the bread-body and blood-wine. Luther recognized that all stations in life offer honorable work that pleases God and benefits the neighbor—the milkmaid as much as the farmer, the mother as much as the priest, the wife as much as the magistrate. The schools he established enrolled both girls and boys so that all could read the Bible and Catechism. His affection for Katherine von Bora and their children was enthusiastic; their household modeled the Christian home as a school for faith. Nonetheless, the benefits of granting spiritual value to women's domestic responsibilities and providing basic religious education must in retrospect be weighed against the loss of monastic access to theological study and religious leadership for a smaller number of women. A very small number of women with high social position were patronesses of the Reformation, and wives of pastors had opportunity for a new sort of ministry, but the orders of creation restricted women's arenas of activity. The mixed resources Luther's theology and reforms offer to feminist historians and theologians require discerning appropriation lest the dangers overwhelm the gifts.[3]

Lutheran women's access to advanced theological study and public church offices were often restricted in subsequent generations. After authoritative statements of doctrine were gathered into the *Book of Concord* (1580), orthodox theologians labored to systematize the Reformers' insights. Using philosophical tools and concerned to secure the objective claims of theology, they highlighted the specialized nature of theology as an enterprise generally closed to lay people and consequently to women. Because evangelical Pietism strove to restore personal experience of the gospel to a central place and granted spiritual significance to the home, women's activities, particularly as mothers, were given greater value. Without rejecting infant baptism, Pietists encouraged personal awakening, whereby the believer became aware of her sinfulness, received assurance of God's love, and determined to live in a manner worthy of that love. Lay preachers—men and women—were granted authority on the basis of spiritual gifts rather than educational credentials or official positions. Women were authors and readers of devotional literature, including hymns such as Lena Sandell's (1832–1903) still beloved "Children of the Heavenly Father." Pietists established charitable institutions such as hospitals and orphanages where women engaged in works of love.

Lutherans in the United States

The entire range of European Lutheranism was carried to North America by several waves of Scandinavian and German immigrants, beginning in the colonial era. Without the support and constraints of state sponsorship, Lutherans in the United States formed churches distinguished from each other by religious and cultural characteristics. Well into the twentieth century, the combination of the high value placed on polity, styles of piety, and confessional matters by many Lutherans and the stress some maintained on ethnic ties and use of non-English languages served to insulate Lutherans from other American Christians. Even Lutherans' internal debates about how much and how best to adapt to their shared American context contributed to isolation and inhibited outreach and discouraged productive interaction across denominational lines. From the late 1800s into the 1980s several rounds of institutional mergers consumed enormous resources and focused the attention of theologians (most often male clergy) on confessional issues that had little resonance with feminist concerns. Likewise, Lutherans' pioneering involvement in bilateral ecumenical dialogues was more likely to cast feminism and women's full participation in the church as a problem than as an opportunity for new insight. By 1988 two bodies—the newly formed, composite Evangelical Lutheran Church in America (ELCA) and the Lutheran Church–Missouri Synod, rooted in mid-nineteenth-century German immigration—encompassed nearly all Lutherans in their membership. That the ELCA ordained women and had over one thousand women on its clergy roster was among the significant differences between the churches.

American Lutheran Women before 1970

Once in the United States, Lutherans continued to limit most women's religious roles to the home and congregation, some to the present day. Catechetical instruction prepared girls with a minimal level of theological knowledge. Family devotional practices gave mothers an educational role that could extend to teaching children in congregational settings.[4] By the late nineteenth century, women's organizations provided members with Bible study materials, opportunities for leadership, and connections to the larger Lutheran church and its missions around the world.[5] Early on, some men objected to these groups as subversive and giving too much autonomy to women who were prohibited from ordination and usually from holding office or even voting in congregations. The structure and purposes of Lutheran women's organizations paralleled those in

other Protestant churches, but the groups were a bridge to ecumenical coopera-
tion for only a few leaders. Emmy Evald (1857–1946), longtime president of the
Augustana Synod's national women's organization, was active in woman's rights
activities including the Woman's Suffrage Association in Chicago; however, she
stands as an exceptional rather than a typical case.

Beginning in the mid-nineteenth century Lutherans established colleges for the education of both young men and women. These institutions of
higher learning offered students freedom mingled with constraints. Programs
promoted conventional notions of woman's nature and women's roles. Young
women were directed toward teaching or nursing or returning home as better-
educated potential wives and mothers. But at these Lutheran colleges young
women could also catch a glimpse of possibilities for careers in public arenas.
The histories of these colleges includes exemplary, inspiring teachers such as
Rosa Young (1874–1970) at Concordia College Selma, a Missouri Synod school
for African Americans, who encouraged both women and men to follow their
calling into church and society.

Barred from ordination and seminary training, Lutheran women found other
ways to answer their vocations. Some became deaconesses, some taught subjects such as English, history, or music at Lutheran colleges, and some were lay
professionals in the local and national church. On the forefront of the churches'
confession through works of love, deaconesses also reflected upon the religious
basis of their ministry and its theological significance. Sister Ingeborg Sponland
(1870–1951), director of Deaconess Hospital in Chicago, observed:

> To us as deaconesses truth cries out that all human beings have a soul
> which has been bought by the blood of Jesus Christ for the Kingdom of
> heaven. There can be no discrimination as to nationality or creed when it
> comes to serving our Master. He served all humanity and bids us to follow
> in his footsteps. In modifying our methods so as to be able to serve people
> of various nationalities and creeds we gain a broader vision and a deeper
> sympathy and understanding—a compassion and love for souls that are
> without Christ.[6]

This expansive view of the church's responsibilities in the world was a challenge
to these churches' narrow focus upon their own members and to an emphasis
on right belief without action. Sister Elizabeth Fedde's (1850–1921) comment
that the deaconesses were themselves the Bible their patients read, calls such a
distinction into question, particularly if word and sacrament are elevated above
or separated from works of love.

Lutheran women in the twentieth century also were particularly active in
campus ministry and social service. No doubt many women found their work

personally rewarding and religiously significant. Nonetheless, the church was not always prepared to receive their gifts. Mary Markley (1891–1954), executive for student work in the United Lutheran Church (ULC), described the difficulty in 1939:

> I grant you that the church-related colleges may be in a dilemma. They are educating not females, ladies, or women, but personalities. They are sending these personalities—Christian women with initiative and a sense of responsibility—back into churches in which outmoded practical methods persist from the individual congregation all along the line to national boards and church bodies.[7]

Her colleague Mildred Winston's (1900–1980) experience illustrates the situation. Following graduation from Susquehanna College in the 1920s she pursued advanced study at Biblical Seminary in New York. When no Lutheran college was willing to employ her, she joined Markley as a lay professional with the ULC. For three decades Winston encouraged young women to answer callings within the church; in the 1950s she organized programs that provided young women with practical work experience, theological training, and opportunities to meet professional women in a range of occupations. Cordelia Cox (1901–1997), for example, brought her training and experience as a social worker and college instructor to her work as the first director of Lutheran Refugee Services, where she oversaw the resettlement of 57,000 displaced persons and refugees. Women such as these produced workshops, newsletters, and reports rather than volumes of systematic theology; they were reflective about their work directing the church's ministry in the world and deeply engaged in what today we call practical theology.

Lutheran Women from the American Second Wave to the Third Wave

In the second half of the twentieth century Lutheran women continued their involvement in women's organizations and their work as lay church professionals. At the same time, the emerging second wave of the American women's movement exacerbated the tension between Lutheran theology that made no distinction between women and men with regard to God's grace and Lutheran polity and practice that restricted women's use of their talents and training. Increasingly Lutheran women turned their energies to reflect on their own experience and religious heritage; like women in other traditions they criticized Lutheranism's shortcomings, retrieved its resources, and reconstructed its treasured messages for themselves and the church. As in other Christian churches, inclusive language, worship leadership, and ordination were early pressing issues. Feminist leadership came from women's organizations, from wives of clergy, from women students and faculty on college and seminary campuses, and from women academically trained in theology and called to pastoral ministry. Decisions in 1970 by the American Lutheran Church (ALC) and the Lutheran Church in American (LCA) to begin ordaining women expanded women's access to Lutheran theological education. By the twenty-first century Lutheran women were deeply engaged participants and publicly visible leaders in church and academy. Access to theological education and the presence of women at Lutheran seminaries and other institutions contributed to the development of a feminist Lutheran theology that addresses practical matters such as liturgical language, ethical issues such as domestic violence, and systematic matters such as those included in this volume.

Leaders of the ALC and LCA women's organizations were in tune with feminism and advocated for women's ordination. Margaret Wold, then executive director of American Lutheran Church Women (ALCW), is an extraordinary but not unique example. She served on the ALC's committee to study women's ordination; her book *The Shalom Woman* (1975) offered a gentle push toward feminist theology. In the 1980s, led by Bonnie Jensen who had earned an M.Div. from Wartburg Seminary, ALCW programs focused on social conditions affecting American women and fostered personal connections among Lutheran women around the world. Having raised their consciousness of the overwhelmingly white membership of the church, in 1983 the national board appointed three women of color as members-at-large: Annie Briggs, Maria Gomez, and Barbara Tucker. Association of Evangelical Lutheran Churches (AELC), LCA, and ALC women's group leaders cooperated in sponsoring a series of theological conferences for women that featured women theologians. Together they insured that when the Evangelical Lutheran Church in America was formed in 1988 the organizations' common commitments to expansive ministry by and for women continued through both Women of the ELCA and the Commission for Women. The latter was charged to promote "the full participation of women; to create equal opportunity for women; to foster partnership between women and men; to assist the church to address sexism; to advocate for justice for women in the church and society."[8]

Feminism and Lutheranism also met on campuses. Wittenberg University historian Margret Sittler Ermath published *Adam's Fractured Rib: Observations on Women in the Church* in 1970. Students were introduced to feminist ideas through the publications of Catholic theologian Rosemary Radford Ruether and Letty Russell, one of the first women ordained in the United Presbyterian Church, as well as other theologians. A contributor to this volume spoke at a St. Olaf College chapel service during Women's Week in 1976. The student newspaper, referring to her as "little Krissie Kvam, 'Christian Feminist,'" reported that her talk included "gentle prodding" toward the "continual social and self-criticism" Christ stressed.[9] Women involved in campus ministry already were engaged in theological work and were among the first ordained. Among them Constance F. Parvey assumed international, ecumenical responsibilities with the World Council of Churches' program "The Community of Women and Men in the Church." The women hired by religion departments at Lutheran colleges were not all Lutherans; moreover, Lutheran women, including several authors in this volume, followed their academic vocations to non-Lutheran institutions. Gail Ramshaw, who taught religion at LaSalle University in Philadelphia, is but one notable example. If her deeply Lutheran and feminist identity is not immediately evident in her prolific publications on liturgical language and worship or in her widely used lectionary editions, it is clear in her autobiography, *Under The Tree Of Life: The Religion of a Feminist Christian* (1998).

At Lutheran seminaries feminism arrived slowly. Adjunct instructors and faculty wives were among the first to engage the conversation. Wives of the faculty who walked out from Concordia Seminary in 1974 were among the founders of the Lutheran Women's Caucus, a pan-Lutheran group with explicitly feminist objectives. Lois Snook, wife of a faculty member at Luther Seminary, St. Paul, Minnesota, edited *In God's Image: Toward Wholeness for Women and Men*, published by the Lutheran Church in America in 1976 and distributed by other church bodies. After ordination was opened to women, they enrolled at Lutheran institutions in growing numbers.[10] Their presence and their activities pressed feminist concerns. Luther Seminary students, for example, organized a conference on Christianity and feminism that featured speakers including Lutheran ethicist Mary Pellauer, then on the faculty of Union Theological Seminary, New York.[11] Other women chose to attend non-Lutheran schools such as Yale Divinity School. Some took the long path through ordination and parish ministry prior to further graduate study; others went directly into academic programs in ethics, biblical studies, church history, theology, or other fields. Lutheran seminaries began to hire women into full-time, tenurable positions in the 1970s. The first two appointments were both in Christian education: Jean Bozeman, a laywoman, to the faculty at Lutheran School of Theology at Chicago (LSTC) in 1971, and Pastor Margaret Krych at Lutheran School of Theology at Philadelphia (LSTP) in 1977. The following year, church historian Faith Burgess (now Rohrbough) was appointed at LSTP to teach and as academic dean. Pastor Norma Cook Everist, a deaconess consecrated in the Lutheran Church–Missouri Synod, was appointed at Wartburg Seminary, Dubuque, Iowa, in 1979. Through the next decade the number of faculty women grew as did the range of subjects they taught. In 2004 Phyllis Anderson became president of Pacific Lutheran Theological Seminary, Berkeley, California, the first woman president of a Lutheran Seminary in the USA.[12]

Women who combined Lutheran theological commitments and feminist goals worked to change the church as well as to articulate their beliefs. They found partners among like-minded Lutheran men and other feminists. In 1978 the *Lutheran Book of Worship* incorporated inclusive language in reference to human beings while retaining conventional forms in reference to God. In the 1980s and 1990s Lutheran journals—*Dialog, Word & World, Currents in Theology and Mission*—published special issues devoted to feminism.[13] In 1988, when Lutheran ethicist Karen Bloomquist and systematic theologian Mary Knutsen reflected on feminism as a potentially new starting point for theology, they each emphasized their hope that feminist theology would foster renewed and freeing expressions of the gospel.[14] To the degree that feminism coincided with Lutheran themes and was not made explicit, some audiences were unaware of it. Opponents of feminism, however, were vigilant in their criticism, sometimes leveling personal attacks on women labeled as feminist. Indeed, a search of the American Theological Library Association's standard index of religious periodicals returns many anti-feminist articles in Lutheran publications but relatively few articles that combine feminist and Lutheran concerns. Even work by authors who identify themselves as both Lutheran and feminist seldom is labeled as such unless the title makes the connection obvious. This may be an oddity of the indexing process, but it also points to the difficulty in recognizing this hybrid and varied sort of theology and in distinguishing it from other Lutheran or feminist theology, particularly when the approach rather than the topic is feminist and Lutheran.

Practical reforms were evident in the policies and practices of the ELCA, formed in 1988. Advocates of women's full participation in the church and of an inclusive church (the goal referred particularly to people marginalized by race, ethnicity, or language) supported the ELCA's representational principle requiring the membership of churchwide and synodical boards to have gender balance and be racially diverse. In addition to Women of the ELCA and the Commission for Women, other units of the so-called "new church" were led by women whose qualifications included advanced theological degrees. Mary Pellauer, Coordinator for Research and Study in the Commission for Women, brought a combination of academic credentials and social activism on behalf of women to her responsibilities. Phyllis Anderson, Director for Theological Education of the Division for Ministry, had experience in a parish, on a synodical staff, and at LSTC in addition to her advanced degree. Karen Bloomquist, Director for Studies in the Division for Church and Society, had similar preparation. Later she took a comparable position in the Lutheran World Federation. Positions like these demanded a great deal—time, energy, creativity, wisdom, and patience; they also provided the women who held them with opportunities to encourage ministry to and by women, to advocate for women, and to advance feminist theology.

Women who had jobs in church offices, in congregations, and on campuses gave significant support to younger women by a variety of means. Particularly relevant to this volume was their early and consistent commitment to the Lutheran Woman's Pre-meeting to the American Academy of Religion (AAR) and Society of Biblical Literature (SBL). This group, now called Lutheran Women in Theological and Religious Studies (LWTRS), has met every year since a brief gathering in advance of the 1987 AAR/SBL national meetings in Boston. Without formal membership and often led by women early in their careers, the group gathers to explore shared convictions, concerns, and challenges. Its purposes are religious, academic, and social. Discussion of academic papers, announcement of publications, and advice about jobs take place alongside requests for prayers, worship, and meals. The study and practice of religion are not divided; rather, they are mutually enriching and nourishing of personal relationships. These are not women who agree on every point, and not every Lutheran woman who might come chooses to do so. Nonetheless, those who gather agree that participation brings precious gifts that include both the experience of being recognized as simultaneously Lutheran and feminist and the joy of companionship in the work of articulating this double identity. Continuing that work, this volume articulates systematic theology that is at once Lutheran and feminist in the third wave. We now turn to an identification of a number of central theological themes when feminist and Lutheran convictions come together.

Theological Themes

In the preceding narrative, DeAne Lagerquist focused on the women theologians who have already contributed to the *semper reformanda* ("always reforming") work of Lutheran theologies. Historical study and recollection illuminates why they could do what they did and where they did their work. In the following, I focus on four key theological themes that emerge from this narrative to ground transformative Lutheran theologies and consider their specific resonance with feminism: vocation, authority, paradox, and grace.

VOCATION

History shows that Lutheran theological reflection on vocation remains a mixed resource of the tradition for women. It names a spiritual value for socially undervalued work, while accepting the orders of creation mandating a limited arena for women's work. Lois Malcolm, one of the authors of this volume, suggested in 1995 that a "Lutheran understanding of vocation as that which one does (whether in the home, at work, as a public citizen, and so on) for the good of the neighbor to enact God's creative purposes in the world" is an important point of resonance with feminism because it affirms "God's ongoing presence and transforming activity" in the world.[15] Scholarly reflection on Luther and vocation is extensive. With some feminist focus and criticism of that tradition of reflection, we can see how the doctrine of vocation in Lutheranism provides a particular resource for feminist theology when it comes to understanding the relationship between God and human beings.

Feminism focuses on securing and protecting women's ability to shape their own lives and relationships. In this way, it focuses on the social and political realms of human life. Lutheran theology holds that women and men have the freedom to shape their own lives because their primary relationship is with God. God calls women and men to the various roles and places that shape their lives, thus no man-made institution has the inherent right to limit those offices and places. This adds a theological component to understanding social and political human life. Luther understood that institutions of this world are inherently sinful and flawed because they are human creations; God's ability to work through them comes from grace. What Luther did not understand—indeed, the late medieval world did not yet appreciate—was that patriarchy was and is one of those inherently flawed and sinful institutions. A contemporary understanding of systems of oppression and privilege that comes with feminism helps us to deconstruct the problematic elements in a Lutheran idea of vocation and reclaim elements that are particularly resonant with feminist theology.

Swedish theologian Gustaf Wingren has been one of the most influential thinkers on vocation in Lutheranism, in part due to his 1957 book *Luther on Vocation*. In it he discusses at length "the concept of man as a fellow-worker with God," an idea worth considering, while he rejects outright the claim that this means the human being is "an independent ethical subject." Like Luther, Wingren insists on maintaining absolute human dependency on God. Nuancing this idea of dependence with a careful construction of human agency is necessary.[16] Wingren's own analogy that follows this claim and informs his discussion of "co-operation" with God makes plain its limitations. He uses the master-serf relationship as parallel to the God-human relationship: "The serf is free, for example, to move his hands and feet; the master does not decide their movements in detail." The larger situation and condition of the serf's life is, of course, bondage: "When the slave . . . does what he is commanded in field and meadow, he is his master's 'fellow-worker.' This is about the way Luther conceives of man as a 'fellow-worker' with God."[17] Whether or not we agree that this is what Luther meant when he suggested that God calls human beings to participate in the ongoing work of creation, Wingren's interpretation that a slave is a master's fellow worker because she carries out the master's order, without any meaningful agency, is both imperialistic and paternalistic.[18]

The initial suggestion that humans are called to be God's fellow workers in the world, however, is one that resonates with feminism insofar as it can contribute to an understanding of shared power and interdependence in the God-human relationship. Further on in his writing, Wingren suggests that "Creation, the work of God, is carried out through the person who, being faithful to his vocation, is a coworker against the devil."[19] A similar and more relevant discussion of such a model of the God-human relationship comes from systematic theologian Philip Hefner and his detailed construction of the created co-creator: "The term *created* indicates that the human species did not design its own nature or role in the world."[20] This preserves the sovereignty of God as creator that grounds the Lutheran tradition. "The noun *co-creator* corresponds to the freedom of the human being."[21] This preserves the real agency embedded in the human condition. Hefner points out that this freedom is not mere liberty or sheer power to do as one wishes without constraint. It is about decision making and choices that have real consequences within human existence.

Hefner and Wingren both emphasize in Luther and the Lutheran tradition a foundational relationship wherein God calls the human being to carry out God's work in the world. This understanding of vocation has been foundational for the emergence of Lutheran women's theological work. The type of shared power and interdependence implied and illustrated by Hefner corrects the limitation of Wingren's interpretation of vocation and provides one key theological basis for Lutheran feminist theology.

AUTHORITY

Feminists have long understood that the patriarchal presumption that men have authority over women because of the socially constructed privileges of the male is a fundamentally flawed and genuinely dangerous idea. Lutheran theologian Marc Kolden points out that the Lutheran tradition understands two ways the sin of unbelief manifests itself in human life: when we overvalue our human nature and try to flee from finitude, or when we sink into it and undervalue our human nature *imago Dei*. In this way he has learned from Valerie Saiving's groundbreaking feminist critique of the classical Christian notion of sin as pride.[22] She shows that under patriarchy, the problem for men is that they presume too much authority, where the problem for women is too limited a sense of authority. The way in which authority is rethought and even reimagined using Luther's idea of the priesthood of all believers provides a second theological basis for a Lutheran feminist theology in the twenty-first century. We see how women throughout the history of the tradition have built on this idea in forming organizations, doing ministry, and teaching long before their ordination by the church body was allowed.

Luther speaks extensively about spiritual power and authority in his 1520 treatise "The Freedom of a Christian." Authority in this sense is God's alone. This was an essential element of Luther's reclamation of justification by grace through faith and rejection of works righteousness: the priest or bishop does not have authority to forgive; God forgives. In claiming that "we are all equally priests," and that "as priests we are worthy to appear before God to pray for others and to teach one another divine things,"[23] Luther elevated the worth of ordinary Christians and provided the seed for what Lutherans speak of as the priesthood of all believers. This egalitarian impulse provides a basis for retooling a theological understanding of authority in a Lutheran and feminist theology. The authority of one human being over another is not part of this picture, and where Luther's emphasis was on deratifying the tyrannical authority of the church in his day, feminist theology deratifies the implicit authority of men over women in patriarchy.

The feminist work of Muslim scholar Amina Wadud provides a helpful image that captures a view of authority resonating with this idea. Wadud describes in detail the *tawhidic* paradigm for her work. *Tawhid* refers to the oneness of God and is a foundational concept in Islam. She also describes it as "the operating principle of equilibrium and cosmic harmony."[24] She imagines the oneness of God as the top point in a triangle and human beings as the two bottom points of the triangle. They relate to God as their spiritual authority and relate to each other as equals along a horizontal plane. Submission in Islam is only to Allah, Wadud argues, not one person to another. Similarly, Gustaf Wingren states plainly that "before God all are equal, for before God we have no office occupied in relation to our neighbors on earth and the basis of distinction and difference there."[25] In relation to each other, human beings are equal and authority rests with God alone. Any attempts of a person to exert authority over another person, whether it be master and slave, rich and poor, or man and woman, is symptomatic of the fallen creation in which it takes place. This was a crucial basis for the Lutheran reformation of the Christian tradition and is a fundamental claim of feminism.

We see how women in the Lutheran tradition have claimed authority in a variety of ways throughout its history: the pastor's active wife, the liturgist writing hymns, the teacher of music at a Lutheran college, or the author of a groundbreaking book on Luther, feminism, and the cross. They were empowered to do this in part because of this theological understanding of authority wherein all are called to be priests to one another regardless of gender. That human beings do not inherently possess authority over one another on the basis of race, gender, social class, sexuality, or any other distinguishing characteristic is a second key theological basis for Lutheran feminist theology.

PARADOX

The ways in which Lutheran theology inhabits and preserves paradox establishes a third basis for Lutheran feminist theology. Whether it be in recognizing human beings as both justified and sinners, God as both hidden and revealed, or Christians as citizens of both heaven and earth, the Lutheran tradition maintains a "both–and" structure and methodology that provides a third theological basis for Lutheran feminist theologies. Indeed, it enables theologians to be both Lutheran and womanist, mujerista, or feminist. This "twoness" is claimed in different ways by all of the authors collected in this volume, and it has shown itself throughout the traditions informing them. Paradox is then not a convenient excuse for holding contradictory truths in tension; paradox is the way in which both Lutheran and feminist theologies recognize the complications of human life in the world and in relationship with God.

Feminism in the twenty-first century works with an intersectional methodology, taking seriously the fact that human life is lived at the intersection of identities. These identities emerge from the socially constructed meanings of race, gender, social class, age, ethnicity, sexuality, and many other things. Living in the tensions that often emerge when one is, for example, simultaneously oppressed and oppressor on the basis of different axes of identity (gender and race, perhaps) is what feminists, womanists, and mujeristas work to make sense of today. The Lutheran theological idea of one person as both saved and sinning can ground exploration of privilege and oppression in a new way.

Similarly, feminist reflection on God finds resonance with the Lutheran idea that God is hidden and revealed. Theologians who are also feminist have made a commitment to engage a religious tradition, despite the patriarchal baggage it has accumulated over the centuries. This represents a conviction that God can work in and through unlikely things like patriarchal institutions. Luther maintains that "the invisible things of God are virtue, godliness, wisdom, justice, goodness, and so forth,"[26] and that these things are not always perceptible to theologians. In addition, a foundational Christian claim emphasized by Luther is that God is most fully revealed in the most unexpected places. This includes a young unmarried woman, a Jewish itinerant teacher, as well as suffering and the cross. Claims that revelation and truth can be found in unexpected places and in the margins holds particular meaning for women who are making sense out of their experiences of marginalization and pain in a patriarchal world and church. God could be and is present even and especially there.

One final example of paradox made plain in the Lutheran tradition is the way in which Luther appropriates Augustine's ideas about the city of God and the city of this world, insisting that the Christian inhabits both. The claim that human life on earth is part but not all of the story for Christians resonates with feminist eschatology and sparks discussions of hope. The promise that God works in the world despite broken and sinful human structures and institutions answers feminist anger at injustice and violation. All of the ways in which paradox is a characteristic of Lutheran theological thinking enable feminist reflection on the intersectional reality of human life in the twenty-first century.

GRACE

The final and perhaps most all-encompassing basis for a Lutheran feminist theology is grace. Grace is the reason that God calls each human being. Grace is
the reason that humans need to submit to no spiritual authority other than God.
Grace is the force that holds many things in tension and paradox. Grace claims
us and our webs of relationships, including broken human beings and sinful
human structures with the ability to conceive of justice and the capacity to bring
it more fully into reality. A Lutheran feminist theology understands the gift of
grace that was incarnate most fully in the person of Jesus and continues to be
experienced in the sacramental relationship with Christ.

Luther insisted on reclaiming a deep sense of God as present in the sacraments, despite corrupt and wicked priests and church teachings about their
character and effectiveness. When discussing baptism, he states that "it is not
man's baptism, but Christ's and God's baptism, which we receive by the hand of
a man."[27] The sacraments are signs of grace in visible form and ritual. The human
participants merely make visible the invisible grace that comes from God. The
sacraments were central to Luther's reformation of the Christian church and
continue to be central to Lutherans today. A robust theology of the sacraments
provides a basis for Lutheran feminist theology insofar as it emphasizes locations of God's transformative power and presence in the world.

The sacraments of baptism and the Eucharist are central because they are grace
fully present in this world. In the same way, grace continues to be the empowering
spirit of creation which was fully human in the incarnation. Feminist theologian
Ann Milliken Pederson points out that the story of the incarnation is itself wrapped
up in "economic realities, political histories, religious struggles, and formidable
social boundaries."[28] The affirmation that the finite is capable of holding infinite
grace, both in the sacraments as well as in the life and person of Jesus the Christ,
gives transcendent meaning to feminist claims about the bodily integrity of women
and the daily reality of all human life insofar as it is shaped by gender, race, class,
sexuality, and myriad other concrete things. Twenty years ago, Karen Bloomquist
articulated theology's need for a new starting point because of feminism:

> [T]he starting point of feminist theology is deeply pastoral. It begins with
> the concrete experiences of real human beings, not in order to apply time-
> less truths to their lives, but to open up a pragmatic inquiry that seeks to
> understand the pains and contradictions in those experiences.[29]

Bloomquist goes on to add that the starting point is also transformative because
it brings about new possibilities.

This collaborative chapter has reflected that commitment toward new possibilities insofar as it started with the experiences of real women in the Lutheran

tradition and proceeded to consider the theological claims that made both their stories and this volume possible. Claims about vocation affirm that women and men are and have been called by God to a variety of places, from hospitals to congregations to the academy. No man-made institution appropriately limits the location and scope of that call based on gender. Reflections on authority show that the equal relationships of every human being to God deratifies explicit and implicit forms of gender-based authority. Understanding paradox helps women and men see that it is wholly possible to be feminist and Lutheran, especially in a theological tradition of paradoxes about God hidden and revealed. This is feminism grounded in a Christian tradition and inhabiting the margins of that tradition, grounded in contemporary human life and inhabiting the margins of social systems. Finally, because Lutheran theology intentionally focuses on grace as embodied and concrete, Lutheran feminist theology is uniquely possible and indeed transformative.

Suggested Readings

Bengtson, Gloria E., ed. *Lutheran Women in Ordained Ministry, 1970–1995: Reflections and Perspectives.* Minneapolis: Augsburg Fortress, 1995.

Lagerquist, L. DeAne. *From Our Mothers' Arms: A History of Women in the American Lutheran Church.* Minneapolis: Augsburg, 1987.

Preus, Marilyn, ed. *Serving the Word: Lutheran Women Consider Their Calling.* Minneapolis: Augsburg, 1988.

Goldstein, Valerie Saiving. "The Human Situation: A Feminine View." *Journal of Religion* 40, no. 2 (April 1960): 100–112.

Stjerna, Kirsi Irmeli. *Women and the Reformation.* Malden, Mass: Blackwell, 2009.

Wingren, Gustaf. *Luther on Vocation.* Trans. Carl C. Rasmussen. Philadelphia: Muhlenberg, 1957.

Chapter 2

The Elusive Lure of the Lotus

Mary (Joy) Philip

August and majestic, it grows out of the murky water
creamy white petals dancing with pearls of dew;
Leaves glowing like emerald caress the water
its sweet fragrance imbuing the air.
The sun bids adieu but I dare not and cannot
for I am mesmerized by its elusive lure

WHO AND WHERE ARE we as women? More importantly, who and where are we as theologians? What are we all about? Just as every tree has its creed and every tribe its scribe,[1] so it is the case with the script that follows. It is from a particular theological perspective, the point of which is to create cognitive dissonance in our otherwise pedestrian ways of thinking and in the process entertain and engage a thought that, while being alien and disturbing, also nudges our sense of responsibility to challenge and transform the world around us that is out of kilter, so to speak.

Voices from the margins have been speaking for many years, prompting us to ask, after decades of postcolonial biblical interpretation,[2] Are our voices being heard? We might even entertain the question that Indian literary critic and theorist Gayatri Chakravorty Spivak posed: Can the subaltern speak?[3] Does she even have a voice? I would argue that those of us at the margins may not be able to "speak," but we can prophesy. When the world's vision is occluded with idols and lies, God speaks through prophets to open its eyes. We are those prophets with voices that can clear visions, with the power to rouse people from slumber and goad them into action; we are voices from the margins but with a difference. We have the power to shake a few foundations!

Margins do not normally make for cozy conversation. Margins are, indeed, sites of oppression, and all of us have our own stories that we can recount. It brings to mind what it must have been like for my grandmothers to live in a time when they had no voice, especially in India's caste-ridden society. Early in the nineteenth century, women in India, except for those belonging to the high caste, were not allowed to cover their breasts and the upper part of their bodies. They were to bare their breasts for all to see. Imagine how humiliating this was! It is said that men did whatever they pleased with these women, even in the sight of the women's families. Wearing an upper cloth to cover their bosoms was a symbol of privilege granted only to upper-caste women; the rest were left to endure the leers. Ironically, in certain circumstances an uncovered upper body was also seen as a mark of respect, rendered by both men and women. For example, the Maharajah (king) of Travancore and other upper-caste men would uncover their upper bodies when in the presence of a deity, as in a temple, and according to custom, the *pujaris* or priests never wore an upper cloth.

In the mid-nineteenth century a group of women from one of the lower castes, the Shanar women, first dared to wear upper cloths in public. It is moot whether the women regarded the lack of breast cloth as a sign of disrespect and shame or they saw it as a sign of respect that was forced upon them because of their low status. The fact is, the Shanar women decided enough was enough. Their uprising led to what came to be called the "upper-cloth controversy," which unfortunately led to much violence, including rioting and burning and looting of houses. Eventually in 1858, a proclamation was issued granting the right to all women to wear an upper cloth, but it took many more years before the untouchables were able to cover their breasts.

This is just one of the many ways in which women were marginalized in barbarous and evil ways. But were the margins about oppression alone? Did not the Shanar women prove otherwise by their defiance? Did they not offer hope to the untouchables who were still being exploited? Experiences can make one bitter, and anger is not easy to quell at times, but we can choose to look at the margins as places of strength, courage, hope, and promise. This is not to deny that margins are places of oppression, but margins are also about vitality, tenacity, and life.

There is much more to margins than what is generally associated with it. It is a lot easier to cry victim than to stand up to who you are. The sacred lotus, *Nelumba nucifera*, is the national flower of India. It is an exquisite flower that grows in murky waters, making it an apt example of that which grows in what we would classify as "margins." The environment in which it lives gives it every reason to cry oppression and decide not to bloom, but instead it chooses to lift its head high above the stinky, muddy water, fighting against all odds, offering hope, as if saying to all: You may not want to see me but you cannot avoid looking at me. I am majestic! You cannot pin me down. I am elusive, but you cannot help but look at me! The lotus could have said that the water was too muddy and stinky and that it did not want to bloom in such shoddy circumstances. But instead the lotus defies it all and emerges out of the mud and stink and stands tall. How often do we, as women, take the easy way out instead of daring to take a risk?

It is the elusive lure of the lotus that we as women ought to claim. We need to dare to describe ourselves as being "majestic" and having an "elusive lure," even though we might offend in doing so. There will be those who cry betrayal and others who accuse us of co-opting and still others who blame us for flouting our sensuality. But it is not a question of betrayal nor of co-opting or of sensuality. It is about acknowledging and naming who we are and for what we stand. We women, straight or LGBTQ, we are from the margins. We need to see the margins for what they really are.

Life in the Margins: Crossing the Boundaries

Barriers or boundaries—physical, social, psychological, religious—are part and parcel of our everyday life. Blood and oxygen keep us human beings alive. Hemoglobin in the blood is that which carries oxygen to the cells, wherein the mitochondrion they produce energy-rich molecules called ATP that power our bodies. But where does this oxygen come from? It comes through the air that we breathe *in from the outside*. Air enters through our nostrils, which are openings in the barrier called skin that divides our bodies into an outside and inside. Once inside, the air enters the alveolar sacs of the lungs and from there enters the blood capillaries. There is a crossing of boundaries here.

We also live *because of* boundaries. After oxygen enters the blood capillaries, it is carried by the blood to the cells. But think again. Can the blood carry the oxygen if it were not enclosed in the boundary of the capillary walls? Blood is carried by the blood vessels that are bound or encircled by a wall that holds the blood inside. It is not that our bodies are simply bathed in blood. Blood that carries the life-giving oxygen is surrounded by a barrier.

We also know that the brain of a human being is the most highly developed or that human beings are the most intelligent of all of God's creation (or so we claim). But what do you think is responsible for this highly developed nervous system of ours? The nervous system is made up of units called neurons that are responsible for carrying impulses across our body. They have a cyton or cell body and dendrites. Each neuron is connected to the next by the dendrites.

Interestingly, very few of them are actually connected and instead there is a gap between two neurons called the synapse. So, how are impulses carried across if there is a space in between? Transmitters that are found at the dendritic end of the one neuron cross the gap and carry them over to the receptors at the dendritic end of the next neuron, and then the process is repeated to the next neuron and so on until the message reaches its destination and the appropriate response made. Have we ever stopped to think that if it were not for that crossing of boundaries by the oxygen and the transmitters and were it not for the blood enclosed within the walls of the blood vessels and carried to all the parts of the body, we would not have life itself? We need boundaries and at the same time we need to cross them. Is not that an oxymoron? But the fact is having boundaries and margins and crossing them are what gives life, promises life, strengthens life.

To use Luther's language, can we be free without being bound? Borders, boundaries, limits, and margins carry negative connotations. But take a look at Genesis 1. It is all about separation: light from darkness; a dome to separate the water from the waters; day from night; and so on. For crying out loud, the creator itself made definite demarcations, separations, while creating and shaping the universe, be it day and night, heaven and earth, water and dry land. Does this mean that divisions into dissimilar or incongruent categories are a must, a prerequisite for something or someone to have an identity, a name? No, not at all, but come to think of it, I come to know who I am when I reach the limit of me, that is, when I encounter that which is not me, an "other," someone who is different. It is at the margins, at the limits, that I come to the realization of who I really am, that I have an identity. It is that which confronts me at the margins of my existence that gives me my distinctiveness as a person. It is not that divisions in the sense of isolating and/or discriminating are good, that segregation of black and white, brown and yellow, high caste and untouchable are desirable. God in God's infinite wisdom and the gene pool in its immense diversity gave rise to quite a few of us varied in size, shape, and color. There is nothing wrong with that. We are beautiful. The ugliness or the segregational differences, for that we are responsible. It is we who make segregational differences.

There is an obvious connection between women and the margins, for that is where women often are. We are the voices from the margins. But as I suggested earlier, margins are not just about horror stories. They are not just sites of oppression. Margins are and can be places of communication, determination, resistance, and hope. According to Lutheran theologian Vítor Westhelle, "Margins are the threshold to eschatological experience, and this happens in two ways—as experiences of condemnation or of liberation."[4] Margins define what in the New Testament is called *eschaton* or in the plural, *eschata*. An eschatological experience is one that either leads to death or one that is life giving, and that is precisely what one experiences when crossing a margin or a boundary, be it social, political, economic, cultural, racial, or ethnic.

The eschaton points to a reality that is beyond us and yet is part of our everyday experience. Every time we step out of the familiar and cross the boundaries that safeguard us, we experience novelty. We operate within our skeletons, within what we can control and administrate, not open to the possibility of there being something, be it promising or condemning, outside of the frame. Our inability to cross borders and go out of the familiar is our incapability to look beyond the frame of what we prescribe as the norm. We resist getting beyond the known most often not because we are afraid of what lies there, but because of what it might demand of us. However, we will never know what is on the other side unless we step over. It is not easy, for it can either bring about our annihilation or take us through an experience that fills us with life more than ever before. Stepping out of our space over to another is a frightening experience. By staying within the framework of our comfort zones, within our skin, we preserve ourselves, but at the same time we deprive ourselves of experiencing novelty. Margins are the playgrounds of danger, death, and menace. When we come to the margins we come to that which separates and protects us from whatever is outside. Crossing over is indeed a risky business.

So, What Are Margins?

How can margins be defined or are they definable at all? As mentioned before, in simplest terms, margins bring about a separation, a demarcation into an inside and outside; a division into two sides.

Let me use my body as an example. My skin is the margin of my body.[5] Because of the skin there is an inside and an outside. The skeleton forms the frame for my body, but it is the skin that puts the finishing touch to it. It covers my exposure, my vulnerability, so to speak, while giving me my final shape with all its contours and trajectories. This margin, my skin, when intact, all is fine, but when infringed, the inside/outside division is no longer there and I become susceptible to viruses and germs threatening from the outside. When attacked by germs from outside, the body produces or activates antibodies, which in turn fight the toxins or the germs and restore the bodily functions. Forces that were recessive or subdued or nonoperational are activated and even created anew. The openings or the orifices, as British anthropologist Mary Douglas calls them, be they natural openings or those caused by injuries, represent the most vulnerable points of my body.[6] What comes out of them or goes into them are marginal stuff that is either life giving or life consuming.

The orifices of my body include eyes, ears, nose, nipples, vagina. My eyes are windows that open and close my view of the world, regulating my perception of reality. My ears are the receptacles through which I heard the borning cry of my children and the deafening cries of children in Darfur. They also tell me which way is up and which is down, maintaining my equilibrium. I breathe through my nose, taking in and giving out air, the breath of life. Part of my being uniquely woman, my nipples are the openings through which my children drew their first source of nourishment, and my vagina is the place within which life was conceived and brought forth and also in my culture the site of pollution because of menstruation. The urethra and anus and pores are the openings out of which waste and that which is detrimental is thrown. Finally, my mouth is that which enables me to speak, to name myself, and through which I take nourishment. To quote Mary Douglas again, "these are marginal stuff of the most obvious kind."[7]

So, what does this mean? How does it redefine or reconfigure our understanding of margins? Margins are spaces of contrariness, where there is a constant dialogue/interaction between the opposites, where exists a delicate balance between incongruent entities. They are places of tension, a tension between ends and beginnings and it is this tensility that sustains margins. An imagery that best explains what I am trying to convey here comes from ecology. Margins are like estuaries.

What Are Estuaries?

Estuaries are borderlands that are continuously graced by the rivers on one side and lashed at by the sea on the other. Purity on one side and brackishness on the other. They receive two environments which do not blend and in the process become a hybrid environment. Conditions in estuaries are very different from those in the sea or in the rivers. Estuaries vary greatly in temperature, salinity, and turbidity (murkiness). As a result they are specialized environments. Because of the constant change in conditions, instability or variability is one of the most important features of estuaries. And it is this characteristic that is its strength. The two conflicting environments do not institute in its inhabitants an adaptability but a vitality, a vigor that gives rise to an entirely new environment. It is not a blending of the two environments but instead the new environment created thus brings about a change, a rousing in whoever or whatever comes in contact with it.

Estuaries are crucial transition zones where there is a struggle for existence. They are the burial grounds for a variety of aquatic organisms which cannot tolerate the mixing up, or in other words, they do not survive the crossing over either way. Apart from this, estuaries also serve as the home for a variety of organisms, among them some endangered species. They are the breeding grounds for several species of fish and serve as "nurseries." The productivity of an estuary is estimated to be eight times that of agricultural land because of the rich organic material that the river brings in. However, overdeposition of this organic material leads to algal growth, which depletes the oxygen and pathogen contamination, both of which are detrimental to the life of its inhabitants. These margins or transitional zones are not just life giving but life consuming as well. Life ends and begins as well at these estuarine margins; they are death traps yet a source of life. The incoming water and the ocean tides create a chaos in which life becomes a struggle because of the constantly changing environmental conditions, so estuaries are places where fatality is not rare and yet life thrives here. These are places where there is exploitation of life, but they are also places where there is nurturing and growth. They are the schools where lessons of life are taught, where one's eyes are opened to the reality of the world, which hitherto were closed and protected. They are margins where there is an unveiling; a revelation takes place.

Estuaries also serve as filters. As the water flows through the salt marsh peat, much of the organic matter is filtered out, resulting in cleaner water. Not surprisingly, societal margins too are often thought of and function as filters, filtering out undesirable elements for the dominant society, á la Hitler's purification process, only that instead of gas chambers in remote areas, the dumps are outside societal gates—the south side of Chicago or the slums of India to name a few. Systematic confinement of poor and other socially "undesirable" people in restricted areas are contemporary death-dealing social filters. But these are, in fact, spaces of otherness. And it is precisely there that life really happens.

The life that thrives in margins, as in the case of estuaries, I think is best described by the concept of hybrids. Hybrids emulate the vim and vigor of the margins. Hybrids are entities that are made up of constituent elements that are incongruent and, while having characteristics of their constituents, have identities that are unique to them. One of their distinctive features is that they transgress. Another trait of a hybrid is that the new entity or hybrid must come into existence and remain in existence, despite threats present in its environment, for long enough to be recognized. Have we not remained in existence no matter how much purification has been performed? And don't we transgress?

Margins thus are hybrid spaces. They have characteristics of both constituents for which they form a margin, but the crossing over of terrains does not unify or blend as in a Mendelian[8] hybrid. Instead it results in a reconfiguring and reconstruction of the constitutional geography in order to develop a new identity that enables not just survival but life with a vigor second to none. They do not have stipulated norms but are characterized by constant change/transformation. They are choratic spaces, whose meaning is constantly redefined by its inhabitants, who construct their own meanings in relation to self, identity, and subjectivity in an ongoing and changing process. Margins are spaces where there is movement, where there is constant dissembling and reassembling, where there is always a metamorphosis, the possibility of being and becoming. We, at the margins, are hybrids. But there is one hybrid par excellence for whom margins was home—Jesus. Jesus is a true hybrid, born of the union of the divine and the human. He was born in the most marginal of places, a barn and in the company of animals and stinky manure. His ministry was among the people that were in the margins—lepers, demoniacs, prostitutes, to name a few. Jesus, the godman lived at the margins, in the Galilees, where from, in the eyes of the others, no good could come, but from whither and from whom the "good news" came. How can margins not be the threshold to eschatological experience?

And So, What Now?

How are we to translate to the world around us and especially to the church our understanding of what margins are and our role as women in the margins is? Where, what, and who is the church? What are we to transform? The place of the church is at the margins. The church is to be estuarine in character. It is countercultural, countertyranny. As Christians, as women, we are to be the same. We live in a fragmented, broken world. We are not about perfection but about ruptures. So, how do we bring about transformation, considering the fact that we are in the margins? How do we face this stark reality that is staring at us? Interestingly, our default is to protest, and most often it is by way of crying victim: You do not know what it is to be a woman or you do not know what it is to be a person of color.

But is that how we should protest against the injustice that has been meted to us? No! We cannot wait for someone to come to rescue us, to lift us up from the margins and place us in the center where power is located. We don't need to go to the center. We just need to call the center into question. That is what margins do! To quote Mary Douglas, "All margins are dangerous. If they are pulled this way or that the shape of fundamental experience is altered. Any structure of ideas is vulnerable at its margins."[9] Every society is fragile at its margins.

Author, poet, and activist June Jordan said, "We are the ones we have been waiting for."[10] We are the change; we are the transformation. We at the margins are uniquely placed. We have qualities and characteristics that others don't have. We are those special transmitters and receptors, as in the ends of the neurons; akin to walls of the arteries that carry blood, we cross barriers and penetrate our way into the dark depths, carrying that which is life giving. We have our stories, our memories that can be told and translated only by us. And we have the responsibility of translating and transmitting all that to the next generation. Those of us in the margins are the interpreters of a special kind of language known as the "marginish." We do a special kind of dance that weaves in and out and entices and enthralls like no other can. We cross barriers and penetrate our way into the dark depths, carrying that which is life giving. Our situation may seem hopeless, and keeping one foot in front of the other amidst forces that try to bring us down takes every effort. Do we opt out or co-opt or do we have the guts to step up? We may be a minority, we may be sidelined, we may be colored, we may not speak the language. We are black, brown, white, LGBTQ, but do we have to cry victim or can we be lotuses, symbols of defiance and hope? Can we make our way through the murky waters of suppression, fighting against all odds, and lift our heads, make our voices heard so that others cannot help but look at and listen to us?

According to philosopher Walter Benjamin, it is because of the hopeless that we have been given hope.[11] All of us have power, however weak it may seem. We have power in our experiences, in our stories, and in our memories. Benjamin calls this kind of power weak messianic power[12] that can awaken even the dead and transform desperate situations into songs of hope and joy. Scripture records the stories of Mary, Rahab, the nameless maidservant of Namaan, and Mary Magdalene. They were in the margins, in hopeless situations, but still they were instruments of hope and promise. We may seem insignificant and out of place, but we are a people who know and know better. We know what is to be feared and what is to be dared, and daring we must be. That is the calling of the church.

The church is a storehouse of memories and stories, big and small. Better still, the church is the heir to memories of the past, in a sense, even custodians of history. What are the scriptures, if not a registry or repository of memories? The scriptures are the storehouse of memories of the first witnesses, a collection of memories that have been written down. As heirs we have the responsibility to see that the inheritance is passed on. It should instill in us a sense of awareness that demands justice. I am again reminded of Walter Benjamin for whom the theme of remembrance is central. His characters—storyteller, collector, translator, photographer—are all heirs to the memories of the past; the storyteller through his stories, the collector through his possessions, the translator in translating texts, the photographer through the pictures he captures—all pass on what has been inherited.[13] What is asked of us is to be storytellers of this treasury. What is asked of us is to be translators of these stories. As the Italian adage says, *traduttore traditore* ("translator traitor"), we might become traitors, as history has taught us. Try following 1 Cor. 11:1-16 (covering heads) or 1 Cor. 14:26-36 (silence in churches) to the letter. We will and must be traitors in our translation if we are to be true to our calling as church. We cannot be anything but translators and storytellers. That is how we can be the church; that is how we can bring about justice. What is it if it is not about justice when we come together at the table and hear, "Do this in remembrance of me"? Remembrance is about justice. It paves the way for the kind of justice that brings to sight those faces and bodies that have been kept away, the justice that gives heed to the voices that are being muted, hushed, and not heard.

French philosopher Jacques Derrida had this saying, "The correct place of the heart is where it is best located."[14] We are in the margins, and while we agree that is not always a good thing, there we are capable of doing things others can only dream of doing. We are in those spaces where there is movement, where there is a crossing, where there is constant dissembling and reassembling, where there is always a metamorphosis, the possibility of being and becoming. We can play victims or we can be co-opted or we can be those spaces of contrariness, where there is this constant dialogue and interaction between the opposites, where exists a delicate balance between incongruent entities that keeps the tensility, places where the lotus grows. We are indeed placed correctly to be estuarine, to be transmitters and receptors, to be storytellers and translators, where we cannot help but be noticeable, recognized for who we are and what we do and the difference we make. We are where the church happens. We are the church!

Margins or borders, to quote from *Walter Benjamin's Grave*, are places where "[t]ruth itself lies on trial, and it is the border that defines and redefines it."[15] Truth does not lie in the text but in the interstices of it, in the margins, in the white fire, as the Torah teaches us. And "where truth is spoken, there is the church and where church is, truth is spoken. Where the church is, captives are set free; and where captives are set free, there is the church."[16] If we believe us to be the church, then our theologizing, our voices, ought to be estuarine, marginish. They should put truth to trial and facilitate a stirring, a turning, a moving around—*metanoia*, transformation—that frees ourselves of our captivities so we might surge ahead.

I am a woman from the margins and I want my voice, my words—the marginal stuff that comes out of my most conspicuous and loud orifice, my mouth—to sound like a pistol shot in the middle of a symphony.[17] Yes, margins are sites of oppression, but they are also about vitality, tenacity, and hope. Margins are dangerous; they are the playground of menace but they are also the thresholds to eschatological experiences—if only we dare to cross them.

There is a Chinese proverb that says that birds don't sing because they have answers; birds sing because they have a song to sing. I am a woman from the margins and I don't have all the answers, but I have something to say: *Look at me! I am a woman and I am correctly placed; I feel majestic, and God help you if you resist my lure.*

Suggested Reading

Benjamin, Walter. *Illuminations: Essays and Reflections*. New York: Schocken, 1968.

Minh-ha, Trinh T. *Woman, Native, Other: Writing Postcoloniality and Feminism*. Indianapolis: Indian University Press, 1989.

Roy, Arundhati. *The God of Small Things*. New York: Random House, 2008.

Solberg, Mary M. *Compelling Knowledge: A Feminist Proposal for an Epistemology of the Cross*. Albany: SUNY, 1997.

Watson, Natalie. *Introducing Feminist Ecclesiology*. Cleveland: Pilgrim, 2002.

Westhelle, Vítor. *The Scandalous God: The Use and Abuse of the Cross*. Minneapolis: Fortress Press, 2006.

Westhelle, Vítor. *The Church Event: Call and Challenge of a Church Protestant*. Minneapolis: Fortress Press, 2010.

PART 2

God and Humanity

IN IMPLICIT WAYS, THE two chapters in this section express the Lutheran theological reliance on law and gospel, that God both condemns and redeems. In chapter 3, Caryn Riswold outlines a broadly conceived view of the doctrine of God, arguing that it is only with Martin Luther's understanding of God's act to humble and empower the human enterprise that feminist theology can make sense of the condemnation of patriarchy as a social and religious system and the grace-filled means to support the full humanity of all, no matter our race, class, gender, ability, or sexuality. Kristen Kvam forges into a careful, nuanced reading of Luther's lectures on Genesis in chapter 4, revealing important insights on God's character and human vocation: God's mercy and grace commence in the Garden of Eden, which casts redemption prior to the cross, and at the same time humans are empowered by God to upend the effects of sin.

Chapter 3

Inhabiting Paradox: God and Feminist Theology for the Third Wave

Caryn D. Riswold

A NEW VOICE IS needed in the wilderness of the twenty-first century. In the midst of a powerful and now faltering global economy, multi-issue activism from feminists in the third wave is emerging in every corner of the human community. Intersectional analysis of human identity in feminism talks about where race, class, gender, sexuality, age, ability, education, and appearance meet. But where is the voice where all of that meets religion? Where is the voice when people of faith are unwilling to abandon their traditions to the annals of patriarchal history? Who is talking about a feminist theology for this world, where 25 percent of American women will experience intimate partner violence at some point in their lives, where heterosexism still dictates state marriage laws, and where black children can still expect a lower life expectancy than their white neighbors because the country in which they live doesn't provide adequate resources for their streets, schools, parks, and hospitals?

Setting the Scene for a Third-Wave Feminist Theology

It is time to construct a systematic feminist theology in the third wave. After generations of feminist activism and hundreds of years with various incarnations of the women's movement, sexism remains a powerful social fact and women's lives are still precariously constructed in the midst of misogyny. Abolitionist and suffragist Elizabeth Cady Stanton was a voice of the first wave when she dared to write *The Woman's Bible* in 1898. The form of patriarchy challenged by this feminism limited women's legal rights to vote, to own property, and to have independent lives.[1] The feminism of the late nineteenth century therefore focused on the most basic legal equity between men and women. Feminist theology, inasmuch as it existed, was found in fragments like Stanton's undereducated attempt at biblical criticism, and in sister suffragist Sarah Grimke's reflective challenge to the preacher's readings of Genesis in her 1838 *Letters on the Equality of the Sexes*, and Jarena Lee's 1836 account of her divine call to preach despite the contrary instruction of her African Methodist Episcopal church's minister. Engaging in social criticism based on her study of Christianity, African American scholar Anna Julia Cooper spoke to "the convocation of colored clergy of the Protestant Episcopal Church" in Washington, D.C., in 1886, and stated that "the ground work and starting point of its progress upward, must be the black woman."[2]

Feminist philosopher and theologian Mary Daly cried from the wilderness of the second wave when she wrote *Beyond God the Father* in 1973. The form of patriarchy challenged by this feminism restricted women's freedom to be equitably educated, to work in a safe and harassment-free environment when they could get hired, and to determine the size of their families. The feminism of the late middle-twentieth century therefore focused on expanding women's ability to fully determine the shape of their own lives at home and in public. Feminist theology began to flourish with work like Daly's, Rosemary Radford Ruether's comprehensive look at *Sexism and God-talk* in 1984, and Phyllis Trible's transformative biblical criticisms beginning in 1978 with *God and the Rhetoric of Sexuality*. Social criticism grew out of their theological work as they and others spoke out about ending the war in Vietnam and advocating for an Equal Rights Amendment.

What is the feminist theological voice of the third wave? The form of patriarchy that we challenge today is more subversive in the ways that it limits women's equality and restricts men's lives. It binds itself to and feeds off racism, classism, heterosexism, and global capitalism. The feminism of the early twenty-first century is populated by those of us raised during the second wave, who grew up singing songs from *Free to Be You and Me*, glued to a racially integrated *Sesame Street*, able to play sports in school because of Title IX legislation, and unfamiliar with a time when women could not serve as pastors in many mainline churches. The third wave of feminism brings the strategies and achievements of the second wave to bear on a new generation of social problems. Does it attend to theology with the same attention given other issues?

Thus far, scattered voices and anthologies have emerged, including Deanna Thompson's *Crossing the Divide* (2004), the focused doctrinal theologies of British theologian Mary Grey in *Sacred Longings* (2004) and theologian Serene Jones in

Feminist Theory and Christian Theology (2000), and the authors brought together by Marit Trelstad in *Cross Examinations* (2006). In an article in *The Christian Century*, Reformed theologian Joy Ann McDougall calls Thompson's, Grey's, and Jones's texts "sophisticated saving work," part of feminist theology for a new generation.[3] Their contribution is clear, but focus on church doctrines like justification, church symbols like the cross, and Christian practices like the Eucharist gives them admittedly less appeal to feminists outside of the church.

At the same time, a brief foray into reading feminist theorists and activists of the third wave reveals that virtually no attention is paid to religion as part of the otherwise thoughtful and complex analysis of human identity and social change. Author Rebecca Walker first made the case for and named a "third wave" of feminism, and her 1995 book *To Be Real* begins to "tell the truth" of a generation of women raised on and with second-wave feminist ideas and achievements. However, this important book leaves out the theological work and religious revolution that took place hand in hand with the second wave of feminism. Writer and lecturer Jennifer Baumgardner and editor Amy Richards, in their widely read third-wave feminist book *Manifesta* (2000), mention religion only in passing as one of the quaint and problematic factors in shaping the mind-set of their parents' generation and the status quo. Several key third-wave feminist anthologies like *Catching a Wave: Reclaiming Feminism for the 21st Century* (2003) and *The Fire This Time: Young Activists and the New Feminism* (2004) have compelling and groundbreaking chapters on topics ranging from media literacy to police brutality, global economic policy, human trafficking, and transgender identity. But there is not the same fierce focus on religion.

This chapter contributes to the work of constructing a feminist theology for the third wave by focusing on how the doctrine and concept of God functions in the twenty-first century, reflecting the human communities that shape it as well as guiding people of faith as they respond to layered challenges ranging from global climate change to children living in poverty. In the same way that the theological work of women in previous generations led to engagement in social issues like the abolition of slavery, the vote for women, and antiwar movements, theology in the third wave of feminism provides resources for women and men within Christianity seeking spiritual renewal in a complex world, and contributes to broader efforts to address various contemporary social problems. The concept of God functions both inside and outside of religious traditions, and this chapter shows how a doctrine of God who simultaneously humbles and empowers humanity is a relevant and nuanced resource for those working toward theological and social justice.

As part of a sociopolitical and theological revolution in another time and place, Martin Luther's work is uniquely suited to inform a new generation's demands for change. Luther's theology provides tools and methods for challenging a status quo, and it empowers believers to take responsibility in their relationships with God and the world.[4] The way in which Luther's doctrine of God simultaneously empowers and humbles humanity can be carefully engaged by feminist theologians seeking to empower women as well as humble the human enterprise. This is one example of the various paradoxes that characterize Luther's work, where two divergent or even seemingly opposite things can be true simultaneously. For Luther, theologians of the cross are able to recognize things for what they are rather than what they appear to be. Luther says in the Heidelberg Disputation that the "visible things of God are placed in opposition to the invisible."[5] That which we can see, that which is visible, hides that which is true about God. The true majesty of God, for Luther, is found in the humility of the cross. What appears to be is not always what is.

Luther saw truth when there appeared to be none, and he spoke of the human person as two seemingly opposite things at once—*simul justus et peccator* ("righteous and at the same time a sinner")—showing how they were both true at the same time. Third-wave feminists amplify the fact that all of us live at the intersection of various identities that are simultaneously true, whether visible or hidden: our race, ethnicity, social class, gender, sexuality, age, ability, education, religious tradition, and multiple other factors. Inhabiting paradox is essential for Luther's understanding of God, humans, and the world, while the intersectional analysis that characterizes third-wave feminist work also demands that we understand how multiple identities shape each human life simultaneously.

Constructing Concepts of God

Christians experience God revealed in, with, and under the things of this world.[6] According to Luther, this happens in unexpected and hidden ways. Reflected in a theology of the sacraments, the doctrine of the incarnation, and the theology of the cross is Luther's idea that "you have been visited by the Word."[7] Because of limitations that are a part of all human experiences, there remains a distinction between the thing in itself (God) and the thing as known by and named by human beings (God). In this way, our doctrines and images of God can never fully capture God. Therefore, we must examine how we construct concepts of the revealed God as experienced by human communities. Lutheran theologian David Ratke describes revelation as "that area which rightfully stands at the beginning of most systematic theologies. How can we say anything about God if we do not examine our ways of knowing about God?"[8] Contemporary theories of the social construction of religion remind us that human communities do not just receive ideas about God. We construct doctrines and concepts based in part on experiences of revelation, and therefore have responsibility for shaping them in ways appropriate to our contexts.

Sociologist Peter Berger is a primary voice in a social-construction theory of religion that specifically informs later feminist theologians like Mary Daly and Elizabeth Johnson.[9] Berger describes a dialectical process, wherein human beings externalize, objectivate, and internalize as they create and maintain society. First, human beings externalize reality by creating culture, which includes creating explanations for how things work and why things are the way they are. He says, "the 'stuff' out of which society and all its formations are made is human meanings externalized in human activity."[10] Plainly, society is a human product: the family and the state and the community, along with other institutions and ideas that govern how we act and think, like religion, are things that we have a significant role in constructing.

Second, and very importantly, the "stuff" that we create is objectivated. This means that we as human beings forget that we made the stuff, and it becomes externally real, confronting us as its own objective reality. Berger says that objectivated cultural products take on a facticity of their own: we assume then that "once produced, the tool has a being of its own that cannot be readily changed by those who employ it."[11] This applies to material as well as nonmaterial things: language, values, ideas, institutions, social structures, and so forth.

Finally in the dialectical process, these externalized objects are internalized. This means that human societies reabsorb cultural products. Because we forget that we had a role in constructing the institution or the concept, we feel compelled to obey it and believe it to be fixed. Socialization is the process "by which a new generation is taught to live in accordance with the institutional programs of the society."[12] This is the teaching and the learning of values, beliefs, rules, and all other cultural facts.

Religion is one institution created by human beings, as are the particular concepts in any given religion, like images of God, the metaphor of trinity, and descriptions of the process of justification. Coupled with a robust Lutheran understanding of God as revealed, Berger's elaboration of the dialectical process actually helps preserve revelation by distinguishing it from our concepts and doctrines. Karl Barth distinguished between revelation and religion partly to insist that religion is the human attempt to reach God that will always fail because God is known only through revelation. Martin Luther concurs with Barth's point that God is an objective reality outside of the world that comes to us only through revelation. Where Barth dismissed religion insofar as it was constructed and Luther was satisfied to state that God is hidden and revealed, Berger enables our present engagement with religion by elaborating how the specific concepts and doctrines within it come to exist and to bear authority over our lives.

Mary Daly applied Berger's theory to the problems of patriarchal religion in the early 1970s. Rather than correct his gender-exclusive language that "Society . . . is a product of man," she underscored his point, insisting that "under the conditions of patriarchy, it is indeed *men* who do the externalizing. . . . However it is women who are conditioned to be the internalizers *par excellence.*"[13] The problem as she identified it is that women have no substantial role in the externalizing process, creating cultural products like a concept of God; yet they are the ones internalizing all of it, usually to their own detriment. Daly was at that time part of the second-wave feminist call for women to step up and be co-producers of reality, to be participants in naming and constructing culture, religion, and theological concepts.

Roman Catholic theologian Elizabeth Johnson picked up this task in the early 1990s when she focused primarily on speech about God. Johnson rightly claimed that "the symbol of God functions as the primary symbol of the whole religious system." This is why sustained focus on the doctrine of God is essential in every generation of feminist theology, because "language about God implicitly represents what [society] takes to be the highest good, the profoundest truth, the most appealing beauty."[14] The goodness, truth, and beauty externalized by a patriarchal society has been and will be, therefore, all of the ideals associated with its preferential option for the male. In addition, the preferential options for the white, the heterosexual, the able-bodied, the wealthy, and the healthy have become objectivated as norms and ideals.

The point of this theoretical grounding is first to remember the fact that all societies construct concepts of God. To assume somehow that the image and understanding of God have been absolutely fixed by past cultures or ancient religious councils is to miss a great opportunity. In fact, there is a risk in static conceptions of God; Johnson states that "if the idea of God does not keep pace with developing reality, the power of experience pulls people on and the god dies, fading from memory."[15] The patriarchal image and idea of God has not in fact kept pace with reality, and the experience of fragmented, complicated life in the twenty-first century demands that theologians either speak to the realities of things like 1.1 billion people living in poverty, global human trafficking, daily quests for clean water, and the nexus of race/class/gender/sexuality, or risk a total loss of relevance.

Luther's Concept of God

The particular concept of God that emerges from Martin Luther's theological revolution is clearly part of the patriarchal tradition that I am challenging. Rather than reject it wholesale, or passively internalize it, third-wave feminist theology as I am constructing it follows the tradition of so many feminist, womanist, and mujerista theologians like Rosemary Radford Ruether, Delores S. Williams, Elizabeth Johnson, and Elsa Tamez who mine Christianity for truth and treasure. If tradition is a *trado,* a handing over, as the Latin root of the word suggests, then we are the receivers of something that we are charged with reshaping and revitalizing.

Luther discusses God via the paradoxes that define both his method and his theology. In fact, in the preface to the Heidelberg Disputation, Luther describes his forty theses as "theological paradoxes."[16] This is due in large measure to the type of revealed-where-hidden ideas that define a theologian of the cross. German Lutheran theologian Paul Althaus describes how, for Luther, "God hides himself in his work of salvation." In addition, God "acts and creates paradoxically while camouflaging his work to make it look as though he were doing the opposite."[17] Luther also continually distinguishes between God's own self and God as can be known by human beings.[18] This distinction between the thing in itself (God) and the thing as known by and named by human beings (God) preserves the power of revelation while taking seriously the role that we continue to play in constructing concepts and doctrines of God.

It is true that for Luther God was a subject, not at all something that human beings create and manipulate. The sheer otherness and fact of God overwhelmed Luther, and he would say it forced him to his theological conclusions. He talked at length about the hiddenness of God with the revelation of God. For Luther, knowledge of God is revealed to us most specifically in the incarnate Word, and God is not something over which we have any control. Situating the doctrine of God in relationship to social-construction theory allows us to look critically at how concepts and doctrines come to exist. It also allows us to take seriously what Luther calls the hiddenness of God and what Elizabeth Johnson emphasizes is the mystery that is God. In both cases, we do not know or see or name all that there is. Thus, I am proposing a paradoxical relationship in a doctrine of God between social-construction theory and revealed divine mystery.

Although certain of the hiddenness of God, Luther *is* certain of some things about God. One certainty for Luther is that God both empowers and humbles. At this point in Luther's characteristically paradoxical work does paradox extend beyond methodology and epistemology and into the core of his theology. The specific points he makes about how God empowers and how God humbles resonate well with intersectional third-wave feminism.

GOD HUMBLES

In the "Bondage of The Will," Luther describes "the humbling of our pride," using the analogy of the human being as a beast standing between and at the mercy of two riders, God and Satan.[19] This famous analogy illustrates the lack of capability that human beings have when it comes to meriting salvation and grace on our own that Luther developed fully throughout his theology. This reclamation of Paul's injunctions about justification by grace through faith in Christ effectively stripped away human work to gain or earn salvation in the eyes of God.

In 1960, feminist Valerie Saiving rightly critiqued the modern theological claim by Reinhold Niebuhr and others that the basic human sin is pride. Saiving based her argument in part on her attention to women's experiences in families and societies. An important part of her critique was how the traditional Christian value of humility was misapplied to women when their experiences of humiliation under patriarchy were not already taken into account. This is still true, and yet we might now work to reclaim the notion that God humbles by applying that idea less to individual human beings and more broadly to the human community. What this means is simple: human beings are flawed, and therefore, their work, ideas, concepts, products, and cultures are flawed. This includes religion as a product that humans construct and externalize.

For Luther, the emphasis often stayed here, on the tragic flaw embedded in the human condition. His last recorded words in a Table Talk are "we are beggars. That is true."[20] In order to get over the corruption in the Roman Church of his day, Luther was pushed to insist that humans can do nothing, that everything that humans do is worthless, in order to more clearly lift up the majesty of God's grace and to understand how it was that even he could be saved. In his 1517 "Disputation against Scholastic Theology" Luther states that "without the grace of God the will produces an act that is perverse and evil."[21] This is the beast between two riders, going wherever the rider wills. Not much could be more humble.

It is important to point out, though, that for Luther what was "worth-less" is human work—the products that humans construct, to use Berger's terminology. It is the human enterprise, then, that must be humbled. We as a species cannot do it. We can't do enough work to bring about salvation and lasting peace and harmony for ourselves or for the world. Human beings themselves are not worthless, in part because they were created in the image of God. This leads to the second part of his theological paradox.

GOD EMPOWERS

What does it mean to say that God empowers? To use Paul's words, the person is justified by the grace of God. To use Luther's words, the Christian is freed to serve the neighbor, freed from the weighty responsibility of earning salvation and meriting grace at all. This is an empowering element in Luther's theology, one that has theological as well as strategic implications. In this idea there is also paradox; it is because of the absolute dependence of the person on God for salvation that the person is liberated from earthly and ecclesial tyranny regarding her spiritual well-being. This is how Luther could help to complete the revolution of the availability and use of scripture by ordinary persons. This is how he could undercut the sacramental system that he found to be unbiblical. This is how "all of us who believe in Christ are priests . . . so exalted above all things that, by virtue of a spiritual power . . . nothing can do [us] any harm."[22] What could be more empowering than that?

GOD HUMBLES AND GOD EMPOWERS

Though much of my discussion of Luther here clearly concerns the human person, everything that is said about the person originates with Luther's doctrine of God: God humbles and God empowers.

A feminist gloss on these ideas is crucial before moving on. Saiving's genius point in 1960 was that Christianity tended to value humility when it did not attend to the specific experiences of those whom patriarchy already humiliates.[23] Feminist theologians can now argue that what the sin-as-pride notion got wrong is seeing it individually instead of corporately.[24] As a community, human beings require the humility that Luther spelled out as coming from God. The cultures and religions humans have produced that survive to this day are based on an ideology of dominance and submission that most often privilege men over women, white over "non-white," straight over gay, rich over poor, and so on. Women as well as men have accepted that this is an objective reality to which we all must adapt, thereby giving the cultural product of patriarchy more reality than it has ever merited. Distinguishing between the human community and the human person is key to understanding how God both humbles and empowers.

God humbles the human community insofar as it produces systems of privilege and oppression. To humble the human enterprise then is to delegitimize patriarchy and its dependence on white supremacy, first-world nationalism, heterosexism, and global capitalism. It is to delegitimize the patriarchal concept of God that still pervades Christian theology.

God empowers the human person to resist systems of privilege and oppression. To empower the human person is, then, to legitimate prophetic voices like Martin Luther, Jarena Lee, and Mary Daly and to continue to hear the voices in all of the margins. It is to demand new visions of God and theological systems consistent with life in the twenty-first century.

Bringing Together Third-Wave Feminism and God

A third-wave feminist doctrine of God builds on ideas from the Christian tradition and transforms them for relevance for this generation. It preserves the paradox embedded in Luther's doctrine of God as humbling and empowering and speaks to the intersectional reality of human life in the twenty-first century.

To flesh out with some more precision the way in which God humbles and empowers the human being, I draw on Lutheran pastor and theologian Philip Hefner's idea of the created co-creator. Hefner captures what I described earlier—the dependence as well as responsibility that comes with being human, created *imago Dei*. Hefner describes how "the human being is created by God to be a co-creator in the creation that God has brought into being and for which God has purposes."[25] Both the adjective *created* as well as the noun *co-creator* have specific weight in this concept. As created, human beings are conditioned, dependent, and humbled. As co-creators, human beings are free, independent, and empowered.

Human beings are co-creators not only of the world in which they live, but also co-creators of concepts of God. In the second wave of feminism, Mary Daly's early work built on Peter Berger's theories and insisted that men and women work together to construct all of reality, including theological concepts. Whereas Daly moved beyond the concept and the reality of God altogether, I have concluded that abandoning the concept itself to the patriarchal theologies of the past and present misses the point. If we abandon the concept of God completely, we leave the objectivated old-white-man-god-of-the-sky in his heaven while his minions continue to dominate the lives of the masses on earth. It is still time to engage in the co-creation of the concept itself.

Third-wave feminist theology includes an understanding of God as one who humbles the human enterprise because so much of what human beings have constructed oppresses, restricts, and destroys. Whether it be greenhouse gases, mockery of gay teenagers in middle school, systemic male privilege, white-supremacist death threats for the first black U.S. president, or a disregard for certain human lives that is a prerequisite for war, the twenty-first century is already full of examples of ways that the products of human culture have taken on a death-dealing life of their own. When economies collapse, poor people are disproportionately affected by job losses and a weakened social service infrastructure. When terrorists attack, ordinary working people are often the ones whose lives are mere collateral damage. When floodwaters rise, neighborhoods populated by the most marginalized are the first to go. When an idea of God is used to bash, to ban, and to bomb, it requires humble attention and retooling.

Third-wave feminist theology includes an understanding of God who empowers human persons. In the midst of these terrors and mind-numbing realities, hope emerges in the shape of the Women's Bean Project in Denver, providing education and job-training skills for chronically unemployed and homeless women; on the pages of the bloggers who seize a space and put their voices and stories out there for all to read; in the efforts of 2006 Nobel Peace Prize winner Muhammad Yunus who pioneered micro-loans in Bangladesh for people to buy cows or cell phones to start their own business;[26] and in a feminist faith community serving its neighborhood and praying the goddess rosary every Wednesday.[27]

There is paradox in what I have just laid out: at the same time, the work of human creation requires humbling and empowering. This is why they must be co-created with the help of God. Without God, we seem to construct and create systems of privilege and oppression and those things that oppress more than they liberate. This includes concepts of God. With God, we can envision and create those things that give life, allow for trust, and create justice. The concept of God can be effectively reclaimed by third-wave feminists with attention to the intersectional reality of human life.

The ancient metaphor and doctrine of the Trinity is finally where intersectional analysis of human identity meets an intersectional doctrine of God: God is simultaneously creator, redeemer, and sanctifier. God created human beings to be co-creators of this world, and this allows us to take seriously the power that we have and to trust women and men with that power. God redeems the world and its inhabitants for life more abundant, freeing us from enslavement to sin as well as oppression at the hands of those adhering to a dominating ideology. Living in what President Obama called in his inaugural address "this winter of our hardship," the human community requires a continual source of sustenance not to acquiesce to the constant temptation to despair and anxiety.[28] The spirit of God breathes nonviolent resistance movements into history, whispers a story of love in the worst slums of Mumbai, and makes possible the joy found in creative human work.

Conclusion

Christian theology has been missing a developed third-wave feminist voice, and third-wave feminism has been missing a substantial engagement with religion and theology. I have proposed here a third-wave feminist doctrine of God that draws on traditional resources with contemporary insights. This combination shows how the idea that God both humbles and empowers human beings provides theological substance as well as a strategic resource for social change. Both of these things can be true insofar as theological paradox remains a central characteristic of the Lutheran tradition, and both of these things must be true in order to speak to the experiences of God's revelation in the world which we continually co-create. Challenges to systems of privilege and oppression are empowered by God, while attempts at defining theology and reality once and for all time are humbled. In the same way that we now understand that human beings are not defined by one part of their identity, whether it be race, class, gender, sexuality, sinner or saint, victim or oppressor, God is not defined by one doctrine, metaphor, or set of ideas fixed in time. Being human encompasses multiple aspects of identity, and God as trinity is at the intersection of identity, in the spark of relationship, and in the cacophony of the wilderness. Inhabiting paradox is where we meet this God and where we best understand ourselves.

Suggested Reading

Berger, Peter. *The Sacred Canopy: Elements of a Sociological Theory of Religion*. New York: Anchor, 1990.

Daly, Mary. *Beyond God the Father: Toward a Philosophy of Women's Liberation*. Boston: Beacon, 1973.

Goldstein, Valerie Saiving. "The Human Situation: A Feminine View." *Journal of Religion* 40, no. 2 (April 1960): 100–112.

Johnson, Elizabeth. *She Who Is: The Mystery of God in Feminist Discourse*. New York: Crossroad, 1992.

Luther, Martin. *The Bondage of the Will: The Masterwork of the Great Reformer*. Trans. James I. Packer and O. R. Johnston. Tarrytown, N.Y.: Revell, 1957.

McDougall, Joy Ann. "Feminist Theology for a New Generation." *The Christian Century* (July 26, 2005): 20–25.

Chapter 4

God's Heart Revealed in Eden: Luther on the Character of God and the Vocation of Humanity

Kristen E. Kvam

FOR NEARLY THE LAST ten years of his life, Martin Luther lectured on the book of Genesis to students at the University of Wittenberg. In these lectures, Luther made startling claims about Genesis 3:15, where God addresses the serpent after Eve and Adam have eaten from the tree of the knowledge of good and evil. God says to the serpent: "I will put enmity between you and the woman, and between your offspring and hers; he will strike your head, and you will strike his heel." In his lecture, Luther described these words as "this first comfort, this source of all mercy and fountainhead of all promises."[1] Why would Luther regard this odd verse about enmity between seeds and the bruising of head and heels with such great esteem? Why would he describe it as the "source of all mercy and fountainhead of all promises"? Why would he have told his students earlier in the lectures that this text "contains whatever is excellent in all scripture"?[2]

This chapter examines Luther's discussion of Genesis 3:15 with an eye toward the contributions it could make for how contemporary Christians might read the story told in the opening chapters of Genesis. In exploring Luther's reasons for regarding the so-called condemnation of the serpent so highly, we must take into account Luther's debt to a Christian tradition that interprets God's statement to the serpent in Genesis 3:15 as the first time the gospel was announced and examine the ways Luther developed this tradition in regard to the situations of Eve and Adam before and after this part of the story.

This chapter seeks to present reasons for reclaiming ways that Luther retold the story—in particular, the ways his narrative affords significant insights into the character of God and the vocation of human persons. We will observe how Luther's telling accents God's mercy and grace, especially in the way God reorients the sinful Eve and the sinful Adam by calling and empowering them to fight against sin. Moreover, we will look at how Luther's portrayal of Eve opposes commonplace depictions of her as particularly treacherous, seductive, and disloyal, especially in comparison to Adam. In these ways, Luther's telling of the story in the opening chapters of Genesis offers significant treasures for the Christian imagination.

Story and Christian Witness

Although we might not stop to think about it often, storytelling is an important Christian practice. Frequently Christians tell very personal stories about their own lives and how God has been at work in them. At other times Christians turn to the biblical witness, telling stories from the Gospels or other scriptural texts. Through these and many other ways of telling stories, Christians relate to themselves and to others the meaning of the Christian faith. We use story to talk about the world in which we live and how God interacts with that world. We literally "relate" ways that sin is active in the world, and we testify to ways that God acts to defeat sin.

Theologians influenced by an approach called "narrative theology" help in thinking about the importance of the stories we tell.[3] These theologians often point to the ways that stories function in our family life to nurture—and even establish—our sense of who we are and how we ought to act. They then draw connections between the ways that stories of our families function and the ways that stories of our religious communities function to underscore the point that "story forms identity."[4]

A great advantage of this approach for Christian theologians is that narrative theology coheres well with the textures of Christian scripture. Stories fill the Bible. Often the stories tell about God—about what God has done and what God has promised to do. Time and again the Bible relates ways that God has been active in the stories of Israel and the stories told by Jesus, as well as stories told about Jesus. Also, Christians often read the Bible as telling one large story that overarches the biblical books, from Genesis to Revelation, from Eden to the eschaton. This overarching story guides Christians in understanding how reality is to be perceived and how life is to be lived in light of the beginnings and endings of this larger narrative.

Years of study and observation have taught me the importance of the story told in the opening chapters of Genesis. After all, the story of "the beginning" shapes the stories that follow. For Christians, this beginning has included God's loving creation of a good world followed shortly by Eve and Adam's fall into sin. Further, Christian tellings of this story frequently have blamed the first woman for this fall, associating her with temptation and evil, with inferiority and incredulity.

Moreover, Christians often have drawn lines of connection from the character and activity of the first woman to the character and activity of all her daughters. Christian scripture offers a powerful example of such lines of connection in the words of 1 Timothy 2:11-13, where Christians are exhorted to adopt restrictions on the speech and authority of women: "Let a woman learn in silence with full submission" (v. 11). This patriarchal injunction is followed in verse 12 with another endorsement of women's subordination: "I permit no woman to teach or have authority over a man; she is to keep silent." Important for our purposes in this chapter is to notice that these endorsements of the subordination and silencing of women are grounded in a way of reading the opening chapters of Genesis. The Timothy passage asserts that the submission and subordination of women are grounded in the story of Eve. It interprets this story as grounds for two reasons "to explain" why women are inferior to men. First, maintaining that Eve was created after Adam, it contends that women have a secondary status to men. Second, it asserts that "Adam was not deceived, but the woman was deceived and became a transgressor" (1 Tim. 2:14). This way of reading Eve's story has funded all manner of patriarchal beliefs and practices, grounding women's subordination in God's will for Eve and all of her daughters. The Timothy text is based on this reading of Genesis, outlining two reasons why Christians should "Let a woman to learn in silence with full submission" and why those in authority should "permit no woman to teach or have authority over a man; she is to keep silent."

Popular culture continues to make references to the story of Adam and Eve. The company logos of a giant in the computer industry as well as the opening credits to the television series *Desperate Housewives* draw upon details of the story, even if we don't explicitly recognize them as such. As theologian Theresa Sanders maintains: "You don't have to be religious to know the story of Adam and Eve. Nearly everyone has heard the tale, or at least heard about it. And nearly everyone has absorbed something of its symbolism."[5] While the symbolism may be overt or subtle, it plays across society in the United States and elsewhere. Thus what the symbolism conveys about the character of women and men as well as God's intentions for them, continues to shape attitudes and behaviors, beliefs, and practices.

The significance of Genesis 1–3 for both Christian theology and popular culture urges Christians to reexamine how we tell this story, especially in light of how our telling characterizes God as well as portrays the first woman and the first man. In this chapter, this takes place in conversation with Luther's lectures on Genesis. Our focus will be his remarks on Genesis 3:15. While this is a small section of the lectures that occupied the last decade of Luther's life, this tiny treasure offers a way to read the story that underscores the unmerited grace of God, allowing God's grace and mercy to empower and nurture the vocation of being human.

Genesis 3:15 and the Heart of God

Most readers of the opening chapters of Genesis will agree that God curses the serpent in Genesis 3. Even readers who look at these verses as remnants of folktales could endorse such an interpretation. For them the text explains why snakes do not have legs, since it portrays God cursing serpents to slide on their bellies. In *The New Oxford Annotated Bible*, the footnote to Genesis 3:14-15 states: "The curse contains an old explanation of why the serpent crawls rather than walks and why people are instinctively hostile to it."[6]

More difficult to see is why Luther would say that God's curse of the serpent is "a most beautiful text" that "contains whatever is excellent in all scripture."[7] Luther heaped such accolades on this passage because he followed a long-held Christian way of reading the passage that understands this text to be God's first announcement of the good news. In fact, the name for the tradition—*protoevangelium* or *protevangelion*—comes from combining a Greek term for "first" with the Greek term for "good news" or "gospel." According to this tradition, the important points made by Genesis 3:15 include God's declaration of enmity between the offspring of the serpent and the offspring of the woman, culminating in the announcement that the serpent's head will be struck or, as Luther translated the verb, "crushed." Following this tradition, Luther understood Genesis 3:15 as announcing God's promise for the future victory over Satan, a victory that would be won through Jesus Christ, the seed of woman. On the basis of seeing God making Christ known in Eden, Luther was able to describe this passage as "this first comfort, this source of all mercy and fountainhead of all promises."[8]

What might we make of Luther's reading? Clearly there will be persons who find it problematic. For one thing, the way that Luther understood this ancient text to be a prophesy of the incarnation of Jesus Christ could be denounced for projecting back into the text a meaning it never carried for its original audience. The combination of anachronism with Christians usurping texts of the Hebrew Bible for distinctively Christian purposes will be deemed as dangerous and wrongheaded for many persons.

This line of argument raises important notes of caution. Christian ways of reading the so-called Old Testament have too often disallowed non-Christian ways of interpreting these texts, showing disregard and even contempt for Jewish understandings of scripture. Yet an advantage of our current situation is an increasing recognition that texts in general and sacred texts in particular have multiple meanings. This recognition encourages study and respect for the rich ways that a text has been interpreted. As biblical scholar Phyllis Trible has pointed out, this multiplicity of meanings is at work within the Bible itself: "A single text appears in different versions with different functions in different contexts. Through application, it confesses, challenges, comforts, and condemns. What it says on one occasion, it denies on another. Thus scripture in itself yields multiple interpretations of itself."[9]

Allowing for scripture to have multiple interpretations permits us to consider a *protevangelion* interpretation of Genesis 3:15 as one possible reading of the text. Moreover, in the context of this chapter, it allows us to follow Luther's christological reading of this text to explore some benefits that arise from Luther's way of telling the story.

First, a key benefit is that Luther's narration portrays God as attentive and responsive to the crisis prompted by sin's entry into Eden. Luther's way of interpreting the text clearly relies upon an understanding of God as one who condemns the devastation effected by the introduction of evil. Earlier in the primal story, God had said that eating of the tree would result in death. But once sin erupts in Eden through Eve and Adam's disobedience, God returns to the scene and denounces the serpent, the agent who initiated the crisis, rather than denouncing Eve and Adam. This denunciation coupled with God's promise that the agent of sin would be defeated display the true character of God. According to Luther, the text "reveals God's heart" and shows "the depths of God's goodness" because God announces the good news that the tyranny of Satan will come to an end and evil will be vanquished.[10] Thus, a wonderful theological benefit of Luther's narration is the way it underscores the merciful character and activity of God.

Another benefit arises out of a surprising feature of Luther's telling. Although Genesis does not portray Eve and Adam's response to God's sentencing of the serpent, Luther's telling maintains that God's promise to defeat Satan's tyranny effectively changes the situation for the first woman and first man. Through God's promise, Eve and Adam come to recognize that God does not condemn them. Instead, according to Luther, "[t]heir guilt has been forgiven; they have been won back from death and have already been set free from hell and from those fears by which they were all but slain when God appeared."[11]

Luther's way of telling the story presents God's saving activity as effective already in Eden. Indeed, Luther's narration provides grounds for seeing Eve and Adam as already justified: "Their guilt has been forgiven." Clearly, Luther's description understands that God's salvation and justification of Eve and Adam has an "already but not yet" character to it, in that their salvation is "not yet" fully accomplished. Concerning Genesis 3:15, Luther wrote: "This, therefore, is the text that made Adam and Eve alive and brought them back from death into the life which they had lost through sin. Nevertheless, the life is one hoped for rather than one already possessed. Similarly, Paul often says (1 Cor. 15:31): 'Daily we die.'"[12]

Luther's depiction of Eve and Adam already being forgiven is an unusual way to tell the story. Much more common are Christian narrations that have justification and forgiveness going into effect in relation to the crucifixion or resurrection of Jesus Christ. Often these more usual ways of telling the story present the benefits of Christ's work as reaching back to saints of old like Adam and Eve so that they too become forgiven and justified by the work of Jesus Christ. But typically it is an event in the life, death, and resurrection of Christ Jesus that sets this saving benefit into its retroactive motion.

Luther's narration is distinctive in that Eve and Adam are forgiven and justified in Eden. In this way Luther's telling of the story offers a wonderfully expansive vision of the effects of God's grace. According to Luther's narration, God's grace to sinners reaches across the span of time and space, from the beginnings in Eden to the endings in the eschaton. How fitting that Luther maintained that God's heart is revealed in Genesis 3. Could there be a more expansive way to depict the heart of God?

Noteworthy also is the way that Luther's telling of the story echoes his reformatory insight that God's grace takes effect apart from any human action that would merit it or initiate it. There is nothing that Eve or Adam can do to earn God's forgiveness. They don't even ask to be forgiven. Instead, in the scene prior to the serpent's condemnation, they each have tried to diminish the seriousness of their own participation in sin by blaming someone else for making them do what was wrong. So there is no way that either of them has contributed anything to their justification, certainly neither repentance nor contrition nor even a prayer. Prior to God's announcement that sin will be vanquished, Eve and Adam truly are in bondage to sin. No effort of their own contributes to the great change in their situation. Instead, truly liberating justification is given solely by God. Thus, Luther's way of telling what happens to Adam and Eve illustrates the proclamation of evangelical freedom from the bondage of sin, including liberation from being enslaved to a false estimation of human works. Before Eve and Adam do anything salutary, God graciously reaches out to them with mercy.

Genesis 3:15 and the Vocation of Humanity

In addition to underscoring the mercy and grace of God, Luther's lecture remarks on Genesis 3:15 portray radical changes for Eve and Adam brought about by the revelation of God's grace and mercy. By exploring these changes, we can better understand Luther's insights into the vocation of human persons, male and female, and how this vocation includes trusting in God's mercy and grace as well as living in light of God's grace and mercy. We can also see that humanity's vocation includes having the courage to fight against sin.

In order to see Luther's sense of the tremendous changes arising out of God's curse of the serpent, it is important to lengthen our look at Genesis 3 by stepping back in the storyline to Eve and Adam's situation before God promises to defeat Satan. Luther's depiction of Adam and Eve prior to the revelation of God's mercy provides a stark contrast to the hope and trust that becomes theirs when God promises to crush sin. According to Luther's telling, prior to the revelation of God's grace and mercy, Adam and Eve were literally in a terrible situation: "Nothing is more terrible than to be in sin and yet to be remote from, or ignorant of, the forgiveness of sins or the promise of grace."[13] As long as God's intentions to forgive sin and conquer evil were unknown to Eve and Adam, they were living in a downward spiral of fear and sin that led them to try to hide from God. When hiding from God was no longer possible, they each accused others— Adam accusing Eve, and Eve accusing the serpent—for their own failings.

Luther's telling does not fault Eve and Adam for this downward spiral. Neither does he condemn them for accusing other creatures (and thereby the Creator) for their own misdeeds when God inquired of each of them what had happened. Instead, according to Luther, they actually could not have done other than respond in fear—with excuses and accusations. In his discussion of Adam's response to God's query, "Have you eaten from the tree?" Luther wrote, "Here Adam is presented as a typical instance of all sinners and of such as despair because of their sin. They cannot do otherwise than accuse God and excuse themselves."[14]

Luther made a similar point when describing Eve's response:

> After unbelief follows the disobedience of all [human] powers and parts. After this disobedience follows later on the excuse and defense of sin; and after the defense, the accusation and condemnation of God. This is the last step of sin, to insult God and charge [God] with being the originator of sin. Unless hearts are given courage through trust in mercy, this nature cannot be urged beyond this point if there are successive steps of sin.[15]

According to Luther, Eve and Adam share equally the characteristics of sin.

Significant in each of these lecture remarks is the empathy with which Luther interpreted Adam and Eve's statements of self-defense. This empathy is grounded in Luther's understanding that, at this point in the story, Adam and Eve are living in desperation and fear because they do not yet have full insight into the grace of God. As long as God's intentions to forgive sin and vanquish evil are unknown to them, they do not know the heart of God.

Although Genesis itself does not portray the responses of Adam and Eve to God's sentencing of the serpent, Luther's telling maintains that Eve and Adam understand God's statement in Genesis 3:15 as God's promise to defeat Satan's tyranny. Moreover, Luther's conviction is that God's promise awakens trust and hope within Adam and Eve: "Wholeheartedly they grasped the hope of their restoration, and full of faith, they saw that God cared about their salvation."[16] The lives of Eve and Adam are dramatically reoriented. No longer are they terrified. Instead, once God has promised ultimate victory over sin and Satan, they come to live in the light of this promise.

Luther's discussion of Eve's response to the birth of Cain (Gen. 4:1) presents a wonderful portrait of Eve as a model for living on the basis of God's promise. To see the contours of Luther's portrait, it is important to notice that Eve's statement in Hebrew contains a wordplay based on the association between Cain's name and the Hebrew verb *qanah*. The NRSV translates her response as "I have produced a man with the help of the LORD," and provides a footnote for the verb, indicating that in Hebrew it "resembles the word for Cain." This wordplay did not escape Luther's attention. In fact, according to Luther, Eve not only thought she had produced a man-child, she thought she had given birth to the promised seed—the child who would be victorious over Satan. Thus, Luther's understanding of Eve's trust in God's promise to defeat Satan incorporates the sense that Eve believed Cain would be the one to crush the serpent's head. On this basis, Luther's telling restates Eve's response in a way that underscores her belief that she has given birth to the promised seed: "I have gotten the man of God who will conduct himself more properly and with greater good fortune than my Adam and I conducted ourselves in Paradise. For this reason I do not call him my son, but he is the man of God who was promised and provided by God."[17]

As might be expected, Luther's view that Eve understood Cain to be the promised seed provided Luther grounds for criticizing Eve. At a few points in his discussion of her declaration, she is faulted for having "a false hope," for believing "on the strength of some opinion of her own, without a definite sign and without a definite Word," and for reaching "a hasty conclusion."[18] Luther's criticisms, however, do not condemn Eve. Indeed, each criticism connects with a positive point made about Eve's faith. For example, his reference to Eve's false hope is part of a larger statement about her faith, a statement that praises Eve for her saintliness: "Although this was a false hope, it nevertheless is clear that Eve was a saintly woman and that she believed the promise concerning the future salvation through the blessed Seed."[19] The second criticism—that Eve believed on the basis of her own opinion without a definite sign from God—appears within the context of Luther's discussion of how Eve believed in God's promise even though she was mistaken about the person to whom this promise referred. Luther's discussion opens with an approval of Eve's faith: "Eve does right in holding fast this way to the divine promise and to her faith in the deliverance through her son. Through this faith in the future Seed all the saints were justified and sanctified."[20] Third, the description of Eve reaching a "hasty conclusion" also appears in the midst of ascribing great faith to Eve. Here, according to Luther, "[h]er extreme trust in the promise causes Eve to reach a hasty conclusion."[21]

The larger context of each of these three criticisms demonstrates that Luther's primary emphasis is on the faith of Eve, not on her mistake. Indeed, in Luther's telling of the story, Eve is presented as "a saintly woman." Although she errs in identifying Cain as God's promised seed, her mistake does not disqualify her from being a model of faith. Instead, as we saw in the aforementioned quotation: "Eve does right in holding fast this way to the divine promise."[22]

Luther's presentation of Eve as a saint and a model of faith contrasts sharply with the negative traditions associating Eve primarily with sin and seduction, stupidity and credulity. Later, when discussing Eve's response to the birth of Seth after Cain had killed Abel, Luther's description of Eve continues to be saintly. According to Luther, "Since the pope's church has invented such a vast swarm of saints, it is indeed amazing that it did not give a place in the list to Eve, who was full of faith, love, and endless crosses."[23]

Eve's way of construing her life in light of God's promise provides an example of the human vocation to live one's life on the basis of God's mercy and grace. Eve's response to Cain's birth demonstrates her trust in God's promise that the seed of woman would triumph over Satan. When considering the vocation of being human, this sense that persons are called to live their lives in light of God's intention to defeat sin is a wonderful treasure from Luther. Like Eve, we too are called to be attentive for signs of God's activity in the world and in our lives. Also like Eve, our mistakes about how God's intention is to be realized do not discredit the value of our witness to God's promise.

In addition to depicting the human vocation of trusting God's promise to conquer the tyranny of sin, Luther's lecture remarks on Genesis 3:15 show the understanding he had that Eve and Adam themselves are called to fight against sin. In describing the response of Eve and Adam to hearing God's curse of the serpent, Luther wrote: "They even hear themselves drawn up, as it were, in battle against their condemned enemy, and this with the hope of help from the Son of God, the seed of the woman."[24] His assertion that "Adam and Eve are set into conflict with this enemy to keep them busy,"[25] makes a similar point.

These descriptions of Adam and Eve being called to contend against sin demonstrate Luther's understanding that a dramatic transformation has taken place in the lives of the first man and the first woman because of God's promise to defeat sin. In Luther's telling of the story, prior to God's curse of the serpent, Eve and Adam are paralyzed by their despair and their fear. Indeed, they are terrified. Yet once God promises ultimate victory over Satan, their lives are re-oriented. They come to recognize that God's promise includes conquering sin and evil, and they now live in light of this promise—in faith and trust but also in courage and commitment. Indeed, we see that their trust in God's promise instills them with the courage to contend against sin. Because faith and hope can be misinterpreted as passive virtues, it is important to underscore Luther's conviction that trust and hope encourage believers—even the very first ones—to fight against sin. God's grace empowers them to join God in contending against the forces of "their condemned enemy."[26]

Luther's lectures offer no hint of worry that Eve and Adam might have been tempted by a form of "works righteousness," whereby they would have seen their battles against sin as meriting or contributing to their salvation. Perhaps this is because Luther's understanding that the dramatic transformation from fear, despair, and paralysis to courage, hope, and active opposition to sin was effected by the grace of God. The sequence of the story is important here. Eve and Adam do not set their own transformation into motion. Rather, it is the grace and promise of God that changes their lives.

Conclusion

Our careful examination of Luther's lecture remarks on Genesis 3:15 enables us to notice several contrasts between the tradition of associating Eve with danger and weakness and the characterization of Eve offered by Luther in this section of his lectures. Rather than Eve representing the possibility of sin and evil, Luther's rendering of her embodies the possibility of trust and faith. Moreover, in contrast to the tradition of describing Eve as weak, Luther's remarks maintain that she, like Adam, was called by God to engage in the most rigorous engagement—namely, to actively contend against sin and its consequences.

Our close study of Luther's lecture remarks also shows that his adoption of the *protevangelion* tradition is in no way superficial. Instead, his understanding that God announced the good news in Eden has far-reaching implications for the way Luther tells the story of Eve and Adam. Luther's sense that God promises the ultimate defeat of sin and evil in Genesis 3:15 informs Luther's understanding that the grace and mercy of God are actualized in Eden. God's promise making also influences Luther's understanding of the dramatic transformation in the lives of Adam and Eve and their descendents. Through God's promise, they are empowered to live in hope and trust and they are encouraged to contend against sin.

Suggested Reading

Jones, Serene. *Feminist Theory and Christian Theology: Cartographies of Grace*. Guides to Theological Inquiry. Minneapolis: Fortress Press, 2000.

Jones, Serene, and Paul Lakeland, eds. *Constructive Theology: A Contemporary Approach to Classical Themes*. Minneapolis: Fortress Press, 2005.

Karant-Nunn, Susan C., and Merry Hanks-Wiesner. *Luther on Women: A Sourcebook*. Cambridge: Cambridge University Press, 2003.

Kvam, Kristen E., Linda S. Schearing, and Valarie H. Ziegler, eds. *Eve and Adam: Jewish, Christian, and Muslim Readings on Genesis and Gender*. Bloomington and Indianapolis: Indiana University Press, 1999.

Martin, Dale B. *Pedagogy of the Bible: An Analysis and Proposal*. Louisville: Westminster John Knox, 2009.

Pellauer, Mary, with Susan Brooks Thistlethwaite. "Conversation on Grace and Healing: Perspectives from the Movement to End Violence Against Women." In *Lift Every Voice: Constructing Theologies from the Underside*, ed. by Susan Brooks Thistelthwaite and Mary Potter Engel, 169–85. San Francisco: HarperSanFrancisco, 1990.

Trible, Phyllis. *God and the Rhetoric of Sexuality*. Overtures to Biblical Theology. Minneapolis: Fortress Press, 1978.

PART 3

Sin and Grace

LAYING OPEN THE RICHES of the Lutheran tradition on two central doctrines—
sin and grace—Mary Lowe and Anna Mercedes respectively expand the riches
of Martin Luther's thought by reclaiming it through sharp queer and feminist
analyses. In turn, they explicate sin and grace as subject positions, both of which
are before God and oriented to the neighbor, the other. In chapter 5, Lowe
articulates a doctrine of sin that rightfully and equally adheres to each of us, no
matter our sexuality. She criticizes the all-too-frequent misogynism and homophobia in Western Christian theology, using Luther's concepts of *coram Deo* and
saint and sinner to develop a new model of sin. In chapter 6, Mercedes responds
to multiple critiques of the effects of the cross particularly on abused women
and girls. She evokes the grace of the cross, especially for those who have been
abused, by mining theological treasures that recall the formlessness Christ took
on the cross to call those who have been pressed away from themselves back to
themselves and therefore also to others.

Chapter 5

Sin from a Queer, Lutheran Perspective

Mary E. Lowe

WHY SHOULD A QUEER, Lutheran theologian care about the doctrine of sin? Very simply, because the charge that lesbians and gays are "deviant sinners" has been used for centuries to violently oppress them. Lesbian, gay, bisexual, transgender, queer, and intersex (LGBTQI) individuals have been viewed as the most "unnatural" of sinners and portrayed as disordered in their nature in a way that straight persons have not.[1] However, LGBTQI Christians cannot set the doctrine of sin aside. For Lutherans in particular, confessing one's sins is an important step in justification, and recognizing how one is being sinned against is a vital part of liberation. There are theological and pastoral motives for launching a queer investigation of sin and crafting a doctrine that does not reinforce homophobic theology or heterosexist church policies. In addition, a proposal is needed that explains how and why individuals participate in sinful structures without placing the blame either on the fall in the garden or on the powerful networks that trap humans. A doctrine of sin is needed that provides a space for *all* persons for confession and reconciliation regardless of their sex, desire, or gender.

There are surprising resources in Martin Luther's theology and queer theory to craft this new model of sin. As a Lutheran I am profoundly influenced by Luther's assertion that Christians are saint and sinner (*simul justus et peccator*) and before God (*coram Deo*). As a queer feminist theologian I am indebted to my feminist, womanist, and mujerista colleagues who have crafted new models of sin as brokenness, diffusion, and defilement.[2] The doctrine of sin proposed here

71

is also shaped by queer theory's insights regarding the instability of human identity and the fluidity of sex and gender. Combining Luther's claim that we are *simul justus et peccator* with queer theory's commitment that legal, medical, and economic discourses constitute and constrain persons yields a view of sin that acknowledges how individuals come to be in sinful social and gender discourses and recognizes the character of human existence as bound and free. Luther's claim that humans are *coram Deo* resonates with the theoretical assertion that persons occupy subject positions in relationships, and together these can be employed to define sin as a subject position. A thoroughly relational doctrine of sin emerges from these pairings in which sin exists in the relational nature of the person, is seen in human participation in distorting discourses, and understood primarily in terms of sinful subject positions.

Theologians have long relied on other disciplines to reconstruct doctrines. Feminist scholar Rosemary Ruether has drawn from Ancient Near Eastern history, womanist theologian Delores Williams from slave narratives, and systematic theologian Wolfhart Pannenberg from physics.[3] I borrow the concepts of discourse and subject position from queer theory to craft a new doctrine of sin. However, since this is a work of Christian theology, these theoretical concepts must serve the central claim that humans are created good by God; they sin, but still possess responsibility and limited agency.

What Is Queer Theory?

Not all LGBTQI persons use the term *queer*. For some, queer remains a derogatory slur. For others queer is a powerful way of affirming their identity, or saying, "I am not 100 percent gay or lesbian; my sexuality is fluid and in process." To call oneself queer is to personally challenge the labels. Queer is also a verb—a way of thinking and interrogating common-sense beliefs about gender, sexuality, theology, the Bible, meaning, and identity. Queer theory is a distinct field of critical theory that traces its lineage back through feminist theory. Just as feminists challenged the idea that women have a unique nature or essence, queer theorists reject the categories of gay, lesbian, straight and the assumption that one's biology determines one's desire. According to Lois Tyson, author of *Critical Theory*:

> For queer theory, categories of sexuality cannot be defined by such simple oppositions as homosexual/heterosexual. Building on deconstruction's insights into human subjectivity (selfhood) as a fluid, fragmented, dynamic collectivity . . . queer theory defines individual sexuality as a fluid, fragmented, dynamic collectivity of possible sexualities. . . . Thus, sexuality

is completely controlled neither by our biological sex . . . nor by the way culture translates biological sex into gender roles.[4]

Notice the connection between the critique of selfhood and the rejection of gender essentialism.[5] Queer theorists, along with critical and feminist theorists, challenge the belief that human identity is autonomous, enduring, and isolated from the world. This critique calls into question familiar anthropological claims from Christian theology such as the belief that all persons possess an autonomous essence or enduring nature that exists prior to its constitution in language, endures through time, and is largely unaffected by the conditions and relationships in which the individual exists. In contrast to this autonomous portrait of the subject, queer theorists aver that identity is in process and constituted by discourse, language, and relations.

What's Wrong with the Doctrine of Sin from a Queer Perspective?

The feminist critique of the doctrine of sin has a rich history, and womanist and mujerista theologians have continued the challenge. One of their central arguments is that the inherited doctrine blames woman for the first sin, charges women as more likely to sin than men, and views bodies and sex as dangerous and polluting. These theologians also reject the claim that humans originally existed in righteousness and then fell into sin. There is much to commend in these critiques, but our excavation of sin must dig deeper. From a queer perspective, there are additional problems with these inherited teachings. To begin, queer biblical scholars have shown how negative cultural stereotypes about same-sex relations have been preached as God's infallible word.[6] Informed by Romans 1:28, homoerotic attraction is viewed as the result of a person's failure to acknowledge God, and as a consequence, God gives the individual over to "degrading" passions. In addition, same-sex relations are sinful because they go against nature. Luther echoed this sentiment when reflecting on the Sodom story.

> The heinous conduct of the people of Sodom is extraordinary, inasmuch as they departed from the natural passion and longing of the male for the female, which was implanted into nature by God, and desired what is altogether contrary to nature. Whence comes this perversity? Undoubtedly from Satan, who after people have once turned away from the fear of God, so powerfully suppresses nature that he blots out the natural desire and stirs up a desire that is contrary to nature.[7]

This sin against nature has also been described as the most damning form of sin. John Chrysostom wrote:

> In ancient times this practice appears to have been the law, and one legisla-
> tor forbade household slaves to . . . love boys, conceding this prerogative—
> or, rather, vice—only to the freeborn. . . . I tell you that such people are even
> worse than murderers. . . . Whatever sin you mention. . . . There is nothing,
> absolutely nothing more demented or noxious than this wickedness.[8]

Another problem is that sexual sins are said to pollute and defile the body in a way that other sins do not. Paul wrote, "Every sin that a person commits is outside the body; but the fornicator sins against the body itself" (1 Cor. 6:18). When reflecting on Romans 1, Luther also claimed that certain sexual sins lead to physical pollution: "Those who do not acknowledge God . . . should be catapulted into the lowest and the worst uncleanliness, that they have not only an unclean heart . . . but also an unclean body."[9] Anything outside of heterosexual relations in marriage, Luther thought, led to an unclean heart, which led to an unclean body.

All of these accusations of sin create emotional hardship and physical danger for LGBTQI persons. But the most dangerous problem is also the most insidious. Dominant Christian teachings assume that the sin of same-sex relations is a part of the autonomous essence of the person. Therefore LGBTQI persons have been seen as sinful in their enduring nature in a way that straight "sinners" have not. In addition, same-sex desire supposedly reflects a stable being that is further disordered by homoerotic acts.[10] Numerous queer historians have identified how modern thought makes this connection between sexual acts and identity. While earlier cultures viewed homoerotic relations as *actions* taken by an individual, modern Western cultures assume that same-sex desire reflects the truth about an individual's autonomous essence.[11] Thus, a person who has sex that goes against nature possesses an essence that is unnatural. Theologian and philosopher of religion Mark D. Jordan traces how the sin of sodomy became the *identity* Sodomite in penitential and theological texts:

> All that you need to know about the Sodomites is that they practiced
> Sodomy. . . . A term like Sodomy suggests . . . that it is possible to reduce
> persons to a single essence, which can then be found in other persons. . . .
> As a recurring essence, it would seem to justify recourse to . . . a punishment
> as near as one can get to the divine fires that poured down on Sodom.[12]

Thus the desire, the act, the enduring nature, and the body of the LGBTQI individual are all viewed as sinful. A recent Vatican statement evinces this perspective.

[H]omosexual acts go against the natural moral law. . . . They do not proceed from a genuine affective and sexual complementarity. . . . Sacred Scripture condemns homosexual acts 'as a serious depravity.' . . . This judgment of Scripture does . . . attest to the fact that homosexual acts are intrinsically disordered.[13]

The term *intrinsically* implies that there is an enduring nature that is contrary to the order of creation. To counter this essential understanding of sin, a new relational portrait of the human person can be employed to complement a new model of sin as discourse and as subject positions.

Another critique that queer, Lutheran theology can bring to discussions about sin is that social structures should not be blamed as the primary cause of sin. From a Lutheran standpoint, the theory of social sin places responsibility for sin outside of persons and denies the biblical claim that sin is a part of human existence. From a queer perspective the social-sin approach incorrectly assumes that individuals possess an enduring nature, rather than continually coming to be within language, social location, and material conditions.[14] A queer, Lutheran, relational model of sin and the subject maintains that we are connected in, with, and under sinful structures in a way that actually shapes our identity and language. Thus the connection between the person and sinful social structures is much stronger and more intertwined than that found in the theory of social sin. In order to produce a model of sin that doesn't designate one group of people as more sinful than others and encourages all persons to recognize their sin and claim the gift of forgiveness, we can combine the theoretical concept of discourse with Luther's insight that humans are *simul justus et peccator*, and weave the theological insight regarding *coram Deo* together with the philosophical concept of subject position.[15]

Sin as Discourse

Sin historically has been defined as pride, lust, powerlessness, alienation, and lack of trust. It is in the best spirit of Christian theology that these interpretations spring from the experiences of people in different contexts. For example, Augustine saw sin as a turning from God to the self (concupiscence), while Delores Williams defines sin as the invisibilization of black women. I suggest that we add a new definition—sin as discourse—to the list. Discourse is very difficult to define, but think of it as systems of rules, expectations, and practices, almost like rules of grammar. Each of us exists in a field of competing discourses (just and unjust) that create and regulate the language, identities, and practices available to us. Chris Weedon, feminist cultural theorist, provides this definition:

> Discourses . . . are ways of constituting knowledge, together with social
> practices, forms of subjectivity and power relations. . . . Discourses are
> more than ways of thinking and producing meaning. They constitute the
> nature of the body, unconscious and conscious mind and the emotional life
> of the subjects they seek to govern.[16]

In the 1960s French philosopher Michel Foucault developed discourse analysis
and investigated the way legal, economic, and medical discourses created the
identity that we currently know as mentally ill.[17] Allow me to give an example
of how discourses function to reward or punish identities and practices. Let's say
that a gay couple wants to get married. Numerous discourses (religious, psychological, legal, and economic) are operating to impose rules and interpretations
on the couple. A conservative Christian discourse says that being gay is "unnatural" and condemns the union. The discourse from psychology would allow the
marriage because homosexuality is considered normal. Currently there is no one
legal discourse regarding gay unions. Some states allow it; others don't. There
are also economic discourses at play. A welcoming state like Massachusetts may
benefit financially from gay tourist dollars. Finally, a progressive religious discourse would celebrate the marriage. These competing discourses interpret the
marriage differently and create specific identities for the two men: newlyweds,
sinners, consumers, deviants. This is the constituting character of discourse; discourses don't create individuals, but they generate accepted identities and subject positions such as heterosexual and wife, as well as deviant identities such as
homosexual and lover. And some discourses have governmental and economic
power behind them so that persons deemed deviant, foreigner, or queer can be
constrained, deported, or punished because of their identities.

Some discourses are sinful and distorting, and we sin when we actively or
passively participate in them. In the example above, the conservative religious
discourse that lesbians and gays are unnatural can be considered sinful because it
rejects the diversity of God's creation, it denies that all are *imago Dei*, it impedes
the flourishing of all persons, and it claims that gender is God-given rather than
acknowledge that beliefs about gender are constructed. This sinful homophobic discourse is more than just a belief because legal and economic rules and
practices are brought to bear upon LGBTQI persons. As a lesbian, economic
and legal discourses make it nearly impossible for me to benefit from a legally
recognized marriage, while distorted religious and cultural discourses tell me
that I am an "unnatural" sinner. These unjust discourses operate simultaneously,
placing me in a deviant subject position.

But no one is solely a victim in discourse theory. Each person is constructed
by discourses, but each also has agency to participate in or resist sinful discourses
and structures. For example, as a white person, describing sin as discourse helps

me better understand how my thoughts and actions are shaped by racist discourses, and how I am complicit in them. Racism is more than merely a sinful structure; it is a discourse that shapes my language and constitutes me as a person. The color of my skin earns me economic, employment, and medical payoffs every day, and by participating in and benefiting from dominant racist discourses, I sin. Humans don't just exist *in* sinful structures; they *come to be* as sinners (and saints) in distorted discourses. I can repent from the sin of racism, but because there is no place outside of discourse, I can never fully give up my privileged white subject position.[18]

Conceiving of sin as discourse exposes the sinful discourses of racism and homophobia, illuminates how individuals are constituted in discourse, and explains why it can be so hard to be converted from active or passive participation in sinful structures. There are, however, shortcomings in this proposal. Discourses seem so powerful that human freedom may be compromised, radical conversion appears impossible, and discourse theory does not allow for human openness to the future. Fortunately, Luther's assertion that humans are *simul justus et peccator* can strengthen the weaknesses in this model of sin.

Luther's *Simul Justus et Peccator*

A great deal has been published on Luther's assertion that humans are simultaneously saint and sinner, and many recognize this as one of his most significant insights. In his commentary on Romans, Luther wrote: "Now, is he [the Christian] perfectly righteous? No, for he is at the same time both a sinner and a righteous man; a sinner in fact, but a righteous man by the sure imputation and promise of God that He will continue to deliver him from sin."[19] For the purposes of weaving Luther's *simul* concept together with sin as discourse it is helpful to briefly identify the key elements of *simul justus et peccator*. For Luther, *simul* is natural, paradoxical, relational, and eschatological. When Luther described Christians as saint and sinner he was rejecting the medieval teaching that sin was merely sinful acts or a lack of original righteousness; he was arguing that humans are sinful by nature and that individual sins spring from the tinder of sin in them.[20] Luther identified the basic forms of sin as unbelief and pride and *curvatus en se* in which the human puts her/himself in the place of God.[21]

But Luther does not abandon his readers in sin; the irony is that they are *justified* sinners. He wrote, "In myself outside of Christ, I am a sinner; in Christ outside of myself, I am not a sinner."[22] There is a paradoxical character to Christian life. Rather than being forgiven and never sinning again, humans sin repeatedly and are forgiven continually. This double character is also echoed in Luther's claim that humans are bound to sin but free in Christ to serve the neighbor. "About this kind of love he [Paul] says that though he was free, yet he made himself the servant of all. This kind of servitude is the highest freedom, for it lacks nothing and receives nothing, but rather gives and bestows."[23] This paradox of saint and sinner, bound and free, empowers the Christian for action on behalf of others in the world.

Simul justus et peccator also emphasizes that sin is relational. Sin is not primarily committed against the commandments or the natural order (although this is Luther's main problem with sodomy). Humans sin in relationship to other beings—be it God, others, or the self, and Luther consistently argued that sins against the neighbor are as harmful as sins against God. "He who does right, shows this with fruits, and no longer sins against his neighbor is born of God. And he who does not do right to his neighbor is a false Christian, not a true one. God does not want those Christians who do not do right. God loves righteousness."[24] Luther also framed sin in terms of affiliation when he explained the *coram* relationships (before God, society, and the world). This relational timbre to *simul justus et peccator* reflects Luther's broader commitment that humans should orient themselves toward God and the neighbor, and neither turn in on the self nor away from the future: "And this is the reason why our theology is certain: it snatches us away from ourselves and places us outside ourselves, so that we . . . depend on that which is outside ourselves, that is, on the promise and truth of God."[25]

Simul justus et peccator is not merely an ontological claim about who we are in the present moment; it is also a temporal claim about our destiny as forgiven saints. British theologian Daphne Hampson recognizes this eschatological dimension: "We can express the Lutheran *simul* in another way. . . . The Christian has a double sense of time. He lives 'from' the future, in that his sense of himself now is derived from his sense of Christ. . . . It is in this sense that Luther is future orientated."[26] Luther's description of the exchange between Christ and the believer makes it clear that future salvation is already present. "Thus the soul that trusts Christ and receives him as its bridegroom . . . is free from all sins, secure against death and hell, and given eternal righteousness, life, and salvation."[27] The paradox of freedom and bondage, natural sin and future hope that Luther expressed with *simul justus et peccator* can correct the fatalism in the model of sin as discourse.

Sin as Discourse + *Simul Justus et Peccator*

When evaluating sin as discourse, I suggested that the deterministic influences of discourse may compromise human freedom and leave little room for conversion. In addition, queer theory is highly suspicious of unifying theories such as the eschatological Christian metanarratives that all of creation will be reconciled to God. Fortunately, by weaving *simul justus et peccator* into the discourse model, these limitations can be overcome. Luther's claim that humans are saint and sinner is another way of talking about how persons are free and bound. Remember that Luther, too, had a very limited understanding of freedom: as sinners, persons are bound to sin; as saints, they are free from the law to serve the neighbor. Luther strongly rejected the claim that humans possess any freedom regarding their relationship with God, but he acknowledged that individuals can exercise freedom in worldly matters. "[A] man should know that with regard to his faculties and possessions he has the right to use, to do, or to leave undone, according to his own free choice. . . . On the other hand in relation to God . . . a man has no free choice."[28] This paradoxical freedom in Luther's *simul* provides the freedom necessary to be converted from distorted beliefs and behaviors in unjust discourses and sinful structures. But this freedom does not come from the will or agency of the individual; it comes from outside the person as gift. As bound and free, individuals are given the freedom to resist dominant, unjust discourses.

Another benefit of weaving *simul justus et peccator* into sin as discourse is that conversion is possible. The discourse theory that informs this model of sin cannot explain radical conversion to God or to others, or away from sin because discourses are extremely powerful and human agency is severely limited. Yet a reorientation of one's life to God is central to the Christian story. *Simul justus et peccator* carries with it the idea of always turning, of simultaneity, of a daily remembrance of baptism, and of conversion. "[T]he old creature in us with all sins and evil desires is to be drowned and die through daily contrition and repentance, and on the other hand that daily a new person is to come forth and rise up to live before God in righteousness and purity forever."[29] A radical turning toward God is the work of the Holy Spirit, and although it may not fit in a theoretical framework, it is necessary in a theological one. Luther wrote: "[M]*etanoia* signifies a changing of the mind and heart, because it seemed to indicate not only a change of heart, but also a manner of changing it, i.e., the grace of God."[30] Luther's anthropology and discourse theory both aver that human agency is severely limited and reject the position that the human will or soul is the site of freedom or conversion. Whereas a postmodern perspective limits freedom because of the power of discourse, Luther argued that any freedom (even earthly) and potential for conversion comes from outside the person— from God.

Luther's *simul justus et peccator* strengthens the definition of sin as discourse because it bears an eschatological quality lacking in discourse theory. His claim that Christians are saint and sinner means that they are being drawn into their future in Christ, and this hope constitutes their present. "They are actually sinners, but they are righteous by the imputation of a merciful God. They are unknowingly righteous and knowingly unrighteous; they are sinners in fact but righteous in hope."[31] It should be noted that the eschatological orientation of *simul justus et peccator* does not mean that the Christian is inattentive to the present needs of the world. The opposite is true, because service to the neighbor is the ultimate expression of love for God and trust in God's future.

The strengths of sin as discourse still stand, and now with Luther's insights regarding freedom, conversion, and hope woven into the proposal, it seems that there is much to affirm. Sin as discourse exposes homophobic ideologies as sinful, and explains how sinful discourses shape us.

Sin as a Subject Position

What if sin is understood relationally rather than ontologically? We could redefine sin as a subject position that persons occupy in relationship with God, one another, and creation. Defining sin this way explains human complicity in sinful structures and places the locus of sin in distorted relationships rather than in an autonomous essence of the person. Recall that queer theory contends that individuals become who they are in a network of competing legal, religious, and medical discourses, and each of us occupies multiple positions in discourse. For example, in relationship to my mother I occupy the subject position of daughter. I'm a professor to my students and a mortgage holder to my bank. To say that persons occupy subject positions does more than merely identify relationships; it involves an analysis of social and economic forces and a complex understanding of the way power is exercised upon and taken up by individuals. One cannot merely choose a subject position; instead, discourses constrain persons and regulate subject positions. For example, the 2000 U.S. census questionnaire offered two gendered subject positions (male and female) and fourteen racial subject positions. The government determined how many gender and racial identities were available, and if a person didn't fit these categories there could be political and economic consequences for the individual and their community.[32]

The concept of subject positions also explains how and why individuals benefit from and take up sinful subject positions in discourse. Recall the earlier example of the gay couple who wants to marry. They each occupy numerous subject positions—middle class, gay, consumer, home owner, deviant, white. From one point of view, these men have been regulated into subject positions that constrain them and deny them privileges afforded straight couples. However, they also benefit from occupying such subject positions as white, home owner, and middle class, and enjoy privileges not afforded others. The men are neither 100 percent saints nor 100 percent sinners. Mary McClintock Fulkerson, theologian and feminist theorist, describes this complexity: "[W]e may speak of multiple subject positions. Since subjects are produced in many different discursive games or practices, there are many constructions of subjects—hence complex subject positions."[33] While occupying the gay subject position, the men are sinned against as victims of discrimination. In the subject positions of white, middle class, the men may be sinning against those who do not occupy these positions (African Americans and those living in poverty). Describing sin as subject positions makes it possible to see how the same individual can sin against others while simultaneously being sinned against by others.

What difference does it make to view sin as a subject position occupied by a person who is relationally constituted, rather than to think of sin as a distortion of the stable being of a person? Let's look again at the example of the gay man who hopes to marry. If we employ the traditional definition of sin, the man inherits original sin, possesses an autonomous self, has sinful desires, and is sinful in his enduring nature. However, with a relational anthropology and sin defined as discourse and subject position, the man's situation changes. He does not inherit the sin of his parents, but sin is still a part of his human nature. His nature is continually emerging—not fixed and autonomous—and is profoundly shaped by his relationships. Sin is primarily relational and occurs when the man is taken up by and participates in distorted discourses and subject positions. Because he does not possess a stable being, whatever sin he commits does not reflect back onto his autonomous essence. Furthermore, since all discourses about sexuality are constructed, same-sex relationships are not sinful. Conceiving of sin as a subject position explains why humans sin against one another without appealing to an historic fall or an enduring nature and highlights the fact that we always sin in relationship. But once again, human freedom may be overly determined. Sin as a subject position also does not allow for the Christian claim that God positions us in relationship to Godself. Finally, claiming that subjects are related to one another in discourse does not imply any ethical obligation to the neighbor. Here again, a concept borrowed from queer theory can be strengthened with an insight from Luther: humans are *coram Deo* (before God).

Coram Deo

Luther's concept of *coram Deo* reveals several of his fundamental beliefs about God and human beings. He explains what it means to be regarded by God in his reflection on Psalm 73:

> There is a difference between "before me" and "before God," not in a spatial sense, since we are before God everywhere, and all things are before Him and before us, but according to knowledge and attitude. . . . Therefore in Scripture we frequently find the phrase "in the presence of God," "before God," "with God," "in front of God." We are before God when we acknowledge and love those things that God has chosen. Thus the soul is before God and before His face.[34]

For Luther, God is the creator and initiator of the *coram* relationship. Humans do not bring themselves before God, but God graciously "regards" humans. "One meaning of the Latin word, *coram*, is "before the eyes of," or "to be in the sight of another."[35] To come into the sight of God is a moment of grace and part of justification whereby the human admits that she/he is a sinner, acknowledges God's righteousness, and receives God's salvation through Jesus Christ. Recognizing oneself as a sinful subject before God is a part of the process of being regarded by God. Luther scholar E. Gordon Rupp recognizes the connection between the human sense of affliction or temptation (*Anfechtung*) and the *coram* relationship in Luther's thought. According to Rupp, "The whole meaning of 'Anfechtung' for Luther lies in the thought that man has his existence 'Coram Deo,' and that he is less the active intelligence imposing itself on the stuff of the universe around him, than the subject of an initiative and action from God who employs the whole of man's existence as a means of bringing men to awareness of their need and peril."[36] In the *coram Deo* relationship we see ourselves as we really are—created, forgiven sinners—because God sees us.

Since the most important subject position that humans occupy is before God, all other human connections must be seen in light of the *coram Deo* relationship. Furthermore, the freedom one receives in the *coram* relationship grants freedom to the believer for service in the world. Deanna Thompson, one of the authors of this volume, describes the *coram* relationship this way. "[H]umanity's fundamental situation is defined by its existence before God (*coram Deo*) and, secondarily, by its existence before God and others in society (*coram hominibus*). Living before God defines one's spiritual existence. . . . Before others in society (*coram hominibus*), one then becomes utterly receptive to the needs and wounds of the neighbor."[37] Through God's grace we recognize ourselves as sinful subjects before God, and in the liberation that comes from justification we are freed to love the neighbor. This implies an ought—an obligation to the other. But this service is not done as a work of merit but as an act of love. Another contributor to this volume, Caryn Riswold, concludes, "Luther's idea that humans live *coram hominibus* is neatly tied in to his view of Christian freedom, where the Christian is freed from the anxiety of works-for-salvation, and freed to serve the neighbor as an expression of Christ's love."[38]

It is important to note that the *coram Deo* and *coram hominibus* relationships are simultaneous. One is always a subject in the sight of God and others. And being before others is not only a physical relationship; it is an ethical claim. *Coram Deo* means that individuals are obligated to the neighbor precisely because they are regarded as subjects before God. "In the presence of another I am in some way claimed by him, while he is also claimed by me. It is true both that he is in my presence and I am in his presence."[39] *Coram Deo* describes a kind of ongoing dance—a dance of being before and in service of the other, the world (*coram mundo*), and God. This relationship can strengthen our responsibility to others as we take up subject positions in discourse.

Sin as a Subject Position + *Coram Deo*

Before explaining how *coram Deo* can strengthen sin as a subject position, it may be helpful to point out the similarities between these concepts. Both emphasize the relational character of humans and acknowledge that they are profoundly constituted by affiliations and are in the process of becoming. For Luther, persons are primarily defined in relationship to God and on the way to God. "In whatever way the nature of man may be explained . . . 'becoming,' 'being,' and 'acting' are always in motion—by the new birth he passes from sin to righteousness and thus from 'not being' through 'becoming' to 'being.'"[40] In queer theory, relationality comes from commitments to the fluidity of being and the constituting influence of language and discourse.

Supplementing sin as a subject position with Luther's *coram Deo* means that subjects are obligated to one another. The *coram Deo* relationship goes hand in hand with the *coram hominibus* relationship and involves service to others. "God has given me in Christ all the riches of righteousness and salvation. . . . I will therefore give myself as a Christ to my neighbor. . . . I will do nothing in this life except what is profitable, necessary, and life-giving for my neighbor."[41] We are free to serve the neighbor because we are regarded by God. And when humans see themselves in the sight of God, they can evaluate their own subject positions in light of the *coram Deo* relationship. This creates a space whereby humans may be converted from an unjust subject position to one of right relationship. For example, heterosexist persons may see themselves before God, recognize their LGBTQI sister or brother before God, and be converted from homophobic feelings and actions. *Coram Deo* liberates the individual from fear and makes conversion possible.

The *coram* relationship also grants freedom. Luther wrote, "A Christian is lord of all, completely free of everything. A Christian is a servant, completely attentive to the needs of all."[42] This freedom can also be used to resist and be converted from sinful actions, discourses, and unjust subject positions. Critical and queer theorists state that there is no place outside of language and discourse; the best humans can hope for is to resist oppressive powers. But Luther's insight that humans are *coram Deo* reveals that freedom comes from God, so we can—on occasion—do more than just resist dominant discourses and sinful structures. *Kairos* moments occur, conversion takes place, and unjust discourses are dismantled.

The strengths of portraying sin as subject position still stand. And now that Luther's insight that we are before God, obligated to the neighbor, and receive the gift of freedom through Christ have been woven into the proposal, it seems that there is much to commend in this new model of sin. Recall that the inherited doctrine of sin has taught that lesbians and gays are sinful in their stable being and that this sin somehow springs from—and cycles back onto—the enduring, sinful nature of the individual. It also does not explain how sinful discourses constitute persons or why individuals participate in unjust structures. Sin as discourse reveals that discourses about sexuality and gender are constructed, that homophobic discourses are sinful, and explains why persons are complicit in sinful systems. In addition, conceiving of sin (and identity) in terms of subject position rather than ontological qualities means that it is no longer plausible to declare LGBTQI persons as sinful in their being, desire, or relations in a way that is different from straight persons.

How Can the Queer, Christian Doctrine of Sin Strengthen Luther's Theology?

The conversation between Luther and queer definitions of sin is not only one way; his doctrine of sin can also benefit from listening to the insights of queer theology. There are three points in Luther's theology that can be strengthened by listening to the queer doctrine of sin developed here. The first relates to his anthropology. Does sin exist in the enduring nature of the individual for Luther? Yes and no. On one hand he was influenced by the philosophy of his time. He taught that all people possess a God-given soul or nature, and that the tinder of sin resides in this autonomous essence. On the other hand, Luther's anthropology—and his concept of justification and sacramental theology—reveal a very relational, non-autonomous portrait of the individual who is always constituted by relationships *coram Deo* and *coram hominibus*. Luther's theology could benefit from the model of the subject suggested here—a subject that is relationally becoming and constituted by discourses and material conditions. Some might be concerned that this subject has no nature or essence that bears the tinder of sin, but this is not the case. The queer, Christian anthropology suggested here does not teach that there is no such thing as a human nature or essence; rather, it sets aside the assertion that humans bear an enduring nature or autonomous essence that is fixed, stable, isolated from language and material conditions, and exists somehow outside of discourse. Thus Luther's foundational commitment that sin is *in* us is maintained.

Weaving a relational portrait of the human person into Luther's doctrine of sin has the additional benefit of deepening one's relationship to the neighbor. If I actually *come to be* in relationship to my neighbor, it is less likely that I will treat her/him as an object for my mastery and use. Instead of a subject-object relationship, this affiliation becomes a relationship between two constituted subjects based on mutual recognition and obligation. This sounds surprisingly close to what Luther was describing with *coram hominibus.* He wrote: "Therefore it [righteousness] hates itself and loves its neighbor; it does not seek its own good, but that of another. . . . Because it seeks the good of another, it works love. Thus in each sphere it does God's will . . . justly with neighbor, devoutly toward God."[43] Certainly Luther would applaud how mutually constituting one another strengthens our responsibility to the neighbor.

Luther argued persuasively that all humans carry the tinder of sin within them, and that sin is more than a lack of original righteousness. But he never developed a doctrine of sin that explained how and why individuals are complicit in sinful structures. Rather, Luther blamed Adam and Eve, individuals, others, and the devil for sin.[44] This may have occurred because he did not articulate a fully relational anthropology that explains how ideologies, culture, and language constitute persons. The proposal that humans come to be and take up sinful subject positions in discourses illuminates the depth to which we are each constituted by relationships and material conditions. It helps us recognize our complicity in alienating structures and exposes the seductive power of discourses to create sinful subject positions that we occupy as we participate in unjust social structures.

Conclusion

In the midst of writing this chapter the Evangelical Lutheran Church in America voted to allow its congregations to call lesbian and gay pastors in committed relationships. Perhaps this is a *kairos* moment for queer Lutherans. But as we move towards full inclusion, there is a great deal of work to do. Like feminist, mujerista, and womanist theologians, queer theologians must critically engage the biblical texts and grapple with the theological tradition to separate the promise of God's love in Christ from oppressive discourses about LGBTQI people, as well as women, bodies, and sex.

At this historic moment we could pursue an apologetic strategy and make no changes in our theology, or we could set aside our theological heritage because of its homophobia. I urge LGBTQI theologians and their allies instead to queer Christian doctrines. We need to ask: What might Jesus look like through the eyes of GLBTQI persons? How would a queer ecclesiology function? What shape would a queer doctrine of God take? Our task is not only to make a space for GLBTQI individuals or to offer a narrow interpretation of a doctrine. Rather, it is to articulate the story of God's love in Jesus Christ in a way that extends the ever-widening circle of welcome to *all* persons, regardless of their sexual identity, gender, or desire. I hope this queer, Lutheran interpretation of sin serves as an example of how queer theology can invigorate inherited doctrines and extend welcome and reconciliation to all.

Suggested Reading

Fulkerson, Mary McClintock. *Changing the Subject: Women's Discourses and Feminist Theology*. Minneapolis: Fortress Press, 1994.

Goss, Robert. *Queering Christ: Beyond Jesus Acted Up*. Cleveland: Pilgrim, 2002.

Helminiak, Daniel. *What the Bible Really says About Homosexuality*. San Francisco: Alamo Square, 1994.

Lowe, Mary. "Gay, Lesbian, and Queer Theologies: Origins, Contributions, and Challenges." *dialog: A Journal of Theology* 48, no. 1 (Spring 2009): 49–61.

Stuart, Elizabeth A. *Gay and Lesbian Theologies: Repetitions with Critical Difference*. Burlington, Vt.: Ashgate, 2003.

Wilchins, Riki. *Queer Theory, Gender Theory: An Instant Primer*. Los Angeles: Alyson, 2004.

Chapter 6

Who Are You? Christ and the
Imperative of Subjectivity

Anna Mercedes

"LET THE SAME MIND be in you that was in Christ Jesus," wrote the apostle Paul to the Christian community in Philippi (Phil. 2:5). Paul had been calling the community to peace amongst themselves, and as an exemplary model of the way toward Christian community, he quoted a hymn describing Christ, "who, though he was in the form of God, did not regard equality with God as something to be exploited, but emptied himself, taking the form of a slave, being born in human likeness" (Phil. 2:6-7). Paul's call is to an extreme and potentially hazardous mind-set, as Christ's humility led "to the point of death—even death on a cross" (Phil. 2:8).[1]

Demonstrating his own indebtedness to Paul, Martin Luther's succinct presentation of the theology of the cross in the Heidelberg Disputation of 1518 declares that the true theologian understands God by fixing her attention on suffering and the cross. Where a "theologian of glory" might speculate about God through an understanding of creation, the "theologian of the cross" studies suffering, and thus avoids misunderstanding bad for good, such that she "calls the thing what it actually is."[2]

In their own study of "suffering and the cross," feminist theologians have become increasingly adept at calling it what it has been too often: rhetoric of forced submission and exploitation. Self-sacrifice and servitude have been violently and disproportionately enfleshed in the bodies of enslaved and abused persons who have been told to "bear their cross"—their abuser, their slave master, their colonial invader. Thus, where Christian lives demonstrate sacrifice, it is too often by way of a forcible and unjust incarnation of this potent Christian theme, forced onto bodies whose lips never spoke the yes that turned Mary's submission into the righteous cadence of the Magnificat.[3]

This chapter will explore the possibility of such a yes by drawing upon selections from both Luther and Dietrich Bonhoeffer. In them we find, rather than a theology of righteous suffering, a christology that holds human persons accountable to their full humanity. In Christ, the grace of God comes as power for humanity: power that resists the sinfulness that hinders fullness of life.[4]

Ever mindful of the ways in which the rhetoric of the cross has been contorted for sinful means, a feminist theological lens can claim graceful power in the cross. A study of Luther's commentary on Philippians 2[5] reveals that it is precisely because Christ has been on the cross and not in spite of it that there is a gospel for feminist theology.

Luther's Commentary on Philippians 2

The Christ hymn in Philippians describes Christ as being "in the form" of God. In his reading of Philippians 2, Luther draws a distinction between the *being* and the form of God,[6] claiming that God always has the being or essence of God, and Christ likewise always has the essence of God. This is an ontological reality from which Christ, as God, cannot separate.[7] In contrast, the "form of God" means for Luther something like "godly action." Rather than a noun like "essence," "form" functions in Luther as an *action state*. As Luther explains, "the being *is* something, although the form *does* something or is a deed."[8] To be in the form of God means to be *doing* godly things, or more precisely for Luther, to be doing gracious, healing things for particular others with whom we are in relationship.[9]

Luther's commentary gives three possibilities for the interplay of being and form. First, when God, through grace, reveals the divine presence to us, there is both being and form.[10] But second, when God is angry, Luther imagines that God removes grace and goes unnoticed, such that "there is divine being, although no divine form."[11] In other words, while the essence of God always remains, God's action state may change. This resonates with Luther's delineation elsewhere between the "proper and alien" works of God in law and gospel. It is as though it is the proper form of God to be in both essence and in form, actively expressing grace, while the putting away of God's form (or graceful actions) is akin to God's alien work under the law.[12]

Third, Luther elaborates an interaction between being and form that is impossible for God but is the tendency of humans. Luther writes that humans like to play at God's form, even though they lack God's being. Humans, however, erroneously imagine God's form as one of unyielding power and judgment more than generosity and healing. They imitate a false god. It seems implicit in light of Luther's *theologia crucis* that when humans act out the godly form, "stealing" the likeness of God, they are actually not acting like the true God at all. Rather, they are acting like that which they imagine God to be: a mighty taker.

Exemplifying what feminist theologians would later recognize as his andro-centric bias, Luther preaches that humans—regardless of gender or social location—chronically act out the godly things, attempting to steal the form of God for themselves.[13] It is because of this tendency to feign godliness, explains Luther, that Philippians 2:6 emphasizes that Christ was "in the form of God," presenting a contrast with humanity's stolen and false "forms" of God. Whereas humans take on our approximations of God's form as thieves, Christ is in the form naturally. In Luther's reading, the text is not primarily explaining the truth about Christ, but is instead drawing our attention to the truth about ourselves: namely, that we have been acting like false gods.[14] As elsewhere in his writings, Luther expresses here that the biblical word is primarily a word *for us*, not prima-rily an abstract word about God's nature.[15]

Bringing grace to our sinful reality, Christ empties himself, "taking the form of a slave, being born in human likeness." Luther reads the Philippians letter as indication that human likeness equates to the servant likeness, or literally from the Greek *doulos*, the likeness of a slave.[16] With verse 7, explains Luther, Paul teaches that, unlike people who have the being of servants but steal the form of God, Christ has both the being of God and the form of God but *also activates the form of servanthood*. Again Luther's understanding of "form" involves action. The truly human form is, as with the godly form, an action state; humane action is servant action. Christ is incarnate in human motion. The grace of God ani-mates the form of humanity, empowering us to inhabit the full potential of our bodies to heal and to care, pulling us away from other sinful ways that contort our full humanity.

Luther's understanding of human nature as inherently slavish raises imme-diate concerns not only for feminist and womanist theology, but for also for all contemporary theology guided by either liberation or postcolonial episte-mologies. Christian theology has been used to enslave in so many ways that it is questionable whether Christian theologians can responsibly promote the theme of servitude. I contend that we can and that our tradition bears witness to the ways in which service, though easily exploited, can also be empowering. But the English word *slave* will not convey empowerment in our post-slavery U.S. context. In order to speak to Luther's Philippians commentary, we need a word that invokes something of the action state Luther envisions in the human form of servanthood, along with the power and freedom he understands to be the servant's birthright as a baptized Christian.[17] Rather than an enslaved or shackled state of being, Luther sees the human form in movement and agency: fleshing out the form of care, activating servanthood. The person brought into her full humanity by Christ moves freely in action, not subjugated in passivity. Indeed, where she appears passive, that too may be an active practice of agency, an expression of Christian liberty.

The Greek *doulos*, or slave, from Philippians 2:7, has recently entered into contemporary English with the feminine ending. A "doula" is a woman who assists a pregnant woman in childbirth, helping the birthing woman to know her own strength. Because this wise female companioning in childbirth can call to mind a deeply active and empowering form of service, the word *doula*, instead of the translation "slave," can connote the fruitful, life-giving actions of the Christic human form. I will use this contemporary word as I continue to move through Luther's reading of Philippians.

For Luther, when we act as we falsely imagine God is—when we steal the "godly" form—we attempt to *take*, neglecting our true livelihood as giving forms. Not only do we, unlike Christ, see the form of God "as something to be exploited," but we also miss the goodness of our human form. We mistake God for a mighty taker and strive in this image to be takers ourselves, forsaking our full humanity.

Luther stresses that, in contrast to human stealing, Christ steals nothing in taking up the work of the doula, for the doula form is a giving, not a taking.[18] So in "taking" the form of humanity there is actually nothing to take: one cannot steal the action of giving. In grasping hold of it, one's grasp automatically opens in a gesture of generosity: the gesture of the doula, ready to foster new life.

Meanwhile, the form of God is indeed not "something to be exploited"—it is a set of serving actions, and therefore moves against the flow of exploitation. It also cannot be grasped or hoarded. In this sense the form of God revealed in Christ turns out to be remarkably similar to the form of full humanity. That form of God becomes ours through the power of God's incarnate presence. Luther writes elsewhere that we "ought to be content with this form of God obtained by faith," and this contentment seems intuitive when what it means to be living in the form of God is also what it means to be living as fully human.[19]

Comparing Luther's theology of the cross in the Heidelberg Disputation to this commentary on Philippians, boastful humans act as theologians of glory, confusing the evil thing with the good and acting in an evil way while thinking themselves to be behaving like God.[20] In contrast, the humanity to which Christ as doula beckons us is a true humanity where we can call humanity what it is, and stop putting on the false identity of God. We are beckoned by Christ to be the humans we are, the bodies we are. As with the theology of the cross, Luther in the Philippians commentary teaches that we become ourselves (or in the Heidelberg Disputation, we become theologians) only through encounter with the *humanity* of Christ. Christ as doula shows us how we are meant to thrive as humans, and *meanwhile* also reveals to us the form of *God*, which was not the form of God we had imagined. Through the graceful actions of Christ, actions synchronously both divine and human, we become in form—in action—the doulas we already are in being. We are welcomed to the wholeness of Christian freedom.

Can Sin Be *Even More* than Luther Thought?

Luther was deeply focused on the pervasive reality of sin. And yet, he may not have seen the half of it! A feminist theological lens quickly detects in Luther's commentary the masculinist bias diagnosed by Valerie Saiving in her landmark 1960 essay "The Human Situation."[21] Saiving argued convincingly that too often in theology "sin" has been defined as self-centeredness, while this definition of sin does not adequately describe the fault of many who are "feminized" by society, for whom sin would be more accurately defined as diffusion, as an inability to come into their own or to focus on themselves at all. The doctrine of sin in traditional theology has been short-sighted, conveying a uniform human experience of sin based on the norms of patriarchal masculinity, and thus overlooking the ways in which many women and men sin through perpetual *diffusion* of self, rather than self-aggrandization.

As we have seen, Luther's Philippians commentary envisions grace for the sinfully self-aggrandized, not for the sinfully underdeveloped. How then might the doula Christ serve the ailing condition of those humans, whether female or male, who are distracted from the life that God desires for them, not by their false play at godliness but through a different and often forced evasion of their human dignity through diffusion and a play at nothingness? Read from a feminist perspective, Luther's interpretation of Philippians 2:8, where Christ Jesus "humbled himself and became obedient to the point of death—even death on a cross," may offer grace for those persons who face a perpetual uphill struggle for fulfillment and empowerment. Surprisingly, the same verse that introduces the cross, that crux of contention in feminist theology, may also speak a word of grace to those persons evading liveliness through thieving after nothing, when nothing is not rightfully theirs.

In interpreting verse 8, Luther writes that Christ not only took on human form, as in the incarnation, but also "took on sin, death and the devil and deceit for our sake."[22] Christ lost even the honor a human *deserves* in that Christ was murdered. Luther claims that in his execution "Christ also lost the favor, thanks and honor which *belonged* to the taken-on human form, showing by this that Christ was made unto nothing."[23]

Being "made unto nothing" presses Christ into a form not discussed by Luther—a fourth possibility that seems distinct from the three interactions of being and form discussed above.[24] Now Christ inhabits a further form: the no-form, the state of diffusion and underdeveloped dignity, a state molded by our corporate sin.[25] In inhabiting the form *beyond* that which human dignity deserves, in being violently acted upon and indeed murdered, Christ has suffered, like so many others, the most extreme conditions of the no-form.[26]

Feminist theology has strongly established that cross theology is problematic where it posits that Christ's violent death is what saves us. Such an atonement theology sets the example for us that we should, following Christ, endure violence in the name of salvation. Of course, Luther does not want anyone trying to save herself. Nonetheless, the attempt of salvific suffering has been made by far too many. Oddly, however, in Luther's Philippians commentary, Christ's action is salvific *not* because of his endurance of the violent "no-form," but because of Christ's assumption of the human, doula form, which enables us to be truly ourselves and to be rightly alive. It is the incarnate life of Christ that offers the graceful pull toward fullness of life for the god-actors in Luther's Philippians commentary, not Christ's further descent into nothingness on the cross. Here, it is not Jesus' death but instead the overall form of Jesus' life that exudes grace—grace, at least for those with an overblown sense of self.

If it was Christ's life that speaks the gospel word to the god-actors, might it be Christ's death that speaks the word to the victims of shattering suffering? Might it be precisely the cross that brings good news to them? To further explore this possibility, I turn to the student notes from the 1933 christology lectures of Dietrich Bonhoeffer.

A Graceful Imperative

Bonhoeffer may at first seem like an odd voice to introduce into a feminist reading of Luther, for Bonhoeffer, like Luther, understood one major sinful predicament: that of being bound up in pride.[27] Yet, while he imagined the same christological dynamics as Luther, with a human Christ who calls prideful persons back down to earth where they belong, Bonhoeffer's description of the christological encounter leaves room to imagine how Christ might function on behalf of other persons as well.

Bonhoeffer believed that in encounter with Christ in human form, a person is pressed to struggle with her own subjectivity. He envisioned that the incarnate Christ presents the Christic self in such a direct and personal way that a person is not able to stand at a distance and theorize about *how* Christ is, pondering for example "the two natures of Christ."[28] In this encounter, there is no space for objectivity. This is a subjective encounter: a meeting between two subjects, friend to friend, body to body, flesh to flesh, in a caress of truth, momentary and catalyzing.[29] Rather than speculation about the *how* of Christ, the incarnate one presents us with the immediate matter of the *who* of Christ.[30]

Bonhoeffer's writings teach that, when asked in faith, the who question can be "the question of those who realize, as soon as they ask the question, that they themselves are meant by it, and instead of hearing the answer, hear the question in return: Who then are you?"[31] Our own subjectivity is in question: "Here a new existence breaks into our existence."[32]

It is as though, feeling beside me the touch of flesh, the nearness of a benevolent other, I ask myself, "Who is this person? All I know is that this person seems invested *in me*." In this way Christ's presence marks the false trail that I have been following in search of my humanity. Christ calls me back to my body, my self. I may not recognize myself, but I see another person beside me: Who is this person? This person is *for-me*. Me? Who am I?

I suggest that this line of questioning, this query after the subjectivity of Christ's beloved, carries the potential of a powerful, constructive word for a person whose sense of self is diffuse, pained beyond recognition. In his lectures, Bonhoeffer asks, "Where does Christ stand?," and answers, "For me, Christ stands in my place, where I should be standing . . . I am separated, by a boundary that I cannot cross, from the self that I ought to be. This boundary lies between my old self and my new self, that is, in the center between myself and me."[33] For Bonhoeffer this separation from self was primarily due to self-aggrandizement, yet Christ also stands for those separated from themselves by a haze of diffusion and self-diminishment.[34] Surely Christ crucified particularly stands for those.

The doula Christ descends in search of the pieces of ourselves that have been crushed and ground and lost, proceeding past the level of human respect, as far as the vector of Christ's compassion for us will lead, which is to say: as far as we have gone, as far as we have been forced to go, even into the null and void, the no-self. This one-for-us comes to our aid not only when we are caught up in our ego, but also when—perhaps especially when—we are pressed into the hell of the no-self and have "become nothing."

The Christ of "suffering and the cross" inhabits the form that is no longer defined by action but rather by being acted upon, by being abused and pressed into diffusion and denied self: a form of passivity in an unsafe space. And Christ becomes—oddly, miraculously—a victim-*survivor*.[35]

Because Christ has been pressed beyond human dignity, we who also know such disgrace may hear the humming of Christ's survival song and feel our dignity rekindled within us. Because Christ has been on the cross, Christ's gospel is one of solidarity with those most abused by the maelstrom of sin. Because present-day incarnations of the body of Christ take up the form of the doula and fix their attention on all those crucified in the present moment, Christ comes to those who suffer today and presents them with the graceful imperative of their own subjectivity, their own becoming.

Revealing the experience of our sister victim-survivor, the cross need not mandate further suffering in repetition of Christ's travail. Instead the cross signals the presence of holy solidarity, of a divinity whose own form is intimately enmeshed in the suffering of our world. The cross signals the presence of the doula Christ who persistently offers a still, small voice of companionship in the storm: a particular, contextual word for both the overblown and the dismembered, and for all those caught in various contortions of full humanity—forced and chosen—that lead to spiritual and physical demise. This voice, this word, catalyzes the perpetual reconstruction of our subjectivity. The doula Christ knows the contours of our travail and steadies us forward as we birth our next incarnation of self.

By grace, by the careful and persistent service with which God attends to us, we are given the promise of ourselves. We are continually reminded of our power to give, to heal, to serve, to take up the Godly form, because God will not let us forget. Like a good birth partner, Christ reminds us of the power in our bodies, the power God has chosen to convey through the human form: corporality that serves.

In resonance with feminism's emphasis on embodiment, the self to which Luther and Bonhoeffer beckon return is a human, bodily self. Bonhoeffer understood our embodiment to be particularly emphasized in the Eucharist, which we might consider to be an encounter with the no-form presence of God: the body broken, given for you. Bonhoeffer teaches that "in the sacrament Christ is present to us in the sphere of our body's tangible nature . . . by our side as a creature," as a person beside a person, bringing us to the "restored creation of our spirit-bodily existence."[36]

We are restored to the fully human form, the doula form: the body of Christ. It is Christ who will ensure the vibrancy of our sense of self, not as autonomous individuals equal with all others, but as particular and precious persons knit into form in the fabric of a community which is Christ's victimized, resurrected body in a diverse world. Christ incarnate embodies our resurrected identity, our center.[37]

For freedom Christ has set us free; for freedom we have been restored as doulas. Astonishingly, abundant care for others—even when it is dangerous, even at the foot of our sisters' crosses—may lead to a new incarnation of vibrant subjectivity, to a revelation of the risen Christ: as it did in Jesus, as it does for us when we encounter Christ in our sister, as it does when we come into ourselves in the midst of our love for others. This is the creative cadence of resurrection to which we testify beneath the cross.

Those of us who have been exploited—whether women or men—need not be protected from the gore of our world or our theologies. We cannot leave the cross to be the theological remedy for our abusers, for the powerful, for the overblown, while finding more gentle theologies for ourselves. We can handle the cross.[38] Though our "no" to abuse under the cross has too often been ignored, we often remain capable, sometimes even more vigorously so, of a "yes" to the power of the cross. We who are victims may live, with grace, as survivors.

Let the same mind be in you, exhorted Paul, that was in Christ, who in the form of God, took up the form of the doula—a vulnerable form forced on the cross into no form at all. Christ crucified stands in solidarity beside the one in the formlessness of the no-self, and presents her with Christ's own body in such a way that she remembers her own. "Who am I?" she asks herself, and in the image of the for-her Christ, she answers her own question. Christ her doula goads her back into her own embodied power. And as with Luther's Christ who cannot steal the human form, since as soon as the doula form is grasped it opens out toward others, her own self-possession, her "getting a hold of herself," may converge in Christ with a mercifully relational identity. So then perhaps she comes to you, loving you as it is her joy to do, and in her gracious company you hear the question, "Who am I?" And you remember.

Yet at no point in the rich doula life will this person cease being held accountable to the question, "Who am I?" It may be her (or his) sinful tendency to forget, to think this question unimportant. But the for-her Christ is vigilant, ever there with and for her, always holding before her the question and the imperative of her own subjectivity. "For God wishes that one becomes the [doula] of the other with body, goods, honor, spirit and soul," just as Christ has done for us, writes Luther.[39] And it is God, having made us new as people for others, who will bear the responsibility of saving us, holding us accountable to our selves in the body of Christ.

Suggested Reading

Brock, Rita Nakashima, and Rebecca Ann Parker. *Proverbs of Ashes: Violence, Redemptive Suffering, and the Search for What Saves Us.* Boston: Beacon, 2001.

Crysdale, Cynthia S.W. *Embracing Travail: Retrieving the Cross Today.* New York: Continuum, 1999.

Dahill, Lisa. *Reading from the Underside of Selfhood: Bonhoeffer and Spiritual Formation.* Eugene, Ore.: Pickwick, 2009.

Joh, Wonhee Anne. *Heart of the Cross: A Postcolonial Christology.* Louisville: Westminster John Knox, 2006.

Thompson, Deanna A. *Crossing the Divide: Luther, Feminism, and the Cross.* Minneapolis: Fortress Press, 2004.

PART 4

The Work and Person of Christ

The usual practice in systematic theology is to talk about the person of Jesus Christ first, and the work of Jesus Christ second. Following some practices in the Christian theological tradition, in this volume, we are beginning with the work of Jesus Christ because the nature of redemption tells us something about the person of Jesus Christ.

The two chapters on the work of Christ by Alicia Vargas and Marit Trelstad live in a space of creative theological tension between realistic acknowledgment of rejection and suffering and a hopeful vision of what is promised by God as the last word—a word of life and love. It is the space and tension between the cross and Easter. Arguing through personal narrative that human suffering is related to and redeemed by the suffering of Jesus Christ in the crucifixion, Vargas articulates a clear vision of the mutually shared suffering of the community and the ways in which the body of Christ participates in redeeming each other in concrete and existential ways. In chapter 8, Trelstad unpacks the harmful ways in which we use Jesus' suffering redemption against each other to justify suffering. She then expands our theological vision of the heart of God's atoning love for us—God's covenantal relationship with us.

The latter two chapters by Kathryn Kleinhans and Mary Streufert draw creatively upon the Chalcedonian Creed in order to address feminist criticisms of the ways in which the maleness of Jesus of Nazareth has been misused by the theological tradition. In chapter 9, Kleinhans shifts feminist attention from exemplary understandings of Christ and salvation to the claims of the uniqueness of Christ in the Chalcedonian Formula (that Jesus Christ is at once fully human and fully divine), providing a fresh interpretation of Luther's view of Christ and humanity as bride/groom. From a slightly different entry point, in chapter 10, Streufert addresses the seeming divide between the historical Jesus and the Christ of faith from a gendered perspective and mines not only the christological devotional tradition but also gender studies in order to challenge the ways in which theology maintains a male ascription to the second person of the Trinity.

Chapter 7

Through Mujerista Eyes:
Stories of Incarnate Redemption

Alicia Vargas

THIS CHAPTER BELONGS TO the oral tradition, just like the oral stories written in the books of our Bible. The stories in the Bible relate the incarnate faith of individuals and faith communities. Even God chose to tell us about Godself by becoming incarnate in Jesus Christ. Jesus' story then becomes the story of God's incarnation in our own lives and of our redemption. The story in this chapter is one of those stories. It is the story of God's incarnate redemption in the life of a U.S. Latina.[1]

In the summer of 2009, the voting delegates of the Evangelical Lutheran Church in America, moved by stories of faithful gay, lesbian, bisexual, and transgendered brothers and sisters, chose to take a historic step to dismantle an obstacle for the ordination of lesbian, gay, bisexual, and transgendered (LGBT) persons in monogamous and committed relationships. To tell their stories, many LGBT people had to come "out of the closet"—a closet that must have offered them some kind of protection—into the open vulnerability of publicly telling their stories of pain to this church. Likewise, I have a story of pain to share.

As one of the presenters at the Transformative Lutheran Theologies: Feminist, Womanist, and Mujerista Conference in January 2009, I was challenged by a question posed by Kristen Kvam: "One thing that strikes me . . . is that I hope they might inspire some autobiographical reflections. I am thinking about musings about one's own journey into theologies that place women at the center of inquiry. Might there be time for some storytelling? I ask because I believe in the importance of story as a way to open imaginations." I responded to her challenging question by "coming out of the closet" in a way and telling my story of pain in this church, one that is intermingled with those of others and that of Jesus Christ. It was not an easy thing to do. It was only possible because I knew that I was in a safe space surrounded by women of all kinds and men allies who had their own stories and their own scars of pain. It was possible, ultimately, because the story of God incarnate in the scarred flesh of Jesus Christ embraced all of our stories, the ones to which I referred and each of the stories in that magnificent group of sisters and brothers in that warm conference room on a cold Chicago day.

So, here's my story and that of two of my colleagues. They are part of a contemporary oral tradition, part of the stories that I hear repeated often in gatherings of people at any and all margins of power. They are just three intermingled stories and part of thousands and millions of others. They are not special in any way. They are just three that I know.

In January 2008, my husband took an administrative job at Pacific Lutheran Theological Seminary (PLTS) after being a parish pastor for sixteen years. Suddenly churchless when he moved to his new job, we were forced to start looking for a new congregation to attend. We ended up at a congregation that has been officially "vacant," even though its pastor has been there for more than twenty-five years. He is openly gay and in a long-time faithful relationship with his partner. When he came out, he was officially de-rostered. Because the congregation refused to get rid of him, the then-synodical bishop reprimanded them and listed the congregation as "vacant." Some say that it was all a sympathetic bishop could do, that at least he did not expel the congregation from the synod, as another bishop had done earlier to two other congregations in the same situation.

There was something very good and satisfying in worshiping with this congregation. My husband knew the pastor from a scripture study group for pastors, and they were buddies before we got there. I did not know him that well; I just knew about the story of him and the congregation and our church. However, I felt a strong affinity with the pastor, so much so, that being pastored by him and worshiping in that "vacant" and reprimanded congregation contributed to giving me hope for the resurrection of our church from the death of exclusivity. I felt a strong relationship with that pastor. It seemed that he knew how I felt in this church, not only as the sole Latina professor in one of its seminaries, but as a person—a simple person who heard one day at the beginning of the ELCA that it wanted to be a multicultural church, and who, rushing to leave her nets on the boat, quit her job at a tenurable position at Vassar College and went back to school at age forty-one, dragging pre-teenage kids with her, to get prepared to serve in this new multicultural church. Five years later, after an M.Div. and an M.A. in New Testament, and more student loans to add to the ones we still had not paid from our secular Ph.D.s, and loads of guilt at moving—and moving again—our kids in the middle of growing up, I graduated and was approved by the candidacy committee. And then, I waited and waited and waited—for a congregation that would want me to minister with them and serve Jesus Christ with them.

In the meantime, some prison inmates called me, but that call was not recognized by the synod because, of course, the inmates did not have a Lutheran church council to give me a Lutheran letter of call. After a couple of years of serving in the jail, two congregations that most probably would not have called me to serve their own members decided to call me to serve the inmates as a favor to me, provided that they did not have to pay me a cent. I served the inmates for seven years and I loved that ministry and I even truly got to see Jesus in prison. PLTS, with all its grace, offered me a half-time job too, so for some years I combined my work among the inmates with serving seminarians. The seminary seemed to be more serious about becoming multicultural than were other parts of the church. Hiring me was one more step in that direction, and the seminary has indeed continued to move, hiring two more faculty of color after me and taking up some affirmative action steps to diversify the student body. Most importantly it knows that we still have to move much more toward multiculturality, so I don't feel completely like a mere token. I appreciated the privilege of both calls, to the jail and to the seminary. God does work in mysterious ways, and even though there is a deep pain in my heart and in my soul because no Lutheran congregation in my synod would even interview a Latina, these two other ministries offered me blessed vocational fulfillment.

My pain lingers, though. I felt insulted, offended, and definitely oppressed by a church that did not trust me with one of its pulpits simply because I am Latina. I live with that pain every day. Truly, how many of your congregations would call a person of color? I don't doubt that if you are reading this chapter all the way to this point you personally might, but would your congregation? And I am not the only one that was not called by the ninety-seven-point-something percent of the white ELCA simply because I am, as I am labeled, a "person of color." Not being the only one in that situation does not make the pain easier. It makes it much worse. A well-meaning assistant to the bishop told a wonderfully gifted woman of color who graduated a year earlier than I did to be realistic and not to expect a call in our synod. He meant well; he didn't want her to be disappointed. He knew the congregations in the synod, and it was really the "realistic" thing to say.

After waiting a long time, my super-gifted friend was for a very short time a pastor of a little dying congregation that no one else wanted to serve in another synod. She led that congregation, where some people would scratch her hand in the line on their way out from worship, until she couldn't take the abuse there anymore. No other congregation has called her, even though she is single, has no children, and is 100 percent mobile and could go to any synod in our church. She has had important church desks around the church. No doubt she's doing God's work from her desk and serving our church in very good ways, but she went to seminary to preach from a pulpit that has not been entrusted to her simply because she's a "woman of color."

And, yes, I know that many congregations do not even want to call a woman of any color, even white, simply because she's a woman. I know that that is still a painfully anachronistic struggle in our church. And I also know that we have a small percentage of pastors of color in the ELCA, mostly serving congregations of their own ethnicity. Praise God for that! But there are not enough ethnic-specific congregations for those aspiring pastors who hear the call of God and believe the rhetoric of our church about multiculturality, which supposedly is grounded in our theology. And we wonder why it is so hard to attract people of color to come join us in our pews! Martin Luther King Jr. purportedly said what is worth repeating every day until it is no more, that the most segregated hour in America is eleven o'clock (or ten, or nine, or eight-thirty) Sunday morning. That is no accident.

So that is how I came to feel great affinity with the pastor of that "vacant" congregation who was himself rejected from the ordained roster of our church. We never talked about my pain or the pain that I imagine he carries in himself, but simply because I imagine his suffering, I feel that my pain is redeemed. I am not committing heresy here. I am not suggesting that this pastor is any sort of Jesus Christ and as such my Redeemer with a capital "R." For starters he did not voluntarily choose rejection, nor was he sent by God to be rejected as Jesus was.[2] No, this pastor is just a pastor who was oppressed for many years by my church, just as I was for slightly different reasons, a little more or less out in the open but for the same systemic sin of arrogant exclusion. Still his oppression redeems mine in the old Jewish sense of Leviticus 25:25: "If anyone of your kin falls into difficulty and sells a piece of property, then the next of kin shall come and redeem what the relative has sold." In that way, the honor of the family would be restored after it was weakened by the selling of a chunk of land. As we know, the honor in most honor/shame societies is a family matter, not an individual one. In that type of culture, as in the ancient Hebrew culture, when the individual gets in trouble, the whole family is in trouble too. The honor of one family member is the honor of the whole family. As per Jewish culture in biblical times, my "next of kin" in my "vacant" congregation family—the pastor and all the LGBT and straight brothers and sisters in the congregation too—redeem my honor as a child of God in the ELCA. Their pain "buys back" my pain. They incarnate it. Yes, they are not the official Redeemer with a capital "R," but they redeem my pain nevertheless. Through their pain they restore my honor in that little part of the ELCA family. Hopefully, I can do the same for them.

This is why I decided to put these oral stories into writing, where they usually don't belong. They are good stories in oral and maybe even in written form. They are painful but they are not stories of victims seeking to elicit sympathy— "Oh! *Pobrecitos*" ("poor suffering, oppressed ones"). Far from it! There was and there is not a drop of "poor little old me" in that congregation. To the contrary, the power that emanates from that "vacant" pulpit and from those pews where gay and lesbian and straight ally and black and white and Latino and Asian have come because they feel "at home" is palpable, is strong, is inspirational, and is gospel. I felt empowered there, and I suspect that is why that congregation is contributing to the two-point-something percent of people of color in the ELCA. Gay, lesbian, persons of color—each "buying back" or redeeming each other's honor just as a family member redeems the shame of another member and of the whole family.

As a Latina woman whose mujerista theology emanates from incarnate stories of survival by faith, I see Jesus as that rejected pastor, whose "pulpit" was condemned because he didn't quite fit the temple establishment at the time, who was brought to trial by systems of power that found him guilty of going against oppressive and exclusive and clubbish but powerful systems. The 2009 ELCA Churchwide Assembly delegates made it now official that LGBT pastors in monogamous sexual relationships don't have to be excluded from all pulpits any longer and that the congregations who call them don't have to be reprimanded any longer. But we all know that LGBT brothers and sisters are going to continue to be excluded in all sorts of open or subtle ways from many places in our church, including from the vast majority of its pulpits—even from congregations that are comfortable with the spirit but not the flesh of the latest vote of the churchwide assembly, those who may accept the principle of inclusion but are not comfortable with calling as their pastor people who incarnate it. After all, the official policy of our church is not that people of color be excluded from its pulpits, but they certainly have been, are, and will continue to be excluded for a long, long time!

In such situations as this painful state of affairs in our church, mujeristas cling to the cross, because for us it is a symbol of that oppressive power in relationship with God's redemption through it. The suffering of Jesus, our next of kin, on that cross redeems our own suffering—the incarnated consequence of systemic sin—and restores our honor even within the oppressive systems that surround us and threaten to annihilate us by ignoring, rejecting, and casting us aside as worthless—as worthless as I felt when no congregation would even interview me for a call simply because I was Latina.

That Jesus suffered and died on a Roman cross for the consequences of our sin makes perfect sense to us simply because we feel that suffering every day. We see systemic exclusivist sin most everywhere we look—especially in the church. With the integration of the White House a huge racist symbolic block has come tumbling down in the United States of America, and there is a fleeting sense of promise. But in the Evangelical Lutheran Church of that same America, our pulpits—and because of that our pews—are not yet remotely integrated. I say "yet" and I emphasize it, because the message of the cross does not make sense to us without the resurrection that followed. We will overcome the forces of exclusivist sin in the United States of America and in the Evangelical Lutheran Church *in America* some resurrection day, empowered by our "next of kin" in our God family, who "bought back" and overcame the consequences of our sin on the cross, redeemed our pain and restored our honor as members of God's family. On the cross, Jesus Christ bore the painful consequences of the sin that separates us from each other and from the will of God for God's children to be one with one another. Christ restored our relationship in the family of God, our Mother/Father, and in doing so Christ restored our family unity and honor as God's children. All of us—children of God and siblings one of another—all of us are restored. The oppressed and the oppressor, the excluded ones and the ones who exclude—all are restored as children of the same Mother/Father because the Son took upon himself the suffering of those who suffer oppression and exclusion, the consequence of the sin of oppression and exclusion committed by all of the children in one way or another, at one time or another.

Mujeristas do not romanticize suffering and pain. We just see it and feel it. We cling to the cross openly and proudly, simply because of the suffering that we don't want but that is "realistic" for us, as realistic, indeed, as was what the assistant to the bishop told my talented friend about not expecting a call in our synod. Latina and mujerista theologians, such as Elsa Tamez in Latin America and Ada María Isasi-Díaz in the United States, constantly refer to the reality of the suffering and pain of our sisters. In society in general, as well as in the church, Latinas are ignored and underappreciated. We can turn to the dismal statistics of Latina women's poverty and education deficiencies. We can turn to the dismal statistics of our own church in living out the gospel with and among our Latina sisters. But according to mujerista theology, Latinas are not frozen victims of that pain; to the contrary, in the confidence of the love of God through the cross Latinas are empowered to survive the struggle and suffering and to work and strive for justice and true equality and unity. That is the resurrection part of the Jesus Christ story. Those are also our resurrection stories.

I am weary of sidelining suffering because some women believed the masochistic tale that suffering gained one points in heaven. I want my four-year-old granddaughters not to be surprised by suffering—because they probably will experience it as women of color even in their lifetimes. I want them always to remember that their grandmother felt her redemption coming from the cross of suffering, that she felt a saving affinity with Jesus on the cross "buying back" or redeeming humanity's pain caused by our systemic sins through the same suffering that I feel. I want them to understand how it is that I found a home in a condemned church with a pastor who through his own rejection restores my honor as a member of the same church family that rejected him and me—in the same way as the rejected Jesus restored the honor of his own rejected people and restores the honor of the children of God. For God so loved the world that God gave God's only Son to suffer like we suffer. I want my granddaughters to know that indeed God loves the world and is constantly in a process of embracing it and molding it to God's will. And where there is pain, God's Son was sent by God to share in it because we, God's children, feel that suffering in a very real way as a consequence of systemic sin in the world. God loves us by sharing that suffering through God's Son.

I also want them to know that God's Son suffered on the cross for the systemic sin of which I, like all women, suffer the consequences while at the same time help to perpetuate as both oppressed and oppressor.[3] I am sure that I am not the only one who right now is wearing a piece of clothing that was made in a sweat shop by a miserably paid woman in an impoverished country. I am sure that we recently have eaten or are going to eat soon a piece of fruit or vegetable picked by the hands of poor men, women, and children around the world who work in barely human conditions for the sake of the affordability of the super-abundant diet of the privileged ones in this country.[4] As long as there is even one exploited person in the world, who most probably is a woman, I want my granddaughters to know that God so loved the world that God sent Jesus Christ, yes, to suffer and die on the cross, to buy back the pain caused by our sin, the sin of the *simul* oppressed and oppressor. I want them to know the meaning of new life in relation to that real pain caused by sin, the new life of the resurrection. No pain from sin, no need for the cross. No cross, no need for resurrection. But there is pain; we know there is. There's sin that causes that pain. There is God's love in relationship with that pain through Jesus Christ. But there is also resurrection.

Ada María Isasi-Díaz, the Latina theologian who first coined the term *mujerista*, talks about the "historical project" and the "survival" that are a constant part of Latinas' lives. The historical project of U.S. Latinas is one of securing the fullness of life that God destined for us concretely within the realities and experience of day-to-day living. The fullness of life that is sought by Latinas starts with survival, the satisfaction of both the basic needs to sustain physical life and what makes for a full and pleasant daily existence, as Isasi-Díaz puts it.[5] Jesus Christ's story of crucifixion and resurrection empowers us to engage in this historical project through our own daily stories of our *lucha* ("struggle") to survive the rejection, ignorance, and devaluation of us in an oppressive context in and out of the church. Jesus Christ is for us the motivator for our *lucha* against our suffering and pain from oppression because we believe that he shared our suffering, and we believe that he transcended that very suffering in the resurrection. We are empowered to *luchar* ("to struggle for, to fight for") our honor because we believe Jesus Christ "bought it back," redeemed it for us. In taking upon himself the pain that sin causes in the world, the Son of God liberated both the oppressors and oppressed that we all are. By buying back the pain from the sin of our human systems, Jesus Christ freed us from being crushed by that pain. We are free to thrive as children of Jesus' Mother/Father, with all the honor that that confers upon us. Children of God, redeemed by our enfleshed sibling, God's Son. Thanks be to God because, indeed, God so loved the world.

Suggested Reading

Isasi-Díaz, Ada María. *En la Lucha / In the Struggle: Elaborating a Mujerista Theology.* Minneapolis: Fortress Press, 2004.

Isasi-Díaz, Ada María. *Mujerista Theology: A Theology for the Twenty-First Century.* Maryknoll, N.Y.: Orbis, 1996.

Isasi-Díaz, Ada María, and Yolanda Tarango. *Hispanic Women: Prophetic Voice in the Church.* Minneapolis: Fortress Press, 1992.

Perex, Arturo, Consuelo Covarrubias, and Edward Foley, eds. *Asi Es: Historias de espiritualidad hispana.* Collegeville, Minn.: Liturgical Press, 1994.

Vargas, Alicia. "Reading Ourselves into the Cross Story: Luther and United States Latinos." In *Cross Examinations: Readings on the Meaning of the Cross Today,* ed. Marit Trelstad, 154–63; 294–95. Minneapolis: Fortress Press, 2006.

Chapter 8

Putting the Cross in Context: Atonement through Covenant

Marit Trelstad

I shall die, but that is all I shall do for Death . . .

Edna St. Vincent Millay[1]

BEFORE THE CROSS, THERE was the covenant. And after the cross, there is the covenant. Indeed, God's covenantal love and promise is the whole backdrop from which one can understand the cross. Despite the cross, Easter morning comes and the crucified one is now risen. Death, violence, and hatred fall away. Raise the cross swaddled and conquered in white flowers, because life and love have the last word! These are basic affirmations of the Christian faith through the centuries and yet, when it comes to salvation and atonement, theology has focused mainly on the cross rather than the covenantal story that surrounds it. The message of Easter does not ignore, downplay, or deny the suffering of the cross, but it also does not glorify it.

Theological, biblical, and pastoral reasons press us to contextualize the cross and insist that the significance of the cross be understood within a wider theological setting. The Christian theological tradition offers a wide landscape for atonement models that are often ignored; thus the cross alone becomes theologically synonymous with humanity's reconciliation with God.[2] Likewise, both the New Testament and Hebrew Scriptures offer a variety of atonement understandings. In fact, contemporary New Testament scholars point to multiple atonement motifs present in early Christianity, some of which include the cross as the vehicle for salvation and others that focus on meal and almsgiving (charity), as in Luke, or the self-emptying of Christ who takes on human form in Phillippians 2:5-11.[3] Early Christians struggled with understanding Jesus' death in light of the cultural shame of the cross. Biblical tradition is not monolithic in its approach to atonement; the cross is not the sole focus, even in the New Testament.

This is not to say that one should ignore or deny suffering and the cross. Indeed, the cross speaks strongly to Jesus' solidarity with human suffering, and this message carries enormous significance at certain times of life and in situations of oppression. A clear example of this is the chapter by co-contributor Alicia Vargas on the significance of Jesus' suffering for Latina American Christians. Nonetheless, Jesus' own suffering and death only makes sense when seen within the context of promised life and hope. Without this context, Christians are apt to overglorify the cross such that suffering alone becomes the necessary path to redemption. In addition, it can sound as though it is only in suffering that one identifies with Christ rather than in sharing in the promises and resurrection life of Jesus as well.[4] In line with this, Vargas is clear that suffering is not the intended state in which Christians should live. She claims that sharing Christ's suffering bolsters a revolutionary impulse to challenge oppressive structures. Nonetheless, some feminist theologians have been hesitant to endorse any connection between suffering and salvation; in particular, the *necessity* of suffering has been the source of many legitimate criticisms of atonement models from feminist theology in the past twenty years.[5]

I seek to ground atonement in a wider biblical and theological context, that of God's covenantal nature. While all the diverse books of the Bible cannot be forced to adhere to a single pattern or theme, God's covenant relationship with humanity is indisputably a primary emphasis throughout the Bible. God continuously offering God's self in covenant relationships, promising to accompany humanity over and over again, best illustrates God's unswerving steadfastness.

In theology, atonement is defined, first, as reconciliation with God and, second, as amelioration of sin or wrongdoing. An emphasis on God's covenantal love suggests an approach to atonement and soteriology that puts the cross into its larger biblical and theological context. Thus, atonement theory begins in the doctrine of God rather than the cross event. Atonement and reconciliation with God are not achieved solely through penal substitution, moral influence, Christ's recapitulation of Adam's sins, or a cosmic battle of good and evil. Atonement originates and concludes through God's nature and will to love.

This understanding of atonement is born from the interstices among feminist, process, and Lutheran theologies. Feminist theology informs it in two ways: first, in adopting its assumption that reality is, at its core, relational and second, by taking seriously the multiple critiques Asian-feminist, womanist, and feminist theologians have raised concerning the message of the cross for women. Process theology furthers feminist theology's emphasis on relationality by claiming that all of reality is ontologically composed within a matrix of interdependent relationships. Thus, it understands the very being and nature of God as relational love. Process theology and Lutheran theology bolster one another in offering complementary understandings of the primacy of relationship and God's trustworthy promise of love and grace. Process theology provides the metaphysical and theological explanation of the primacy of relationality. Lutheran theology provides an emphasis on justification rooted in God's unswerving love and promise. Lastly, Lutheran theology and heritage clarify that love and grace spur this-world experiences of salvation in three ways: eliciting *metanoia* within the very identity of humanity; bringing accountability and judgment; and emboldening defiant actions toward justice.

Covenant here describes the fundamental promise and reality of relationship God offers to creation. It does not argue a supercessionist or exclusionary notion of election and covenant since it assumes, ultimately, that covenantal love is essential to God's nature and thus this relationship is extended to all creation. This atoning relationship does more than correct wrongdoing. It offers a wider vision of salvation as wholeness and beauty; it provides creative possibilities for new forms of becoming. Grace and truth meet together in God's continual offer of love to the earth and God's enfolding of creation back into God's self. Atonement itself may be understood within an ontological covenant that indelibly knits humanity to God.

Atonement is an ontological issue in the sense that who we are, in all avenues of our lives, is created in and by relationships. And if God is the fundamental relationship from which we live, move, and have our being, then this covenant shapes our being and existence. Let me be clear that "ontology" is evoked here in terms of existentialist and process understandings of being—that one is shaped and created through action and relationship—rather than having an essential, static core or being that defines one's self.[6]

A review of the various atonement models in Christian theology reveals the breadth of atonement models in the tradition. These include, but are not limited to, cross-focused understandings. All in all, I argue that a covenantal model aptly addresses both aspects of atonement: reconciliation with God and amelioration of sin. In addition, it responds adequately to feminist and womanist critiques of traditional atonement models, particularly the concern over connecting the concepts of necessary suffering and redemption. Ultimately, putting the cross's significance into the overall context of God's repeated insistence on life, love and relation tempers a theological glorification of suffering that has all too often reinforced further suffering and death.

The Cross in Context: Traditional Atonement Models and Feminist Critiques

In *Saving Paradise: How Christianity Traded Love of this World for Crucifixion and Empire*, Rita Nakashima Brock and Rebecca Ann Parker tell the story of their search for the cross, like the women of Jesus' time—coming to mourn, to understand. Nevertheless, they could not find its dominance in early Christian art or imagery, and when the cross was imaged at all, it was entirely surrounded in the waters of paradise, in images of verdant life. They were puzzled by its absence and curious about what a paradise-centered Christianity could offer to Christians today, particularly women. They argue that the Christian emphasis on the cross grew over time and the connection between violence and redemption grew in Christian theology commensurate with Christianity's increasing relation with the powers of empire.[7]

While I do not seek to argue with or for Brock and Parker's claims, I am likewise unsettled by current Christian theology's sole focus on the cross when it comes to matters of atonement and salvation. Despite the dominance of crucifixion-centered atonement models, Christian theology includes a variety of interesting understandings of how God enacts reconciliation with humanity. Traditional atonement models have been based on various foundations, including the incarnation, the crucifixion of Christ, and God's love as moral example.

An example of the variety of atonement models in Christian theology comes from the writings of Irenaeus in the second to third century. Irenaeus taught that humans were atoned through Jesus' blood, but he also stressed that it was Jesus' incarnation into a human body and life that atoned through the "recapitulation" of Christ. Through Jesus, creation regained the image and likeness of God, erasing Adam's sins and restoring creation to a pre-fall existence. Christ's obedience to God trumps our/Adam's disobedience. Medieval mystic Julian of Norwich likewise included an emphasis on the incarnation as the means by which humanity is reconciled with God. Norwich stated that Jesus joined humanity by falling into Mary's womb, to be born and to reconcile God and humanity through his incarnation, suffering, and resurrection.[8] According to Julian, because of Jesus' dual nature as God-human, he "falls" alongside humanity into our very experience of life, suffering and death.

Perhaps the most prominent example of an incarnational atonement model comes from Athanasius's (c. 297–373) theology. The Eastern orthodox theological tradition continues to carry Athanasius's incarnational emphasis in atonement theologies.[9] Within these incarnational atonement models, the cross is understood as following from the incarnation and a part of God's overall goal of reestablishing the union between God and humanity. Incarnation, the union of God and humanity in Christ, is the context for understanding the cross. While

Eastern Orthodoxy has juridical elements to its atonement theories, they are far more prominent in Western theological traditions, particularly after Anselm.

The classic 1931 book *Christus Victor* by Swedish theologian Gustav Aulén provides a synopsis of the atonement models more familiar to Protestants and Roman Catholics within the Western theological tradition. Reviewing centuries of theology, Aulén asserted that all atonement theories fell under three main understandings of Jesus' role in reconciling humankind to God: Anselm's satisfaction theory, Abelard's moral example theory, and the *Christus Victor* (Christ the Victor) or "classic" theory, to use Aulén's words.

Within the work *Cur Deus Homo* ("Why God Became Human"), St. Anselm of Canterbury (1033–1109) proposed the "satisfaction" atonement theory that Jesus, through the cross, reconciled humanity to God by satisfying God's honor. Human sin is irreconcilable with God's righteousness and perfection but Jesus' self-sacrifice on the cross is able to compensate God's honor. Reformers in the sixteenth century often adopted Anselm's model in their depiction of "forensic justification," which imagines atonement through legal metaphors: humanity is proclaimed guilty of sinning against God and yet Jesus stands in for the accused, taking the blame as well as God's rejection and punishment for this crime.

Peter Abelard (1079–1142) rejected Anselm's idea that Jesus' death was necessary for the forgiveness of human sin. According to Abelard, God could have reconciled humankind to God's self in another manner and had done so in the past through the forgiveness of sin without any sacrifice. Thus, Jesus was not required to die to satisfy either the devil's dues or God's own honor or system of justice. God instead chose this particular mode of reconciliation or atonement, Jesus' death, in order to demonstrate the great depth of God's love for humanity. In response to this demonstration of God's love through self-giving, humans would be inspired to greater acts of love and tender charity. Therefore, Jesus' death serves as a moral example or influence that elicits human faith and conversion. Neither Anselm nor Abelard understood Jesus' death on the cross in terms of God's owing the devil a ransom because to do so would have granted the devil too much power in relation to God.

The *Christus Victor* model takes two different forms. The first, following the work of Origen, sees God as paying a ransom to the devil for human sin. Another version of this first form depicts God as offering Jesus to the devil as a "payment" for the release of a captive and sinful humanity, but the offer is like a worm being offered on a hook. Only God knows that the bait holds the barb that will undo the devil when it is taken. A second form of the *Christus Victor* model depicts Jesus' death in light of a battleground between cosmic forces of good and evil, where the death of Jesus suggests the conquest of evil, but the resurrection affirms the ultimate sovereignty of God.

All of these examples illustrate the variety of atonement models within the Christian theological tradition, with a variety of contexts and interpretations within which the cross is understood. One can see that most atonement models begin soteriological reflection within their overall assumptions concerning the nature of God. Indeed, they propose very different understandings of God. A review of atonement models in Christian theological history supports the idea that the early Christian church viewed the cross's role in atonement in a wider context.

The various atonement models also tell us much about the operative theology and central concerns in each time or tradition. For example, the theological backdrop of the cross for Athanasius is incarnation and theosis. For Anselm, the cross is interpreted in light of an overall divine honor system and, for *Christus Victor* models, the backdrop of the cross is defined by a cosmic, dualistic battle between good and evil. Thus, today we can learn much about a person or group's overall interpretive lens through their predominant concept of God and their explanation of the atonement. For example, there is no doubt that Anselm's substitutionary model is a very common model for United States Christians today. Knowing the honor/shame and punitive theological landscape that elicits this understanding of soteriology and atonement could perhaps tell us quite a bit about the Christians for whom this model is the most persuasive.

The Cross in Context: Feminist Theological Critiques of Atonement Models

Over the past two decades, womanist and feminist theologies have offered sustained, insightful critiques concerning traditional models of atonement, and these have shifted the theological conversation of atonement in irreversible ways. The role of the cross in atonement, in particular, is contested. Of course, there is great variety within women's theological approaches to the cross. On the one hand, some Lutheran feminist and mujerista theologians have appreciated Luther's theology of the cross because it depicts God as the one who struggles alongside the oppressed. On the other, some feminist, womanist, Asian, and Asian American feminist theologians have criticized soteriologies and atonement models centered on the cross because the cross symbol has been used to legitimize passive suffering, and this has disproportionately affected women; the weight of the cross is shouldered particularly by those most vulnerable. For these theologians, the cross cannot effect salvation if it simultaneously reinforces the oppression and suffering of women. Something cannot save that oppresses; the concepts are mutually exclusive.

If we glorify passive suffering as redemptive through the image of the cross, we may inadvertently justify abuse and convey the impression that it is women's Christian responsibility to bear silently suffering, abuse, or torture. Considering that 25 to 30 percent of women will be beaten or abused within their lifetime, this is a substantial concern.[10] "This is my cross to bear" is a common justification women give as to why they cannot leave an abusive situation, and this sentiment is sometimes reinforced by pastors who counsel them. Suffering and abuse are understood as necessary, unavoidable, and potentially redemptive because they model Jesus' suffering on behalf of others—where the "others" are often children or even the abuser.[11] Rebecca Ann Parker and Rita Nakashima Brock's book *Proverbs of Ashes: Violence, Redemptive Suffering, and the Search for What Saves Us* recounts a myriad of women's stories that confirm this lived, damaging connection between theological atonement models and the abuse of women.[12]

Feminist critiques of the cross symbol and atonement theories coordinate in four major issues. First, glorifying the cross potentially treats suffering as though it is God-given and inevitable. This makes the loving character of God in relation to the world dubious and also models God-human relations on a patriarchal model of relationship that idealizes the roles of hero and helpless victim. Second, it valorizes passive suffering as redemptive. Third, the weight of "redemptive" suffering is borne primarily by the oppressed and disadvantaged and it is most often promoted and preached by those who stand to benefit from others' suffering. Finally, it may lead to a human neglect of our individual and collective responsibility to end suffering and hold perpetrators of violence accountable.

Rebecca Parker writes of her own theological shifts:

> I could see that when theology presents Jesus' death as God's sacrifice of his beloved child for the sake of the world, it teaches that the highest love is sacrifice. To make sacrifice or to be sacrificed is virtuous and redemptive.
>
> But what if this is not true? What if nothing, or very little, is saved? What if the consequence of sacrifice is simply pain, the diminishment of life, fragmentation of the soul, abasement and shame? What if the severing of life is merely destructive of life and is not the path of love, courage, trust and faith? What if the performance of sacrifice is a ritual in which some human beings bear loss and others are protected from accountability or moral expectations?[13]

Womanist theologian Delores Williams likewise criticizes traditional atonement theories that interpret Jesus' death as vicarious suffering in light of black women's historical and contemporary experiences of surrogacy and suffering in her famous article "Black Women's Surrogacy Experience and the Christian Notion of Redemption."[14] In light of these biblical, theological, and feminist discussions of atonement, I argue that the cross must be understood in a wider context, that of God's covenantal grace and promises, or our theological and ethical understanding of suffering can become narrow, distorted, and potentially abusive.

A Brief History of Covenant Theology

Covenant theology is certainly no new emphasis in Protestant theology. Covenant or Federal theology has been a key emphasis within Reformed theology since the beginning, particularly within the Zürich theologians, Bullinger and Zwingli, who offered that Christian life be centered on the concept of covenant.[15] Wesleyan theology has also emphasized the centrality of covenant, particularly for pietism and liturgical practices such as John Wesley's Covenant Service.[16]

Beyond guiding Christian practice, covenant would also become a key locus for Reformed systematic theology. The term *covenant* was interpreted to refer to multiple, successive biblical covenants by seventeenth-century Reformed theologians in England.[17] They refer, for example, to covenants forged with Adam and Eve, with Noah, with Israel at Sinai, with Abraham, with David and with Jesus. Most Reformed covenant theologies, however, unify these multiple covenants under these major categories: the covenant of redemption, the covenant of works and the covenant of grace, most commonly the two covenants of works and grace. Essentially, one can simply state that the covenant of works is the prelapsarian covenant with Adam and Eve, specifying the rules by which the covenant of God is maintained: "do this and live." But, after the fall, humans are unable to maintain the commands of God, so God offers a covenant of grace.

Reformed theologian Karl Barth, however, collapsed all discussion of covenant into a single covenant of grace. In Barth's work, God's covenant with humanity is viewed strictly through the lens of christology and God's sovereign decision to love precedes all human work. He wrote that God's "primal decision" is an act of free love, "God's eternal election of grace" through Christ.[18] God's freedom, for Barth, is witnessed to by God's sovereign *choice* to elect, to extend grace and love to creation—to move, through Christ, to humanity.

Recognizing Luther's own emphasis on *sola gratia* (only grace), one can see how Barth's understanding of covenant as grace and election is amenable to a Lutheran adoption. Luther himself, however, avoided the term *covenant* and preferred to use "promises of God." Luther's avoidance of the term *covenant* could be due to his own anti-Semitism, illustrated in his infamous treatise "On the Jews and their Lies," wherein he slanders the Jewish claim to be God's covenant people. However, Luther's reaction to nominalism, particularly the work of William of Ockham, is the primary theological reason for rejecting the term *covenant*. Ockham described covenant as a relationship of mutual obligation between God and God's people just as a political covenant describes the rules of a relationship between a king and servants. In his fervor to distance himself from any form of works righteousness and due to his wariness with the idea of holding God slave to obligation, Luther preferred the word *promise*. I hold, however, that a Lutheran reclamation of the term *covenant* is consistent with justification by grace alone, and it is far more adequate for describing the inherent relationship of grace which Luther intuited so strongly.

The Ontological Covenant Atonement Rooted in Radical Relationship

For more than a century, we have learned from the biological sciences and physics that our very self and, likewise, all of reality is composed of interdependent relationships. Sociological, theological, and philosophical models have followed, trying to incorporate this fundamental insight. In a process worldview, where there is no posited beginning or end of time, the relationship between God and creation is also fundamental; it is simply the way things have been, are, and will be.

At its very foundation, a covenantal understanding of ontology assumes that relationship itself is the radical root of existence. I use the following paraphrased conversation as an illustration. This question was offered by Steve Scher, a National Public Radio radio host, to his guest, a local expert on spiders: "I've had this question for years—I don't see any other bugs in my basement, so what are the spiders eating?" "Other spiders," replied the expert. "You mean it is spiders all the way down?" "It's spiders all the way down."[19]

Analogously, reality itself is "relationship all the way down." I am proposing that we begin to formulate our understanding of atonement through a common assumption of contemporary relational theologies. Feminist theologians have likewise emphasized the thorough interconnectedness of all creation. For example, theologian Catherine Keller claims that the human "self" is composed of its relationships to other humans and all of creation.[20] This emphasis on reality as created and sustained through interdependent relationship has become an assumed tenet of most feminist theologies today. We may suspect that we can fall out of relationship or that being in relationship is based on acceptance or choice, but in process and feminist theologies this is not so. Process theology in particular affirms that humankind and all of creation are forever in relation to God and God is forever in relationship with the world.

Process theologian Alfred North Whitehead described the relatedness of God in terms of the primordial and consequent natures—God's "dipolarity." Whitehead defined the love of God in terms of God's constant commitment and offering of creative possibility to the world.[21] According to Whitehead, God's action and love toward creation always precedes humanity's response, and it is neither controlling nor dependent on the moral worthiness of people. Correspondingly, there is freedom in each moment to respond and offer creativity back to God. The relationship between God and humanity is one of cooperative creativity. God is constantly giving and receiving from the world, regardless of its decisions.

One is assured a relationship with God simply because of who God is and who we are in relation to God. While human analogies are invariably faulty, this idea of atonement may be illustrated by a parental or friend analogy. Why do I love my son? Because of met requirements? Because he does good actions? No—it is simply because he is my son—it is because of his relationship to me. This is where it starts—the relationship itself precedes any Hallmark feelings I may have for him. Likewise, God loves us simply because of who we are in relation to God and this relationship shapes who we are ontologically, literally making our existence and future possible.

With this radical relatedness in mind, one begins atonement in the doctrine of God and the model of a God who continuously, and invariably, reconciles the world to Godself in every moment of time. Because God offers the best possible vision for each moment and because God is abidingly present, God can be said to be loving: present and encouraging, empowering the best that is possible for the beloved. God is trustworthy, not capricious, in God's perpetual offer of love. It is a part of the very nature of God to love, to be in relation with others. There is no "opting out"—for God or for us. Our own *experience* of reconciliation with God, however, takes many forms, such as penitence, satisfaction of justice, empowerment, healing of relationship, and liberation from the grips of sin or evil. Thus the wide variety of atonement models offered in the history of Christian theology may reflect our own experience of God's persistently atoning action.

An Ontological Covenant

In contrast to Reformed theology's covenant of grace and covenant of works, I offer that the divine covenant is an *ontological covenant*—a covenant that describes simply the way things are. In an ontological covenant, relationship with God and with others is a given, even though the quality of the relationship can vary enormously. The work of Catholic existentialist philosopher Gabriel Marcel provides a description of God's relationship with the world that mirrors the convictions of process and many feminist theologians. Marcel viewed relationships with God and other humans as providing the fundamental basis for reality. Reality, he held, is best described as "being-in-society" (as opposed to Jean-Paul Sartre's "being-in-itself"). Additionally, that love, grounded in God, is "the essential ontological datum."[22] God is the fundamental relationship from which we live, move, and have our being, and this covenant shapes our being and existence. With Marcel, all ontology or being is rooted in our relationships with God and each other.

Within the Reformed and Wesleyan traditions, the term *covenant* is commonly assumed to contain a sense of mutual obligation.[23] I argue that this is only one form of covenant—a contractual covenant—which differs from a more foundational, ontological form of covenant also present in the divine-human relationship. This ontological covenant describes an unconditional form of relationship which is offered gratis, irrespective of merit, worth, or acceptance. These relationships are offered preceding and in spite of any response we may have to them. We do not get to control who loves us. This does not mean, however, that we are powerless in our response to them.

In terms of God's covenant nature, God offers relationship to the world without ceasing, regardless of its condition. There are certainly times in the Bible when God offers covenants prior to any response by the recipient. Paul emphasized that God's promises and grace precede God's gift of the law (Romans 4) by centuries. And Jesus, in the Last Supper, offered a new covenant to those whom he knew were moments away from betrayal. In these instances, covenant does not seem to be dependent on worthiness, mutual promises, or obligations. In fact, in the case of Abraham and in the case of Jesus, the covenant was simply declared. I am your God and you are my people. This is the new covenant offered to you. The living out of this relationship follows the declaration of covenant.

As mentioned above, the other form of covenant relationship entails a chosen contractual agreement wherein two parties agree to a relationship of mutual obligation and expectation. These interactions of rich, consensual responsibility can be found in both God-to-human and human-to-human relationships. This form of covenant is also represented well in the Bible—between God and God's people, between individuals, and between tribes—in the form of laws and regulations that guide the religious life and honor the terms of the relationship. In everyday life, such covenants are also exemplified in relationships such as marriage or long-term partnership or even one's job contract.

In examining the nature of God in both process and Lutheran theologies, I am clearly emphasizing a form of atonement built into the very nature of existence, giving preference to the first, ontological type of covenant as the primary definition of God's relationship with humanity. In a process model, one could add that conscious choice of a relationship with God in response to the givenness of God's love, like that described in the second form of covenant, enhances one's experience and one's incorporation of God's vision in one's life. But, in a Whiteheadian model, consciousness and choice are not always present in every moment of becoming; they are "higher levels" of experience that are subsequent to the more basic form of relationship with God. Therefore, it is right to prioritize the first form of covenant as this is the predominant shaping relationship in which we live, move, and have our being.

Like Barth, Luther's doctrine of justification makes grace the primary act of God, preceding all others. God reaches out in love and grace. Luther insisted that this grace is not contingent upon our works, and a covenantal ontology insists that we take this conviction down to the deepest level when we consider atonement. God's grace is contingent upon neither works nor choice. We are ultimately reconciled with God because God is love. An inviolable covenantal relationship of love and acceptance, of God's promising again and again to accompany humankind, is the very meaning of grace.

Barth maintained that it is, ultimately, God's sovereign choice to elect humanity. For Barth, God must be able to choose to love or God's freedom is lost. An ontological understanding of covenant, however, challenges this interpretation of freedom. Freedom is not, ultimately, about choice. On this very topic, German theologian Jürgen Moltmann has challenged Barth's definition of divine freedom by invoking Augustine's distinctions between forms of freedom. Augustine did not rank freedom of choice as the highest form of freedom, even if it was absolute. To develop his own understanding of God's power, Moltmann steers us toward definitions of liberty that describe freedom *in* relationship not freedom *from* relationship. This type of freedom is seen in community, in love and openness to one another. Moltmann argues along Augustinian lines that the highest form of freedom, perfect freedom, would be *to desire* and *do* the good that is within one's nature and to communicate this good to others.[24] Thus Moltmann states, "[God] does not have the choice between being love and not being love. If [God] is love, then in loving the world, [God] is by no means '[God's] own prisoner'; on the contrary, in loving the world [God] is entirely free because [God] is entirely [Godself]."[25] Divine freedom is revealed as persistent love and presence to the world. God is love and, along Thomistic affirmations, God's act and being are one and the same. God cannot choose not to love.

The Atoning Power of Covenant Love

I scratch one place on my back
And my whole back wants scratching
I love one person on this earth
And the whole world wants loving
    —Charles Chase[26]

Certainly Luther's confidence in God's grace elicited radical, real change within his own life and, consequently, in all of Western Christianity. Luther was boldly clear that humans are not saved through their own actions or merit but God's fundamental grace. Nonetheless, he taught that we are moved to respond to this grace, honing our life and service to the neighbor. Likewise, in the forms of covenant I have described above, the reception of God's grace is fundamental and relationships of mutual obligation are subsequent though not inconsequential. Living into an atoning covenant with God can have a great impact on one's life and the lives of others. First, a realization of foundational grace can lead to ontological change or *metanoia*. Second, God's love brings graceful judgment and motivation toward better forms of relationship. Lastly, confidence in grace, love and the promises of God leads to bold accountability and action.

ONTOLOGICAL *METANOIA*

Opening oneself to love and relationship, even divine love, can be an enormous challenge. It is risky to crack open one's shell in a world where, yes, spiders eat spiders. The film *Babette's Feast* depicts a group of pietistic Christians who are so closed off to lavish grace that they literally refuse to taste the feast in front of them. In a similar light, C. S. Lewis described heaven as a great feast to which all were invited, even those in hell. For those who had accustomed themselves to finding comfort in distrust, dislike, and distance from others, heaven's open graciousness is painful. When they are in "hell," they are comfortable, but it is actually the context of love that challenges them to such an extent that many simply board the bus back to hell. Heaven is defined by welcome, loving relationships and a common table graciously laden with the most lavish feast offered freely. For those arriving fresh from hell, this love is felt as judgment in the sense that it calls for a whole new way of seeing and living, requiring an ontological change of their entire person, and this process is difficult. As Alicia Vargas's contribution to this volume makes clear, living into grace and being Christ to the neighbor is neither neat nor easy.

In his treatise "The Freedom of a Christian," Luther described the result of God's grace as ontologically transformative; it changes one's very identity. One is no longer a slave but, rather, through God's grace, one is king, priest, and bride of Christ.[27] All that is Christ's is now the Christian's. While a claim to ontological change within human nature could stand in seeming contrast to Luther's work in The Bondage of the Will, where he claims that humans are simultaneously justified and sinner, here it is clear that there is a deep saturation of the Christian's very soul by the grace of God: "[T]he Word imparts its qualities to the soul."[28] Even if the power and impetus comes from outside the Christian in God's love, Luther describes a real change within the very being of the Christian:

> Since these promises of God are holy, true, righteous, free and peaceful words, full of goodness, the soul which clings to them with a firm faith will be so closely united with them and altogether absorbed by them that it not only will share in all their power but will be saturated and intoxicated by them. If a touch of Christ healed, how much more will this most tender spiritual touch, this absorbing of the Word, communicate to the soul all things that belong to the Word.[29]

According to Luther, "a Christian is perfectly free lord of all" and, as a result, is moved to respond in a life of service and love to others.[30] In his opening letter to Pope Leo X, Luther went so far as to state that all of Christian life is summed up in this. While the terms he used are undeniably patriarchal, he described how God's gift of grace changes one's very understanding of oneself. This realization of grace elicits a life of service—not because works merit grace but simply because the neighbor has real needs. It would be foolish to claim that Luther was an anti-authoritarian social radical, but it is clear that he understood the social and ecclesial implications of his theology and wrestled with them. A radical doctrine of grace has real implications for the rest of one's life; it brings about renewed work for the good of the neighbor.

GRACEFUL JUDGMENT

Perhaps one could protest that all this love-based theology could provide an easy, cozy, or comfortable idea of God that ignores suffering or real injustice. In Lutheran terms, there is the fear that it is all gospel with no sense of the law, either civil or theological. After all, Luther's own atonement model could be argued to be a forensic system, akin to Anselm's, where Christ takes our place and receives the punishment of a wrathful God. Luther's own relationship with his father and his theological context supported this understanding of honor, shame, wrath, and punishment as the terms of reconciliation. Indeed, the title of Jonathan Edwards's 1741 classic book *Sinners in the Hands of an Angry God* could be seen to echo Luther's own earlier fear of such a wrathful God. When he understood that Jesus has taken this wrath in our stead, Luther found himself incredibly released.

There are times, however, when I wonder whether Luther was not able to incorporate the radicality of his idea of grace despite merit. If the promises of God truly precede the law, if grace is ultimately not based on merit, then what sense does a legalistic, forensic atonement model make? Grace precedes judgment and suffering. In fact, covenantal love is the only context wherein judgment and suffering make sense. Against the backdrop of loving, abuse and oppression stand out, accentuated. The theological sense of the law, to illumine sin in our world, is much stronger when one begins with justification by grace and gospel.[31]

Whitehead understood God's nature to be both loving and evaluative; judgment emerges from love. Within process theology, one can claim that each movement of God's nature, primordial and consequent, performs an atoning function, enacting God's grace as well as God's justice or judgment. In reference to the atoning function of the primordial aim, one can state that human relationship with God is reconciled and restored simply because God creates, loves, and redeems creation. But God's consequent nature (God's reception of the world) into God's being has another atoning function besides revealing God's presence and patience to accompany us no matter what. Whitehead also wrote about God's judgment because, as God feels what the world has become, God reconciles human actions with God's nature. When God receives and feels the actions of the world, God feels these in light of what God envisions as the best possibility that could have been; the felt discrepancy between the two is a form of judgment. This is not a wrathful judgment. According to Whitehead, "It is the judgment of a tenderness which loses nothing that can be saved. It is also the judgment of a wisdom which uses what in the temporal world is mere wreckage."[32]

Divine love, fully offered again and again, regardless of our attempts to reject or kill it, carries with it a form of graceful judgment that is stronger, ultimately, than all our acts of retribution or forensic adjudications of right and wrong. An external power may force or require obedience, but only a trustworthy relationship elicits our deepest desires for right relationship with God and with others. We hold ourselves most accountable to those whom we love and trust.

BOLD LOVE

> [T]he elemental love of the Gospels, in an unconditional radiance that embraces the neighbor, stranger, or even enemy, suggests something utterly different from the self-demeaning, abuse-accepting passivity so many have mistaken for Christian love. Through the passion that issues in compassion, love *persists*. And therefore justice in our world has a chance.[33]

Luther's clinging to God's promises and justification made him bold in the face of both civil and religious authority. Indeed, a reading of his sermon "On Preparing to Die," reveals the need to cling to God's promises so fiercely that hell, sin, and the devil are not able to gain purchase in one's heart, life, or home. Keep in mind, for instance, that Luther wrote about all Christians being perfectly free lords and priests in the face of very real, powerful lords, bishops, and priests, including the pope. One year after Luther's treatise on Christian liberty, he was excommunicated. The church got the message. Coming from a different basis, professor of preaching Christine M. Smith's book *Risking the Terror: Resurrection in this Life* emphasizes that a resurrection emphasis is certainly not naïvely optimistic or idealistic but, rather, boldly confronts the violence and suffering of this world because it believes in the power of God's promises.[34]

By rooting atonement within the overall covenantal relationship with God, the threat that we can fall out of relationship with God disappears. This relationship is part of the very nature of both God and the world—this cannot be undone. Atonement rooted within covenantal relationship grounds our soteriological reflections in the persistent, grace-filled love of God that precedes all of our actions or acceptance. Reconciliation is through loving relationship and this is the context within which the cross must be understood, not as the sole agent of atonement. This contextualization of the cross within an ontological covenant prevents the overglorification of suffering and the cross that can happen when atonement and soteriology focus solely on the cross. For this reason, it may more adequately address the lives of women in abusive relationships, which was the initial concern of feminist theologians concerning atonement models in Christian theology. This shift in focus, however, also has implications for understanding salvation and redemption in other contexts of human suffering. Christianity does not ultimately claim that suffering and abuse is redemptive; rather, redemption and reconciliation begin and end in covenantal love brought to fulfillment.

An atonement grounded in covenant restores the biblical emphasis on the promises of God, the offer of covenant relationship again and again. In both the Hebrew Scriptures and the New Testament, God's offer of a covenant relationship leads to a broader vision of salvation and atonement that includes restoration, peace, and justice for all creation. Covenant and God's Being as love, not punishment, is the informing landscape within which atonement is ultimately understood. Atonement becomes a perpetual experience of the nearness and vision of God, a presence in which our lives are shaped and empowered. We are invited to live into a covenant relationship with God, and we are called to surround the crosses of this world and insist they stop.

Suggested Reading

Brock, Rita Nakashima, and Rebecca Ann Parker. *Proverbs of Ashes: Violence, Redemptive Suffering, and the Search for What Saves Us.* Boston: Beacon, 2001.

Brock, Rita Nakashima, and Rebecca Ann Parker. *Saving Paradise: How Christianity Traded Love of this World for Crucifixion and Empire.* Boston: Beacon, 2008.

Darby, Kathleen Ray. *Deceiving the Devil: Atonement, Abuse, and Ransom.* Cleveland: Pilgrim, 1998.

Hall, Douglas John. *The Cross in Our Context: Jesus and the Suffering World.* Minneapolis: Fortress Press, 2003.

Love, Gregory Anderson. *Love, Violence, and the Cross: How the Nonviolent God Saves Us through the Cross of Christ.* Eugene, Ore.: Cascade, 2010.

Terrell, Joanne Marie. *Power in the Blood? The Cross in African American Experience.* Maryknoll, N.Y.: Orbis, 1998.

Trelstad, Marit, ed. *Cross Examinations: Readings on the Meaning of the Cross Today.* Minneapolis: Fortress Press, 2006.

Chapter 9

Christ as Bride/Groom: A Lutheran Feminist Relational Christology

Kathryn A. Kleinhans

FEMINIST THOUGHT HAS POSED several important challenges to Christian theology and praxis. These challenges are perhaps most famously expressed by the following:

If God is male, then the male is God.—*Mary Daly*[1]

Can a male savior save women?—*Rosemary Radford Ruether*[2]

Is it any wonder that there is so much abuse in modern society when the predominant image or theology of the culture is of "divine child abuse"— God the Father demanding and carrying out the suffering and death of his own son?—*Joanne Carlson Brown and Rebecca Parker*[3]

In these passages we see the dynamic interrelationship between christology and soteriology, two classic theological loci that are distinct but closely intertwined. Christian language about who Jesus is and Christian language about what Jesus did and does are two sides of the same coin. The christological and soteriological debates of the first four ecumenical councils attest to the concern that what Jesus did matters precisely because it was God incarnate who did it.

Hence the problem. As feminist critique has demonstrated, the history of Christianity since Nicaea and Chalcedon is hardly an innocent one. The maleness of Jesus has functioned to support androcentrism and patriarchy in church and society. The image of the suffering servant has been invoked to reinforce both familial and ecclesial patterns of dominance and submission.

Jesus as a Challenge for Feminist Theology

In response to the problems of Jesus' maleness, of Jesus' suffering, and of the ways in which the Christian tradition has used these elements in the suppression of women, some feminist theologians have attempted to decouple christology and soteriology, redefining understandings of Christ and salvation. These revisionist christologies take several forms, but their common thread is rejection of the traditional claim that Jesus is a unique manifestation of God's saving presence and action. Feminist theologians Joanne Carlson Brown and Rebecca Parker envision a Christianity in which "Jesus is one manifestation of Immanuel but not uniquely so, whose life exemplified justice, radical love, and liberation."[4] Similarly, Carter Heyward urges a shift in focus from "the Christ" to "that which is christic."[5] Rejecting "christologies that base themselves in Jesus" as inadequate, Rita Nakashima Brock redefines christology as "the logical explanation of Christian faith claims about divine presence and salvific activity in human life."[6] Given these radical redefinitions, one is hard pressed to understand why it is important for these feminist theologians to name their subject matter in some sense a christology rather than simply a theology. When the historical Jesus is divorced from christology, what is the value of the Christ symbol? If the incarnational baby is problematic enough to be thrown out with the patriarchal bathwater, why keep using his name?

In this respect, I appreciate the frankness of post-Christian feminist theologians who reject Christianity precisely because they understand the uniqueness of Jesus as the Christ to be an essential Christian claim. Some Christian feminists have defended revisionist christologies on the grounds that historical religions change and develop over time. Daphne Hampson, a post-Christian theist, rightly responds that without some affirmation of religious particularity and uniqueness for the Christ event, Christianity ceases to be Christianity and becomes something else instead.[7]

These debates are not only theoretical but personal. I myself am a practicing Christian who regularly recites the Apostles' and Nicene Creeds in worship as an expression of my faith. I am also an ordained Lutheran pastor who has chosen to make promises to preach and teach in accordance with the scriptures and the Lutheran confessions. Given this faith and these commitments, rejecting the centrality, uniqueness, and saving personal work of Jesus Christ[8] is simply not an option for me. To the extent that this is a constraint, it is an informed and freely chosen one. I believe that the Lutheran theological tradition has rich resources with which to respond constructively to the challenges posed by feminist critique.

Much of the critique of the maleness of Jesus as a tool for gender dominance and of the suffering of Jesus as a tool for physical dominance reveals an assumption that the function of Jesus Christ is primarily exemplary. The figure of a crucified male Christ is problematic for many feminists because, seen as an exemplar, it suggests that the appropriate behavior for Christians is to be male (like Jesus is) and to suffer for others (like Jesus did). Thus, upholding the uniqueness of Jesus as the Christ seems to essentialize characteristics that are either impossible or undesirable for women.

But is the uniqueness of Jesus Christ to be rejected because it provides problematic examples for women (indeed, also for men) to follow? Or is there a way to understand the uniqueness that might actually help to free us from the heteronomy of exemplary christologies and soteriologies? In other words, might a fresh feminist understanding of a uniquely incarnate Jesus Christ call us into the fullness of our *own* redeemed uniqueness rather than requiring our conformity to harmful images and behaviors?

Lutheran feminists are well situated to articulate such a christology. Historically, Lutherans have been suspicious of exemplary theologies because of the concern that an emphasis on imitating Christ could lead to works righteousness. In "A Brief Instruction on What to Look for and Expect in the Gospels," for example, Martin Luther warns against "changing Christ into a Moses"[9] when we focus more on Christ as an example for us rather than a gift to us.

Despite both feminist criticism of the damage perpetuated by a suffering male role model and Lutheran criticism of the danger of legalism, imitative theologies continue to flourish. Christ is held up as an example not only for individual emulation but for institutional, ecclesial emulation as well (as, for example, with doctrines of ministry that require clergy to be male in order to represent Christ). Thus, the critical agenda shared by feminist and Lutheran theologians remains both relevant and necessary.

But from a perspective suspicious of exemplary theology in general, revisionist feminist christologies do not solve the fundamental problem. Shifting the focus from Jesus Christ to "the christic" (Heyward) or to "Christa/Community" (Brock) retains the assumption that christology's primary function is exemplary; it simply redefines that which is to be imitated. For Lutherans, neither an imitative christology nor an imitative soteriology will do. The call to live as Jesus lived is no more sufficient than the command to suffer as Jesus suffered.

Is there a constructive alternative to exemplary theologies that takes feminist concerns into account? Lutheran theology has typically relied on forensic language in which the legal verdict of innocence is granted to guilty sinners because of Christ's voluntary sacrifice on their behalf. This classic Lutheran "for you" emphasis counters the imitative "like him" or "like this" model, but it has problems of its own. A theology of "Jesus does it all for us" can reinforce models of passivity, dependence, and submission that are detrimental to women's well-being. Eliminating the call to imitate Christ, however "Christ" is construed, also seems to eliminate the value of human agency. Feminist concerns thus leave Lutherans navigating between Scylla and Charybdis, seemingly faced with the choice either to reject God's saving initiative and action on our behalf or to reject our own agency as created and redeemed women and men.

Relational Christology: Insights from Finland and Chalcedon

In recent years, Finnish Luther scholars have argued that a one-sided emphasis on forensic justification is inadequate to do justice to Luther's theology. They call attention to a neglected theme in Luther: union with Christ, also described as the real presence of Christ in the believer through faith. This Finnish reading of Luther is congruent with language that is present but often ignored in the Lutheran confessions, namely, that forensic justification is also effective justification. The imputation of righteousness effects regeneration in the believer. I find in this recovered insight a useful image not only for talking about Christian faith and life but also for developing a more robust christology that is both Lutheran and feminist.

Like co-contributor Mary Streufert in the following chapter, I also find resources for feminist christology in the christological formulations of the early church. The word *homoousios*, "of one substance," was introduced at the Council of Nicaea as a technical christological term. The creedal statement adopted at Nicaea in 325 C.E. explicitly rejected the Arian understanding that Jesus Christ is *homoiousios*, "of similar substance," with God. A century later, in 451 C.E., the Council of Chalcedon adopted a christological definition that developed the point still further, insisting that Christ is *homoousios* with God and *homoousios* with humans.

It is important to note that the Chalcedonian Definition does not simply define Christ as both completely (*teleion*) divine and completely human. It explains each of the two natures relationally: Jesus Christ is *homoousios* "with the Father" and *homoousios* "with us." The christological claim is not that Jesus is "like" God and "like" humans but that Jesus *is* fully, perfectly, both God and human. These relationships of identification are constitutive for christology. The two natures of Christ are intimately and uniquely joined in an inseparable union, in which, nonetheless, each remains distinct.

What implications does this christology have for understanding how Christians relate to Christ? Might it suggest that the optimal identity for Christians is not to be "like" Jesus, as imitative christologies and soteriologies posit, but to be "with" Jesus in an intimate, even constitutive, union? Might a christology of intimate personal union address the concerns of feminist theologians without sacrificing the Lutheran conviction that salvation is a free gift from God through faith in Christ? I believe that it does.

Christ as Bride/Groom: Reading Luther Constructively

I propose Luther's nuptial description of the union between Christ and the believer as a surprisingly fruitful resource for such a relational christology. The best-known formulation of this image is in Luther's 1520 treatise "The Freedom of a Christian":

> The third incomparable benefit of faith is that it unites the soul with Christ as a bride is united with her bridegroom. By this mystery, as the Apostle teaches, Christ and the soul become one flesh [Eph. 5:31–32]. And if they are one flesh and there is between them a true marriage—indeed the most perfect of all marriages, since human marriages are but poor examples of this one true marriage—it follows that everything they have they hold in common, the good as well as the evil. Accordingly the believing soul can boast of and glory in whatever Christ has as though it were its own, and whatever the soul has Christ claims as his own. Let us compare these and we shall see inestimable benefits. Christ is full of grace, life, and salvation. The soul is full of sins, death, and damnation. Now let faith come between them and sins, death, and damnation will be Christ's, while grace, life, and salvation will be the soul's; for if Christ is a bridegroom, he must take upon himself the things which are his bride's and bestow upon her the things that are his. If he gives her his body and very self, how shall he not give her all that is his? And if he takes the body of the bride, how shall he not take all that is hers?[10]

This nuptial imagery certainly can be interpreted or heard in ways that are detrimental to women. Some feminists reject the bridegroom–bride metaphor itself as intrinsically hierarchical, on the grounds that it defines the woman as an extension of the man's identity.[11] As Luther's comparison develops, the details become even more problematic for women. In Luther's description of the particular attributes each participant brings to the marriage, the believing soul, personified as female, contributes nothing of value. In fact, what she brings into the marriage has negative value: "sins, death, and damnation." Anything and everything good she possesses she receives from her male partner. Given the gendered language of the contrast between Christ and the believer, Luther's nuptial metaphor can easily serve to reinforce both the subordination and the negative valuation of women.

Yet for a theologian in the Lutheran tradition, the passage is not easily dismissed, as it is the source of one of the central soteriological images of Lutheran theology, the so-called happy exchange. Rather than rejecting the nuptial imagery in Lutheran theology—and indeed in the scriptures from which Luther drew it—as intrinsically patriarchal, I choose to wrestle with the tradition, in order to bring forth a blessing.[12] In particular, I propose that reading Luther's nuptial imagery not only as a soteriological expression but as a christological one can generate more constructive insights. What might neglected aspects of the marriage metaphor tell us about who Christ is and about who we are in Christ—not just about what Christ does?

I certainly am not attempting to argue that Luther was a feminist as we understand the term, nor do I claim to respond comprehensively to all feminist critique of Luther. My more modest goal is to offer a constructive reading of Luther, using and claiming his nuptial imagery in a way that yields new insights. I argue that neglected aspects of Luther's marriage metaphor can be positive resources for a feminist Lutheran christology.

On the surface, the language of "exchange" emphasizes a forensic understanding of justification. Luther's description is clearly transactional: the groom takes what is the bride's and the bride takes what is the groom's. But this transactional language appears precisely as an illustration of a reality that, for Luther, is fundamentally relational: faith unites the believer with Christ!

Four aspects of Luther's use of the marriage metaphor are worth examining more closely: (1) the difference between Luther's use of nuptial imagery and late medieval use; (2) the transformational nature of the union; (3) the uniqueness of the union; and (4) the mutuality and full sharing resulting from the union.

THE DIFFERENCE BETWEEN LUTHER'S USE OF NUPTIAL IMAGERY AND LATE MEDIEVAL USE

The use of nuptial imagery to describe the relationship between Christ and the Christian is of course first found in the scriptures themselves. By the late middle ages, such language was in fairly common use among mystics, both male and female. The goal of mysticism was an experience of union with the divine, classically described in three stages of mystical ascent: purification, illumination, and union. For some mystics, union with God was experienced as a vision of spiritual marriage to Christ.

Set against this background, Luther's use of nuptial imagery is noteworthy in several respects. First, the union is effected by faith; it is not the culmination of disciplined human effort. Indeed, Luther reversed the direction of the action, describing Christ as a bridegroom who "spontaneously pursues us"[13] as his bride. Second, because sinners are justified through faith alone, it is not necessary to distance oneself from one's sinful state in order to experience union with God. The believer enters into the marriage relationship precisely as he or she is. Purification is the result of union with God in Christ, not its prerequisite. Third, medieval mystics typically emphasized physical union with Christ in his suffering. Luther, on the other hand, describes this marital union as a happy or joyous exchange, union with Christ in his victory over sin, death, and damnation. Clearly, Luther is doing something new with this nuptial imagery of union.

THE TRANSFORMATIONAL NATURE OF THE UNION

While Luther's use of nuptial imagery rejects the active striving of the medieval mystics, nonetheless it is not entirely passive. As noted above, an understanding of the marital union in which the bride remains entirely dependent on the groom is as problematic as an understanding which emphasizes the need to struggle and suffer to become like Jesus. In his sermon on "Two Kinds of Righteousness," Luther offers a more general, less transactional use of nuptial imagery, highlighting the importance of individual response. He describes a relationship in which the response of the beloved consummates or completes the marriage:

> [T]hrough the first righteousness arises the voice of the bridegroom who says to the soul, "I am yours," but through the second comes the voice of the bride who answers, "I am yours." Then the marriage is consummated; it becomes strong and complete in accordance with the Song of Solomon [2:16]: "My beloved is mine and I am his."[14]

According to Luther, then, the nuptial union does not negate the individuality of the bride; indeed, it requires it.

Luther emphasizes that the marital union is more than transactional, an exchange of dowries. It is also intimate. Precisely in its intimacy, the union is transformational. Luther describes the way in which the gift of Christ's "alien righteousness" engenders a "proper righteousness" in the believer that is truly one's own. But does this marriage union transform only the believer or is Christ also somehow transformed in the relationship?

We recognize that human identity changes as a result of relationships. I am spouse of Alan. I am mother of Chris and Paul. In one sense, I am genuinely and demonstrably still the person I was born and baptized as fifty years ago. But, as a result of these relationships, I am myself differently now than I was before. I am who I am in relationship with others. My identity is defined and expressed in relationship.

Similarly, when the Word of God takes on flesh, the Word remains the second person of the Holy Trinity, who was in the beginning with God and through whom the world was created; but the Word is the Word differently in and after the incarnation, because of the hypostatic union of the divine and human natures. When the Chalcedonian Definition asserts that Christ is fully divine and fully human, it explains these terms not only ontologically but relationally, not only what Christ is but how Christ is, namely, that Jesus Christ is *homoousios* "with the Father" and *homoousios* "with us." As is the case with human identity, so too with the identity of Christ: Christ is who Christ is in relationship. Christological identity is defined and expressed not only in relationship with God but also in relationship with humans.

THE UNIQUENESS OF THE UNION

Feminist scholar Mary Daly aptly and memorably criticized the way in which traditional christology has functioned to ascribe divine status to all men. For Luther, however, it is clear that the uniqueness of Jesus Christ generates a relationship between the Christian and Christ that is itself unique. Indeed, Luther uses nuptial language specifically to criticize the medieval hierarchy of the church in a way that resonates strongly with the feminist critique of patriarchy. He explicitly warns Christians against the danger of "false bridegrooms" and lambastes church officials who falsely present themselves as bridegrooms, usurping the place of Christ.

This critique is not an isolated instance but a recurring theme: in a variety of his writings—biblical commentaries, theological treatises, and polemical treatises—Luther insists on the uniqueness of Christ the bridegroom over against the claims of the institutional church to be Christ's representatives. Several brief examples suffice: "No one is allowed to be both a husband and a bridegroom except Christ alone, as John 3:29 says."[15] Luther asserts even more pointedly, "In their writings the popes claimed that they were the bridegrooms of the Christian Church and that the bishops were the bridegrooms of their dioceses. In reality, they were panders."[16] As these passages demonstrate, Luther's use of nuptial imagery explicitly rejects androcentric generalization. One might say that, for Luther, because God is uniquely incarnate in Jesus Christ, other males dare not presume to assume a divinized status. This aspect of Luther's theology is worth recovering and applying in church and society as a critique of the hierarchical structures of our day that claim to embody divine authority.

The understanding that the uniqueness of Jesus Christ engenders the uniqueness of the Christian's relationship with Christ can be used as a critical principle not only to challenge androcentrism and patriarchy but also to challenge a glorification of suffering. While there have certainly been pieties of suffering and ascetic self-denial in the history of Christianity, the classic Christian affirmation is not that suffering is intrinsically salutary but, rather, that Christ's suffering is uniquely salutary. When Christians do suffer, it is not to be understood as the fulfillment of a command to suffer like Jesus but as an almost organic consequence of union: when one part of the body suffers, the whole body suffers.

THE MUTUALITY AND FULL SHARING RESULTING FROM THE UNION

Feminist reaction against Luther's use of nuptial imagery is, as stated above, related to the way in which the (female) bride is described as having negative worth while the (male) groom is described as having infinite worth which he stoops to share with the female. This critique focuses primarily on the state of the two parties *prior* to the happy exchange. Luther describes the aftermath of the spousal union and the ongoing character of the marriage relationship in ways that are more egalitarian. The bride is not simply the nominal beneficiary of her husband's wealth and status. Rather, she assumes full authority in managing the now joint household.

Luther describes the marriage union between Christ and the believer using the tangible legal image of community property: "For groom and bride have everything in common. . . . She is part of his body, and she bears the keys at her side."[17] Although Luther considered human marriage to be an incomplete reflection of this union, his own marriage provides glimpses into his understanding of the joint authority the believer really shares with Christ. While hardly egalitarian by current standards, the Luthers' marriage was characterized by more mutuality than was typical in the sixteenth century. Luther placed significant trust in his wife's abilities. Katherine ran the Luther household, managing finances, buying and selling property, and generating new income streams. To be sure, Luther's views of human marriage are not without contradiction.[18] On the one hand, Luther shared the common assumption that wives should be obedient to their husbands; yet, on the other hand, Luther could refer to his wife both affectionately and respectfully as his "Lord Katie," and on at least one occasion to himself as her "obedient servant."[19] Luther did not appoint a guardian for Katherine in his will but named her as his sole heir and as guardian for their children. The fact that this decision was not honored by Luther's contemporaries is a testament to how radical Luther's acknowledgment of Katherine as a genuine partner was in his time.

Unfortunately, the mutuality Luther envisions concerning the marriage union between Christ and the believer is sometimes obscured by the patriarchal assumptions of his translators. Consider the following translation:

> Thus the bridegroom also says to the bride: "If you will marry me, behold, then I will give you the keys and all my goods." Now she is no longer merely a woman; she is her husband's helpmate, who possesses her husband's property and body.[20]

The English suggests that the status of being "merely a woman" is negligible while becoming "her husband's helpmate" is something of a promotion. Luther's German[21] is striking on several counts. The German word Luther used to translate the Hebrew of Genesis 2:18, which English translations render as "helpmate," is *Gehilfin*. But the German word Luther uses here is *mennin* (*Maennin*, in standard modern German), a feminine form of the word *Mann* (male person). This is the term Luther used (it may be a neologism) in his translation of Genesis 2:23, reflecting the Hebrew wordplay *ish* and *ishshah* to describe the duality of the first human couple. The use of the deliberately constructed form *mennin* rather than a common word for female or woman suggests a complementary created partnership rather than a diminutive status. According to Luther, the woman is not simply "a female figure" but "a woman" as God created her to be! Moreover, there is no possessive pronoun in Luther's text. She is not "her husband's" helper or "his" woman.

In his commentary on this very passage, Luther further develops a complementary understanding of the union:

> Whatever the husband has, this the wife has and possesses in its entirety. Their partnership involves not only their means but children, food, bed, and dwelling; their purposes, too, are the same. The result is that the husband differs from the wife in no other respect than in sex.[22]

Luther's description of the real relationship between spouses and the full extent of their sharing is much like the classic christological description of the communication of attributes. In Jesus Christ, human and divine natures are fully joined in one person. In the relationship between Christ and the believer, the two are just as fully united, and with just as real consequences, in faith.

Queering the Marriage Metaphor

Nuptial imagery for the relationship between Christ and the believer, whether in Luther or in the scriptures themselves, can be read as a reflection—and a reinforcement—of the lesser status and value ascribed to women. To lift up Luther's description of the attributes each participant (the divine bridegroom and his sinful bride) brings to the union as a model for gender and status in human marriages would certainly be problematic from a feminist perspective. But there are elements within Luther's use of the marriage metaphor that offer resources for reclaiming this biblical image in a more egalitarian way. The key to a more generative reading of Luther is to focus not on the transactional elements in isolation but on the intimate, transformative nature of the marriage relationship.

Christology is not and should not be an abstract doctrine. The study of who Jesus Christ is needs to encompass considerations of who Jesus Christ is in relationship with God and who Jesus Christ is in relationship with us. Constructive engagement with the marriage metaphor can help us understand what this means and also what it does not mean. The goal of marriage is not that I *become like* my spouse. It's that I *be one with* my spouse. This is precisely the distinction between the creedal *homoousios* ("one" or "the same") and the rejected Arian *homoiousios* ("similar").

In challenging role-model christologies and soteriologies, a Lutheran feminist theology can respond to concerns regarding the maleness and the suffering of Jesus by emphasizing an intimate personal relationship with Christ and the benefits and new reality that accompany the relationship. True, the sharing of community property results from a gift, but it is a gift that is now truly ours to use with full authority. Despite Luther's gendered use of the marriage metaphor, the benefits of being in relationship with Christ are no less a gift for male Christians than for female.

The growing reality of legally recognized same-sex marriage adds a new dimension to a re-reading of Luther's spousal imagery. When marriage is understood as an exclusively heterosexual estate, then the maleness of Jesus as bridegroom implies the femaleness of the believer. However, when marriage is understood as a gender-neutral estate, then the focus shifts from the gender of the two partners to the intimacy, uniqueness, and full sharing of their spousal relationship.

While Luther uses the gendered imagery of his day, it is plain that gender is not the central concern in Luther's use of nuptial imagery, either in his description of Christians or in his description of Christ himself. In a series of lectures on Isaiah, Luther uses nuptial language in ways that transgress gender expectations for both parties in the relationship, describing the believer also as bridegroom and describing Christ also as bride. Given the maleness of the historical Jesus, the believer, whether male or female, is typically cast in the female role of bride. Commenting on the nuptial images in Isaiah 61:10, Luther not only makes the expected comparison of Christ and the church to bridegroom and bride but also, quite unexpectedly, identifies believers with the typically male role of bridegroom. In the marriage union of faith, believers take upon themselves the identity and role of Christ. Luther concludes, "Thus all of us who believe are by faith bridegrooms and priests, something the world does not see but faith accepts."[23] The believer is now by faith both bride and bridegroom! Luther also describes Christ with this dual nuptial identity. Reflecting on the maternal imagery of Isaiah 66:9, Luther writes:

> He says that He is the author of begetting. "I, however, do not appear to be fertile. On the contrary, I, God, am sterile, yes, dead and crucified. But

> I keep My method of bearing for Myself. I give others the power to bring
> forth, and I can bring forth too. I am both Bridegroom and Bride. I can
> beget and give birth, and I can give others the power of begetting."[24]

This joining of the typically dichotomized, gendered roles of bridegroom and
bride is nothing less than striking.

I am proposing in this chapter the image of Christ as bride/groom as a rich
resource for a feminist Lutheran relational christology. I use the hybrid form
bride/groom to emphasize that gender is not the point in Luther's use of the
term. The backslash signals not an alternative, bride or groom, but an inclusive rendering in which Christ the bride/groom functions symbolically as both
male and female. While the hybridized term bride/groom resists an either/or
gender dichotomy, it also resists the tendency to exclude gender as irrelevant
by referring to a generic, degendered spouse. Christians relate to Christ in our
particularity, trusting that the relationship both encompasses and transcends our
gendered existence. Indeed, the scriptural and ecclesial language of the church
as the body of Christ seems to confirm this insight. The phrase *body of Christ*
refers not only to the historical Jesus of Nazareth but to the church. Christ is
both male and female in the world today, in the bodies of Christian believers.

The christological question is: Who is Jesus Christ? A Lutheran feminist
response might be: Jesus Christ is the Word of God incarnate. And Jesus Christ
is the one who, as fully divine and fully human, is our most intimate life-partner
with whom we are united and transformed.

Suggested Reading

Braaten, Carl E., and Robert W. Jenson. *Union with Christ: The New Finnish Interpretation of Luther*. Grand Rapids: Eerdmans, 1998.

Hoffman, Bengt Runo. *Luther and the Mystics: A Re-Examination of Luther's Spiritual
Experience and His Relationship to the Mystics*. Minneapolis: Augsburg, 1976.

Kvam, Kristen E. "Luther, Eve, and Theological Anthropology: Reassessing the
Reformers' Response to the 'Frauenfrage'." Ph.D. diss., Emory University,
1992.

Mannermaa, Tuomo. *Christ Present in Faith: Luther's View of Justification*. Edited and
introduced by Kirsi Irmeli Stjerna. Minneapolis: Fortress Press, 2005.

Treu, Martin. *Katharina von Bora: Luther's wife*. Trans. Stephen P. Glinsky. Reformation Biographies. Wittenberg: Drei Kastanien Verlag, 2003.

Young, Pamela Dickey. *Feminist Theology/Christian Theology: In Search of Method*.
Minneapolis: Fortress Press, 1990.

Chapter 10

The Person of Christ from a Feminist Perspective: Human and Divine, Male and Female

Mary J. Streufert

IN 1996 MY SPOUSE and I traveled the expanse of the Alaskan Inside Passage, stopping for several days in Sitka, the former seat of the Russian Orthodox Church on this side of the Pacific. Now a National State Park site, the impressive Russian Bishop's House holds the Chapel of the Annunciation.[1] On the white tongue-and-groove wall of this private chapel, horizontally reposed above the simple altar, I found Jesus Christ, with a gold halo and visibly pregnant. Graceful white cloths parted to reveal that Christ was clearly bearing a fully pregnant womb, upon which his hands rested. Startled, I pointed out what I saw to my spouse and pressed the state park guide for more information, but he would not even affirm that I was seeing what I was seeing. This particular image of Jesus Christ has stayed more clearly with me over the years than any other, perhaps because of the dilemma it embodies for feminist christology: How is Jesus Christ male and female?

Immediately, one may think that I am arguing that Jesus of Nazareth had a body that held both male and female biology, what contemporary activists and scholars describe as intersexual.[2] To make such a claim about the flesh of Jesus would be highly speculative and is not the purpose of this chapter. Rather, I seek to address concerns feminist theologians rightly raise about the christological tradition and to strengthen what I see as some of the weaknesses in feminist christology.[3]

Image and Dilemma

Any number of women theologians speaking from the perspective of the full co-humanity of all people are not arguing about the actual biology of Jesus of Nazareth but are instead arguing against the interpretation of Jesus' maleness in the christological tradition, including the male normativity of the three persons of the Trinity. As numerous feminist scholars have pointed out, Jesus' maleness continues to be the *theological* basis for the exclusion of women from ordained ministry in the Roman Catholic and Orthodox churches, as well as a number of Protestant churches.[4] Some interpretations root this hierarchical theological anthropology in Jesus' actual biology, insisting that the female body's dissimilarity to the biology of Jesus distances humans who are women and girls from "likeness" to God. Another vein of argumentation relies on a hierarchically created order of authority—that Jesus Christ is fully male because God created males to be in authority over females. In either case, readily apparent to feminist analysis is the problematic interpretation of Jesus' maleness. In other words, christology has "a network of symbolic associations" wound through doctrine, biblical interpretation, and symbolism that gives Jesus' maleness a theological weight it does not deserve.[5]

What exactly are the problems that feminist theologians raise? In general terms, the problems over the interpretations of Jesus' maleness fall within three areas: (1) the divinization of maleness and (2) the effects of lining up maleness and divinity on the salvation of females, on the one hand, and, (3) on the other, on the ways on which the Christian tradition has been affected by this male idealism.

Speaking to the first problem area, perhaps the most famous challenge to the theological association of maleness and divinity came from post-Christian feminist theologian Mary Daly, who argued, "If God is male, then the male is God."[6] Indeed, a blurred line between a supposedly male divinity and humanity necessarily excludes females. Second, the theological proposition that God is male by virtue of Jesus' human maleness leads to a crisis in confidently expressing God's redemption of females and in understanding those who are "not-male" as subject within the life of God. In the contemporary cultural and religious rhetoric that attempts to dichotomize biological sex, sexuality, and gender meanings, an active understanding of maleness associated with divinity pushes female bodies at an even farther reach from the body of Christ. This is a christological and soteriological problem. Yet the strength of a christological understanding that associates maleness and divinity also carries ecclesial and social problems. To whit, women are yet to be understood as equally called, equally authoritative church leaders, and women and girls have yet to be understood as equally valuable in mind and body to men and boys.

Finally, feminists urge the church to be loosed from the androcentric (male-centered) interpretive or hermeneutical positions upon which it continues to rely. Androcentric interpretation has led to several problems. The inheritance of Platonic dualistic metaphysics within the Christian tradition has allowed for further dualism in the areas of sex and gender, providing the means for patriarchal ideology to infuse the Christian tradition and thereby leave its mark of dualism across the body of Christ: male is to reason as female is to body.[7] For instance, feminist theologians criticize androcentric interpretations within the theological tradition that have excluded the female as subject.[8] Additionally, the androcentric hermeneutics by which we interpret Jesus' life, death, and resurrection have been questioned, and feminists, among others, have begun to offer alternative hermeneutics with which to interpret the person and work of Jesus the Christ.[9] With this representative legacy within christology, feminist theologians have had significant work to do.

Over the past forty years, feminist theologians have raised crucial questions and offered rich and varied answers. However, as feminist theologians have rightly tried to untangle maleness from divinity, feminist christology has encountered problems. Feminist christology often arrives at an Ebionitic or thoroughly human christology, declaring Jesus the one whom we should emulate.[10] I suggest that feminist christology can claim the divinity of Jesus Christ without divinizing maleness. This is in response to what I see as a significant shortcoming of feminist christology that rejects the faith claim of Jesus' divinity and offers no viable alternatives to remaining within the Christian confession that Jesus Christ is God incarnate. Feminist christology also has continued to struggle with a thoroughly male Jesus, either by rejecting Jesus as unique savior or by arguing for a commonality in suffering by lifting up the suffering of scores of women who are also "crucified."[11] In response to what I see as a problematic diffusion of the physical body of Jesus, I suggest there are ways within feminist christology to allow both maleness and femaleness to be recognizable in Jesus Christ.

Ultimately, these two particular problems in feminist christology are rooted in its theological inheritance of historical criticism, upon which feminist christology depends as it seeks to constructively answer its own rightfully lodged criticisms against the patriarchy and androcentrism of the theological tradition. Briefly explained, the rise of rational thought in theology and biblical studies especially during the nineteenth and early twentieth centuries influenced how scholars interpreted religious meaning and texts. What was not rational—explained by the best of human reason—came to be seen as a burdensome weight to Christianity. As one example of this thinking, German theologian Adolf von Harnack argued that who and what Jesus was as the prophetic man in the Gospel accounts needed to be freed from all cumbersome symbols, including the layers of the church's theology.[12] Harnack's suspicion of the symbolic should only be seen within its historical context, however. The strong stream of historical criticism in which he stood carried not only challenges to theology into the twenty-first century, but also gifts, including the practice of reading biblical texts as related to their specific ancient contexts. Still, an overreliance on historical criticism can lead us into focusing on the "fact" of Jesus as a man. The problem is that feminist christology is then stuck, because from the perspective of historical criticism, it is obvious that Jesus was human and male, leaving poorly or unanswered for feminist christology how Jesus Christ is divine or female.

How can feminist christology work through these problems and simultaneously maintain feminist commitments to the flourishing of all creation and remain connected to the Christian tradition? Relying upon the broad boundaries of "no division" articulated at the Council of Chalcedon in 451 C.E., I offer here a provisional christology. Both a contribution to ongoing constructive work in christology and to the church, what I am exploring is symbolically expressed in the painting in Sitka: it is possible to understand Jesus Christ as fully human and divine and fully male and female.

My argument is guided by three seeming paradoxes. The first is that which is represented by the tension between historical criticism and the symbolic. The second paradox is outlined and confessed in the Chalcedonian Creed: Jesus Christ is fully human and fully divine. Finally, less articulated in modern christology is the "paradox" of male and female, the third set on which I rely to forward development in feminist christology.[13]

Divine but Not Divinely Male

The Council of Chalcedon in 451 C.E. laid down a principle for christology that has defined its development ever since: "[W]e unanimously teach and confess one and the same Son, our Lord Jesus Christ: the same perfect in divinity and perfect in humanity, the same truly God and truly man. . . . We confess that one and the same Christ, Lord, and only-begotten Son, is to be acknowledged in two natures without confusion, change, division, or separation." On the one hand, Chalcedon is understood to outline parameters for christology by a paradox. Christian theologian and apologist Alister McGrath summarizes it as such: "[P]rovided that it is recognized that Jesus Christ is both truly divine and truly human, the precise manner in which this is articulated or explored is not of fundamental importance."[14] Given the political climate of the debate, McGrath stipulates, consensus led to the agreement that Jesus Christ is at once fully human and fully divine, but the consensus also involved a lack of specification regarding exactly how the two natures were related. The result over the centuries of Christian theology is that within every cultural context, there are different expressions of what the divinity and humanity of Christ mean. Here is the context and the resource for feminist christology that seeks to answer how Jesus Christ is both human and divine.

Although understanding Chalcedon in this manner is helpful for furthering constructive feminist christology, it is likewise prudent to heed a different view on the importance of the tension of the human and divine natures expressed at Chalcedon. British theologian Frances Young argues that the agreement reached at Chalcedon was not only a political compromise and a paradox that offered boundaries for christology, it also was a positive theological statement on two levels. First, the Chalcedonian Creed defined one thing to be two things,[15] a radical and decisive move because it was commonly understood that where there is no *hypostasis*, there is no *physis*, whereas Chalcedon affirmed that in Jesus Christ, there is one *hypostasis* and two *physeisis*. In other words, the Council needed to affirm that in one "countenance," Jesus had two natures: Jesus is God and Jesus is human, both of which are necessary for redemption. Such a conception went against how "being" was understood; the common understanding was that you had to have one "countenance" for each nature. Second, Young argues, Chalcedon needed to show that we understand the divine nature from the perspective of human nature. In so doing, the following dialectic is preserved: God is completely other and humanity is made in the divine image. Thus, the paradox that Chalcedon itself is keeps this tension in the forefront.[16]

Young argues that the paradox of Chalcedon pushes us to remain in divine mystery, through the emphasis on divine otherness and the realization that human concepts of God will be inadequate. Human expectations of the divine are always disrupted! As Young concludes, "And that means that Chalcedon is more than paradox and more than mere parameters."[17] Even while relying, on the one hand, on the creative space open to feminist christology in the "paradox" Chalcedon presents, feminist christology likewise is wise to heed Young's urgency to think theologically about divine otherness.

How is Jesus divine? I think that nineteenth-century German theologian and philosopher Friedrich Schleiermacher offers a helpful way for feminist theologians to affirm Chalcedon without divinizing maleness. Although Schleiermacher engaged Chalcedon in his comprehensive tome *The Christian Faith*, he did not begin his christological explanation with the person of Jesus Christ; rather, he started with the work of Christ by answering what we know about redemption first. Simply put, whereas the preponderance of the tradition begins with a theory of sin, Schleiermacher begins with a descriptive understanding of grace—and then concludes what sin is—in order to understand the person of Christ. In other words, Schleiermacher described what we know of redemption and then asked what the experience of redemption leads us to know about the redeemer. Schleiermacher was convinced that we know the work of Christ first.

Because of this interpretive move, Schleiermacher was able to say, first of all, that we are redeemed *for* relationship with God, rather than being redeemed *from* sin. Likewise, because redemption is relational, it is developmental. Succinctly expressed, "Redemption is the development of Christ's God-consciousness within us."[18] Because redemption entails our relationship with God, then sin is best understood from Schleiermacher's point of view as whatever impedes or interferes with our developing relationship with God. Jesus redeems us because he has a total effect on us; he takes us into his influence.[19] Knowledge of redemption, Schleiermacher argued, precedes knowledge of the redeemer. In other words, we only know something about the person of Christ because we have experienced the work of Christ.

What we know about the person of Jesus Christ, Schleiermacher concluded, is that Jesus is not simply an ethical model for us but the one who opens the relationship with God for us. In this way, Jesus Christ is truly unique; he is the only one who has the effect of transformation on us, into intimate relationship with God.[20] Jesus Christ is able to have this effect on us due to Christ's own intimate relationship with God. The gift we receive is that we are drawn to God through Christ.

More specifically, Schleiermacher described Jesus Christ's own intimate relationship with God as "perfect God-consciousness" and "sinless perfection."[21] To understand the humanity of Christ, Schleiermacher relied on an analysis of the way in which humans experience reality. As Schleiermacher scholar Catherine Kelsey notes, "In [the] immediate awareness before thinking or acting, we sense that things outside of us influence us and that we influence them in return, even if slightly." Furthermore, we "sense that one being influences us whom we do not influence in return (prop. 4) We are utterly dependent on that one."[22] God-consciousness occurs in the "moment" of immediate awareness before thought or action; this is where God has influence and power.[23] On the other side, in thinking and acting, we have power to change. While humans also have God-consciousness, Jesus' God-consciousness is perfect.

Perfect God-consciousness is therefore continuous and unaltered translation of God's influence on the immediate awareness of one's life into all thought and action.[24] Perfect God-consciousness is the unbroken divine influence on immediate awareness so that thought and action are "sinless." Such is the uniqueness of Jesus Christ. Schleiermacher went so far as to say that what is supernatural about Jesus Christ is that Jesus Christ's *perfect* God-consciousness developed within a life of sin without a community of faith. In essence, then, Jesus Christ, although fully human, is different from humanity.[25] Although *Jesus* is divine, the implication is that God is present with us in the same way as to Jesus Christ. Affirming Chalcedon, Schleiermacher argued that Jesus Christ is alike to us in all things except that his translation of God in his immediate awareness is perfect. "He is like us in all things excepting sin," as Chalcedon states. Jesus is human. Jesus is divine. Jesus' *maleness* is clearly not the ground of divinity, yet Schleiermacher's own theological answer to Chalcedon offers one alternative for a feminist christological affirmation of the divinity of Jesus Christ.

Human, Beyond the Divide

The boundaries of no division set by Chalcedon invite us into a theological and a practical stretch in the paradox of the incarnation—that Jesus Christ is fully human and fully divine. I suggest that Chalcedon offers us yet a third way of knowing Jesus as the one who is exclusively neither but fully both. Such a theology of the incarnation cuts across rational sensibilities and pushes our thinking beyond the "divide" between male and female in the body of Christ.

Unfortunately, as feminist theologian Eleanor McLaughlin notes, liberal theology dismisses Jesus' gender as non-important, that his historical maleness is secondary to his "universal" humanity and thus not soteriologically restrictive. Unlike theology that stresses the centrality of Jesus' maleness to God's identity and the gospel, liberal theology represents the cultural impatience that feminist theology faces when it raises Jesus' sex and gender as issues. Moreover, theological imagination is impeded by the historicized worldview that curbs the power of the symbolic, even in feminist christology. One problem resulting from our cultural impatience with feminist theology's insistence that there is a problem is that we avoid seeing that women are not included in cultural symbols of maleness or in the generic humanity the legacy of Aristotle provides. To this problem McLaughlin answers that constructive feminist christology must include "woman as well as man in the icon of God," for we are all made in the image and likeness of God (Gen. 1:26-27).[26]

Through tension between the historical and the symbolic, McLaughlin works to reclaim the scandal of the body for Christianity, most specifically, for feminist christology. As the apophatic tradition affirms, symbolic reality does speak truth, truth that testifies to the experience of Jesus the Christ in the body of believers/followers. By pointing to the scandal of the incarnate God for first-century Jews and Greeks, she argues, "A feminist Christology must seek just such embodiment, female embodiment, with all the outrage and erotic energies which that *kenosis* of male privilege arouses."[27] The lead to make this apparently outrageous claim comes from Chalcedon itself, for it was through this council that the paradox of the divisionless divine *and* human God was affirmed. So, too, in and through christology, shall the paradox of male and female be made into a third way.[28] "Therefore," McLaughlin urges, "we have to argue what seems apparently as nonsensical as the Chalcedonian paradox of full divinity and full humanity in one person. How is Jesus Christ a person[29] whom we can experience as either man or woman?"[30]

McLaughlin points out that feminist christology has too easily dismissed the body. When working with the "fact" of the historical Jesus as a male person and how this historical maleness is used in the Western christological tradition to hierarchically order humanity, feminist christologies have focused on the Christ event of the present. Succinctly stated, feminist christology often "loses" the body. McLaughlin holds that feminist christology is therefore missing the point that Chalcedon was talking about a real body, the incarnation, as the site of "no division," lest we forget the scandal of this paradox. Feminist christology must take this scandal into the next paradox of the tradition: male and female in order to enlarge the theological tradition's capacity to embrace and support the full co-humanity of all in Jesus Christ. Full co-humanity is inherent to the gospel message. As Lutheran systematic theologian Lois Malcolm notes, the promise God gives to us through Jesus Christ is that we are justified by grace through faith; the entire cosmos has been and is being saved. The concomitant judgment that accompanies this promise is a judgment against "any human attempt at self-deification that would negate or refuse the very gift-like character of the promise."[31] In other words, justification by faith means that we are critical of any thought or practice that sees Christian faith joined to "social structures and ways of thinking that sanction male privilege."[32] Lutheran dogma itself, Malcolm argues, supports the *full* humanity of all in Jesus Christ.

The second problem is that a feminist christology that remains bound exclusively to the historical loses the testimony to the real that the symbolic opens up in understanding our human relationship with the divine. McLaughlin therefore proposes we "remythologize and resymbolize, with the help of the pre-Reformation spiritual tradition, to discover a Jesus who is for humanity, very God, very man, and very woman, or perhaps never simply God or only man."[33] Resymbolizing is necessary if Christianity will move from androcentrism to the gospel, she argues. But is this just pleading for what women want? No, she firmly answers from a theological position, "The feminist requirement that women be genuinely included in Jesus' humanity could be seen as a faithful response to the evangelical promise, 'God so loved the world' not merely an exercise in 'secular humanism' or modernist heresy."[34] Such theological grounds are likewise fully supported by theologian and Luther scholar Deanna Thompson's feminist theology of the cross.

Thompson addresses the seeming divide between Martin Luther's teaching and feminist theology, adroitly responding to criticisms of Luther's theology while simultaneously claiming his theology of the cross as a radical keystone between feminist and Lutheran theologies. Although Thompson remarkably defends Luther's teachings on a number of points, she nevertheless argues that "to bridge the divide" between feminist and Lutheran theological commitments means that "Lutheran categories" must be reformulated in order to clarify the gospel.[35] Thompson's claim is similar to McLaughlin's claim that religious symbols must be reformulated in order not to be androcentric.

The theological basis for the very theological reform Thompson proposes lies in the hidden God Luther explicated in his theology of the cross. As Luther argued, the God hidden in our world not only disrupts the very expectations we humans have of God, but also changes the way we create and live theology. As Thompson states, "A theology of the cross serves as a critical, negative principle. To question and chip away at status quo theology and ecclesiology was, Luther believed, the vocation of all those who follow Christ."[36] Like Martin Luther, Thompson argues, feminist theologians of the cross can be critical of theology in order to deter theologies of glory "that suppress and oppress women."[37]

Conceptualizing Jesus Both Male and Female

Largely hidden from the view of American modern and contemporary Protestant theology, medieval iconography and theology holds a complex view of Jesus Christ as both male and female. Two recent studies by British feminist philosopher of religion Janet Martin Soskice and American medieval scholar Carolyn Bynum make the following points clear: medieval understandings of sex/biology and gender[38] were quite fluid and this fluidity itself assisted in understanding and communicating how essential the actual body of Jesus Christ as God Incarnate is to salvation.

First, a medieval medical understanding of human bodies saw all human bodies on a scale; to think in terms of dichotomous sexes—like our contemporary term, "opposite sexes"—was not a normative medieval understanding. Although I am not proposing that we return to the male-identified version put forward by medieval natural philosophers—that women are inferior versions of men—their thinking led to interesting influences on theology.[39] Because males and females were understood to exist on a scale of biology in medieval thought, rather than as two extreme biological opposites, human bleeding belonged to all bodies; it simply worked better in women. In fact, men were encouraged to apply leeches to their ankles on a regular basis in order to bleed periodically, since bleeding was thought to be necessary.[40] Given these medical views, it should be little surprise that "it was easy for writers and artists to fuse or interchange the genders and therefore to use both genders symbolically to talk about self and God."[41]

Not only were actual human bodies seen to be "fluid" along a scale, but the characteristics of what it meant to be a man or a woman also were fluid in medieval Christian writing. For example, Bynum points out, a number of male medieval writers mixed gendered meanings when they referred to "mothers as administering harsh discipline or of a father God with souls in his womb."[42] Such gendered mixing is also found, for example, among Paul's writing, which may be seen as a reversal that is central to the Christian tradition.[43]

This fluidity of sex/biology and gender speaks to one central point Bynum makes: medieval art and writing tended not to eroticize the human body, unlike contemporary habits. For example, some medieval paintings depict the baby Jesus' circumcision, including the blood from the wound. One painting in particular depicts the crucified Jesus, with blood flowing from his side to his crotch, an image that has nothing to do with sexuality and everything to do with the connection between the fleshly suffering of circumcision and crucifixion.[44] Medieval writers often referred to the "humanation" of circumcision and the cross. Yet, as both Bynum and Soskice amply demonstrate, medieval iconography and texts also highlighted the "humanation" of Jesus Christ in the acts of nourishing or feeding. In these images and texts, the breasts of Jesus Christ focus our attention. Jesus Christ feeds the church, feeds believers, actually nursing them in various scenes. As Bynum astutely points out, Jesus Christ's body is depicted as both "fertile and vulnerable,"[45] fertile enough to give life and vulnerable enough to suffer pain.

Medieval images communicate, therefore, that to bleed and to feed—to suffer and to nourish—marked the incarnation of God in Jesus Christ. As confessed in Chalcedon, the incarnation is essential to salvation. Bynum states, "It is true that medieval and Renaissance texts increasingly and movingly emphasized the humanation of God as the salvation of us all. And by 'humanation' they often meant enfleshing."[46] Not focused on an exclusively physiological male body, medieval theologians offer us a gift, not only to see Jesus Christ's body as vulnerable and nourishing, but also to see all of our physical bodies connected to the body of Jesus Christ.[47]

A fascinating connection to the medieval understanding of a biological and gender continuum is contemporary social-cultural reaction to people born with either combined physical features of male and female or with genitalia that is deemed by doctors not to fit a standard norm of "biological presentation." Biologist Anne Fausto-Sterling points out, "While male and female stand on the extreme ends of a biological continuum, there are many other bodies . . . that evidently mix together anatomical components conventionally attributed to both males and females."[48] For example, sometimes someone with chromosomes XY does not develop "male" physical features, but identifiably "female" physical features, or a person may have both male and female physical features. Contemporary American and European culture relies on biological dichotomization, she argues, which is supported by the state and the legal system's demand of a rigid two-sex division. However, Fausto-Sterling points out, "Sexual difference, [early medical practitioners] thought, involved quantitative variation." In other words, biology occurred in "different degrees."[49]

The number of all babies born with some degree of intersexuality, which can include chromosomal and biological features, is estimated to be around 1.7 percent. To grasp what this number means, according to Fausto-Sterling 5,100 people out of a city of 300,000 would be identified intersexual to some degree. This is far more often than babies born with Albino features, which is just one in 20,000.[50] Our culturally operative assumption that there are two extreme sexes influences our responses to intersexed people. Fausto-Sterling further argues, "Our conceptions of the nature of gender difference shape, even as they reflect, the ways we structure our social system and polity; they also shape and reflect our understanding of our physical bodies. Nowhere is this clearer than in the debates over the structure (and restructuring) of bodies that exhibit sexual ambiguity."[51] I would take her argument one step further—that "our conceptions of the nature of gender difference" shape theology, including christology.

I think that her study allows us to see two things. First, the actual members of the body of Christ, the church, live with a rich variety of biological variance. Their very bodies challenge our conceptions of polar opposites. We are all fully human. Moreover, when seen in relationship to the central christological message of salvific humanation in medieval imagery, our gender-dichotomized christology is also loosened up. As Fausto-Sterling reflects, "Knowledge of biological variation . . . allows us to conceptualize the less frequent middle spaces as natural, although statistically unusual."[52] We are invited into a middle space, socially, biologically, and theologically.

Insights from Galatians: Gender and Bodies

"There is no longer Jew or Greek, there is no longer slave or free, there is no longer male and female; for all of you are one in Christ Jesus" (Gal. 3:28). Although this passage is sometimes interpreted to be a pre-Pauline baptismal formula or to be an uncharacteristic addition to the entirety of Galatians, New Testament scholar Brigitte Kahl sees it differently. Kahl's work reveals the sundering of dichotomies in Galatians 3:28 as a radical hinge for the entire Galatians text, wherein Paul redefines difference and unity "in Christ." Kahl's exegesis supports McLaughlin's assertion that gender becomes unfixed in Christ and is therefore a rich resource for feminist christology. In short, "the baptismal reclothing and unification of male/female [Galatians] proclaims relates to Paul's discourse on 'naked' maleness already described as central to Galatians."[53] Kahl argues that Paul shifted the meaning of difference from a hierarchical meaning of superior difference "over" others to a unity in difference without hierarchical oppositions, both theoretical and social. Paul answered the Galatians' questions over circumcision and being clothed with Christ by saying, in essence, that "'in Christ,' difference has become different."[54]

In a community focused on the disparity of Jewish and Gentile identity, to dismantle the social meanings of these two categories into pluriformity was exceedingly transgressive. Although, as Kahl points out, "Paul's religious and ethnic identity as a Jew" did not change, he came to have "a different perception of being Jewish."[55] It is likewise with the uncircumcised Gentiles who are now clothed with Christ. They remain uncircumcised. They are different. To be "in Christ" now means that these differences do not carry the same meanings that they did "outside" of Christ. In one sense, identity in Christ is a third way between two previous opposites. This radical reconfiguration of difference in unity is veritably apocalyptic. Kahl notes, "In a divine revelation of the messianic event—the resurrection of Israel's crucified Messiah—Paul 'sees' that the binary oppositions and hierarchies (male-female, master-slave, Greek-Barbarian), which the Greeks thought to be the basic cosmic structures on which the world rested, are no longer valid."[56] Positions of superiority, marked by difference, are now simply that: different *in Christ*.

How Paul reconfigured the meaning of either having been circumcised (Jewish) or having not been circumcised (Gentile/Galatian) also affects the meaning of male and female. In other words, according to Kahl, the issue Paul made over ethnic identity also implies gender problems.[57] The position of maleness and femaleness in the world are changed. Kahl's most remarkable point for the sake of my argument here is that the meaning assigned to the physical demarcation of the Jewish male was taken away when what it means to be "in Christ" was made physically pluriform.[58] Males in Christ became both circumcised and "of the foreskin." The status of the male was altered through the changed meaning of the physical male body. There were now three different forms of humans—the uncircumcised male, the circumcised male, and the female. Kahl raises a question over the meaning of male and female bodies in the community at Galatia: "Being a Jew and being uncircumcised—wasn't that a description exclusively for Jewish women?"[59] Indeed, the pluriformity of the two kinds of male depolarizes the sexual dichotomy between males and females, challenging the status of male superiority.[60] In more anachronistic terms, a treasure in Galatians, as Kahl makes clear, is the disruption of identities, both social/religious and gendered, "in Christ."

Further reflection on the book of Galatians, especially in respect to baptism, surfaces the helpful image that God's act in baptism does two important things. Baptism takes us "beyond the divide" of differences, and it makes us one person, a central connection to Chalcedon's expression of the incarnation. Feminist theologians and biblical scholars have struggled with and criticized the male metaphors and masculine grammar forms in Galatians. However, as Sandra Hack Polaski, professor of New Testament and author of *A Feminist Introduction to Paul*, argues, "[I]t is also possible to read the masculine grammatical constructions and male metaphors in this passage as pointing to a reality that is, indeed, beyond the divide between male and female—even though that division is inscribed in the very language in which the text is written."[61] Polaski urges readers to listen to Paul beyond his gendered language and gendered images for the baptismal promise "beyond the divide." Practically, the differences among bodies hold no power "in Christ"; symbolically, Polaski's phrase echoes Chalcedon's confession of no division in the incarnation. In fact, Paul's declaration of oneness in Christ—that the church is a body—does not mean sameness but pluriformity. As Polaski states, "As one person we are not to model sameness . . . but diversity, mutuality, and interdependence."[62] The same diversity is what Chalcedon upholds: humanity *and* divinity—beyond the divide.

Conclusion

What does this mean in worship and praise of Jesus Christ? It means that feminist christology can claim not only male and female in Jesus Christ but also the divinity of Jesus Christ while it continues to articulate important and necessary constructive criticism of the theological tradition from which it came. Stretching to find the constructive spaces of paradoxes and testing the boundaries of Chalcedon afford further feminist articulation. To confess that Jesus Christ is divine must not necessarily be out of bounds for serious feminist thought. Schleiermacher's own theological discoveries through Chalcedonian engagement give feminist christology a foothold out of an ethical christology through at least two christological interpretations: the synthesis of the work and person of Jesus Christ and the perfect God-consciousness of Jesus Christ. Unlike Rudolf Bultmann and the stream of the tradition that followed, including significant feminist work, within Schleiermacher's system, divinity is not accorded to the resurrection or a post-Easter event. Rather, the nature of Jesus Christ is divine, and divine mystery remains what it is—mysterious, but not male.

Furthermore, to see Jesus Christ as fully male and fully female carries significant anthropological, christological, and ecclesiological implications. First, when we think about what it means to be human from a Christian perspective, made in the image and likeness of God, we are freed from thoroughly polar understandings of human biology and gender meanings (what it means to be "a man" or "a woman"). Taken together, our sources here were pre-Reformation iconography, the fact of human intersexuality, and Paul's exhortations to the Galatians as they tried to make sense of what it meant to include Gentile male bodies, which carried different social and religious meaning from Jewish male bodies, in the baptized community. All three instances help us to see that gender meanings are disrupted in Jesus Christ.

Second, taking Chalcedon's paradoxical claim that Jesus Christ was fully human and fully divine, exclusively neither but fully both, deepens the possibilities in feminist christological symbolism. Again, medieval iconography encourages us to loosen symbolic understandings of the person and work of Jesus Christ from a thoroughly androcentric interpretation, one that is exclusively identified with maleness. Although further study is warranted on the medieval focus on maternal images of the female in Jesus Christ, this reminder of different symbolism within the Christian tradition encourages the church to reevaluate its christological symbolism.

Third, such a christological disruption of identities leads to central ecclesiological implications. In short, the symbolic fluidity of sex and gender in Jesus Christ means that our identities are disrupted in Christ. Baptism could never be more radical than this—that all of humanity is redeemed in Christ, no matter the physical form of our bodies or the social and religious meanings assigned to our bodies. As Kahl and Polaski so forcefully point out, Paul's urgency with the Galatians comes right to us: our differences are different in Christ. That is, the many variations of who we are, even physically, no longer hold the same power of exclusion when we are clothed with Christ in baptism.

Radical as all of these ideas may seem, as a feminist Lutheran theologian, I return to Luther's theology of the cross, which affirms the critical element of theology. As Thompson points out, a feminist theologian of the cross works to deter theologies of glory "that suppress and oppress women."[63] If the theological tradition's interpretation of Jesus' maleness suppresses and oppresses humans who are "not-male," then there is cause to chip away at it and to embrace a theology of the cross, wherein our human expectations of God and the way we theologize are disrupted. I hope that this provisional feminist christology assists in chipping away and being confronted by God through Jesus Christ in ways we do not expect, for the promise that we are all justified by grace through faith means that all humanity is found in Christ Jesus. May the image of Jesus Christ in Sitka—fully human and divine, fully male and female—remain with all of us.

Suggested Reading

Baker-Fletcher, Karen. *Sisters of Dust, Sisters of Spirit: Womanist Wordings on God and Creation.* Minneapolis: Fortress Press, 1998.

Braaten, Carl E. "The Person of Jesus Christ." In *Christian Dogmatics,* vol. 1, ed. Carl E. Braaten and Robert W. Jenson, 465–569. Philadelphia: Fortress Press, 1984.

Fausto-Sterling, Anne. *Sexing the Body: Gender Politics and the Construction of Sexuality.* New York: Basic Books, 2000.

Grant, Jacquelyn. *White Women's Christ and Black Women's Jesus: Feminist Christology and Womanist Response.* Atlanta: Scholars Press, 1989. No. 64 in the American Academy of Religion Academy Series. Ed. Susan Brooks Thistlethwaite.

Kahl, Brigitte. "Gender Trouble in Galatia? Paul and the Rethinking of Differ-ence." In *Is There a Future for Feminist Theology?*, ed. Deborah F. Sawyer and Diane M. Collier, 57-73. Sheffield: Sheffield Academic, 1999.

Schüssler Fiorenza, Elisabeth. *Jesus: Miriam's Child, Sophia's Prophet: Critical Issues in Feminist Christology*. New York: Continuum, 1995.

Streufert, Mary J. "Maternal Sacrifice as a Hermeneutics of the Cross." In *Cross Examinations: Readings in the Meaning of the Cross Today*, ed. Marit Trelstad, 63–65, 283–85. Minneapolis: Fortress Press, 2006.

PART 5

Spirit and Body

THE TWO CHAPTERS IN this section bring feminist and Lutheran theologians into conversation with each other, arguing that they share similar concerns that could contribute to the current theological discourse about the Holy Spirit's transforming work in people's lives. In chapter 11, Cheryl Peterson maintains that both perspectives share a concern for the embodied means by which the Spirit works, not only through the means of sound and voice, but also through the relationships within the community that the Spirit creates. In chapter 12, Lois Malcolm offers a reading of Luther's commentary on the Magnificat that seeks not only to deepen themes in feminist spirituality, but also to broaden the scope of Lutheran pneumatology in ways that are, in fact, more congruent with the apostle Paul's depiction of the Spirit's work. In different ways, both chapters propose that a conversation between feminist and Lutheran theologians presents fresh possibilities for understanding even more fully how the Spirit's transforming work brings about a new creation not only in our own lives, but also in the world around us.

Chapter 11

Spirit and Body:
A Lutheran-Feminist Conversation

Cheryl M. Peterson

WE ARE LIVING IN a period of time that is distinguished by widespread interest in spirituality, in which the fastest growing Christian movements are those that emphasize the transforming work of the Holy Spirit, in particular new Pentecostal movements both in the United States and in the southern hemisphere. Even in non-Christian discourse, those persons who claim to be "spiritual but not religious" and who often borrow liberally from various religious traditions, talk of the spirit is most often related to transcendence. It may mean freedom from certain strictures and structural or personal oppressions, for example, addiction to drugs or alcohol. Certainly it means for most of these a kind of transformation, whether that is, for example, becoming a better person or experiencing a greater sense of peace and well-being.

Both in and outside of the church, people are seeking spiritual transformation. In a recent survey of pneumatology, theologians Andrea Hollingsworth and F. LeRon Shults state, "Pneumatological interpretation always occurs in the context of dealing with experiences of transformation."[1] Whatever else can be said about the Spirit in Christian theology, this much is true: the Holy Spirit is the agent of new life and transformation. In the words of the Nicene Creed, the Holy Spirit is "the Lord and giver of life."

Although the last several decades have witnessed a revival of interest in pneumatology by theologians, feminists and Lutherans for the most part have not been at the forefront of this theological renaissance.[2] In spite of this, both

perspectives have constructive contributions to make to the wider pneumatological discourse that, I propose, are mutually enriching. While at first glance,
these two perspectives seem to have little in common, they have shared concerns—particularly relating to the embodiment of the Spirit in the means of
grace and in the community that is created by the Spirit. Further, I propose that
a conversation between these perspectives offers fresh possibilities for understanding the transforming work of the Spirit as the "giver of life," particularly if
one considers the work of the Holy Spirit primarily not in light of creation or
redemption, but new creation.

A New Paradigm for Pneumatology: Critiquing Western and Lutheran Traditions

Many of the constructive proposals made by feminist theologians challenge
certain aspects of the inherited Western tradition.[3] The over-individualization
of the Spirit's work is one concern; another is related to dualisms that tend
to equate spirit and transcendence with maleness, and bodiliness and sin with
female experience. Feminist theologians seek to interpret the transforming
experience of the Spirit in relation to "embodied action, egalitarian community,
and emancipating power."[4]

Most of these feminist offerings in pneumatology can be viewed as contributing to a new paradigm for pneumatology in the West that is beginning
to take shape, but that, according to German theologian Jürgen Moltmann,
has not yet fully emerged. Feminist theologian Molly T. Marshall concurs with
Moltmann when he states that we are "witnessing a transition from an anthro-
pocentric to a holistic pneumatology, one that embraces the whole of creation and recognizes in the Spirit the symbol of wholeness, relatedness, energy
and life."[5] This new paradigm has shifted focus from the individual and the
Spirit's work as connected to faith and sanctification (resisting the flesh, often
described in dualistic terms that are body-negative) to the whole cosmos and
the Spirit's work as connected to the renewal of creation (not only body- but
earth-affirming).

This new paradigm challenges many of the tendencies in traditional Western pneumatology, which tends to interpret the life-giving work of the Holy
Spirit in terms of a doctrine of redemption in Christ and to relegate the Spirit's
work to bringing the believer into a relationship with God working through the
means of grace. In traditional Lutheran theology, the proper work of the Spirit is
to make available the new life won by Christ's victory on the cross. The Spirit's
work is to subjectively apply the benefits of Christ to the individual by bringing her to and sustaining her in faith.[6] Another distinctive Lutheran emphasis
is on how the Spirit works to create faith and its benefits. In his debates with

Karlstadt and the "enthusiasts," Luther insisted that the Spirit does not work apart from external means, by which he meant the word and sacraments.

These traditional Lutheran emphases are charged with subsuming the Holy Spirit's work under christology and limiting it to the present application of the past event of the cross and resurrection and narrowly focusing the locus of the Spirit's work on the individual.[7] The insistence that the Spirit always works through the means of word and sacrament is also seen as unnecessarily restrictive, hierarchical, and unbiblical. The robust pneumatology proposed by feminist theologians and others such as Moltmann begins not with the Spirit's work as relating to Christ and the promise of salvation as mediated by the church, but with the Spirit's work in all life forms, creation itself. In this schema, the Spirit is, as ecofeminist theologian Mary Grey puts it, the "the depth principle of life—human and non-human,"[8] the vitality and energy that is at the source of all of life and wholeness.

One might surmise from this brief overview that to bring classic Lutheran theology (and its concern with the Holy Spirit's role in salvation and the life of the believer) into a conversation with feminist theology (and its concern with liberating the Spirit from the strictures of church structures and seeing the Spirit's movement in embodied, empowered, liberating activity) might simply be impossible. However, as one who lays claim to both of these perspectives and many of their concerns, I propose that it is not only possible but desirable, and that the best way to begin such a conversation is not with creation or redemption, but new creation. Here I follow Methodist theologian D. Lyle Dabney who calls for a "theology of the third article," which begins "neither with human possibility nor impossibility as do theologians of the first and second articles, but rather with the Spirit as the possibility of God."[9]

The Holy Spirit as the Giver of Life

A consideration of the work of the Holy Spirit as the "giver of life" from the perspective of the promised eschatological new creation incorporates both the traditional Lutheran emphases and also addresses the concerns of feminist theologians. The promise of a new creation includes both reconciliation of sinners to God and to one another in a new household or kingdom (or as some feminists prefer, kin-dom) of grace. The work of the Spirit is not oriented toward the past by which the benefits of Christ are applied to the believer; the work of the Spirit is oriented by the future in a proleptic movement in which all things *are being made* new. The Holy Spirit is the relational divine reality who brings creation, redemption, *and* new creation into being. The Spirit opens up the future, creating a community that not only experiences that new life through the forgiveness of sins and the reconciling of relationships among its own members, but one that is also opened up by the Spirit to work for justice among peoples and the healing of creation.

The rest of this chapter addresses some of the concerns and constructive proposals lifted up both by feminist theologians and the Lutheran tradition regarding the person and life-giving work of the Holy Spirit as an eschatological gift that is experienced in and through the community, the church created by the Spirit. There are various approaches one might take to address pneumatology in the classic Lutheran sources, including Luther's writings. I primarily consider the writings of Martin Luther contained in the *Book of Concord* (the Smalcald Articles and the Catechisms) because they are regarded as offering "valid interpretations of the faith of the church" and thus are authoritative for the life and teaching of Lutheran churches.[10]

Both Lutheran theology and feminist theology contribute to an embodied theology of the Holy Spirit over and against two common tendencies in the Western tradition: the tendency to disembody the Spirit's work and the tendency to individualize the Spirit's work. In different ways, both traditions affirm (1) that the Spirit works through *embodied means,* including word and sacrament but more specifically human speaking and hearing, and the community in which this speaking and hearing occurs; and (2) the work of the Spirit includes the creation of a community of life-giving relationships nurtured by the forgiveness of sins and fruits of the Spirit, and that the Spirit opens this eschatologically oriented community to the needs of the world.

Speaking and Hearing in the Spirit

Feminist theologians are concerned to challenge the trajectory in Western theology by which "maleness has become associated with those spiritual and intellectual pursuits that seek to transcend the limitations of embodied experience, naturally associated with carnal, earthy femaleness."[11] Roman Catholic feminist theologian Elizabeth Johnson is among those who have shown how this trajectory has supported hierarchical dualisms within the Christian tradition.[12] Thus, a central project for feminist theologians has been to overcome the dualisms of mind/body, spirit/matter, and male/female. Rather than draw us out of our bodies and the creation, the Spirit draws us more deeply into our human reality and into the interconnections of all living things. I should note that overcoming these dualisms is a concern not only of feminist theologians. The introduction to a recent collection of essays on the Holy Spirit states that one of its goals is to serve as a "corrective to disembodied discussions of the Spirit that ignore the nitty-gritty details of planetary life."[13] The essay by constructive theologian David H. Jensen begins with the startling phrase: "Holy Spirit seeks bodies."[14] Even though this is clearly how the Spirit works in the Old and New

Testaments, such an affirmation of the Spirit's embodiedness startles us because of the long-held tendency in Western theology to separate spirit from body, a tendency which inevitably elevates the former while degrading the latter.

The Spirit that "seeks bodies" is the very same Spirit that raised Jesus from the dead. Moltmann describes the proleptic work of the Holy Spirit in realizing the eschatological hope in the present: "If according to the Christian hope 'the transfiguration of the body' consists of the raising from death to eternal life, then it is already experienced here and now in the Spirit of life, which interpenetrates body and soul and awakens all our vital powers. Eternal love transfigures the body."[15] In *Sensing the Spirit*, the first full-length feminist constructive treatment of the Holy Spirit (and spirituality), feminist theologian and author Rebecca Prichard explores the body-transfiguring work of the Spirit in the embodied lives of Christians using the fivefold imagery of human sense. Prichard intends the word *sense* to refer both to the human senses of hearing, seeing, feeling, smelling, and touching, and also to the task of hermeneutics, the task of making sense in terms of appropriating meaning in a text and/or context.

It is the sense of hearing that offers the possibility of fruitful engagement with Lutheran theology. For Prichard, the Spirit is the "voice" who gives "both prophetic utterance and faith-filled hearings."[16] The Holy Spirit enables us to hear the divine speaking in language we can understand, while also bearing witness with our spirits, enabling our voices to speech, to testify, to proclaim and praise the God who liberates. This includes naming and resisting oppression wherever it is experienced. Prichard's title for the chapter on the sense of hearing is "Spirit, Speech, Silence." By including "silence," she acknowledges the ways that women's voices have been excluded in the record of scripture and tradition. The fact that any remain at all is evidence of "breath of the Spirit who inspires our speaking, who bears witness with us and within us."[17] She holds up the women in every era who spoke out in spite of the prohibitions against doing so. Because of the historical exclusion of women from the clergy and other positions of public leadership, these women found other ways to "find their voice," many through writings. Prichard cites Teresa of Avila as one example of a woman who used the pen to be "heard and understood" in a misogynist context.[18] Here the Spirit acts as a liberator for those who have not had a voice, "freeing the tongues of those long-silenced and filling the lungs of believers whoever and wherever they may be."[19]

Philosopher of religion and theologian Stephen Webb credits feminist theologians with developing the notion of voice as a complement to the more traditional theological category of the Word.[20] "Voice" connects the speaking of the Word to a body; when we hear a voice, we hear a person. The scriptures testify to a God whose revelation comes to us "not in a vacuum but through the medium of living, breathing creaturely existence."[21] Because God does speak through bodies, it is important to listen for the voice of the Spirit in all bodies, especially those marginalized bodies and in the silences of history so that the whole "truth" can be told and heard. Nelle Morton, feminist activist and educator, famously described this movement as "being heard into speech."[22] Women and other marginalized persons find their voice only as they are truly heard by others. The Holy Spirit is the voice of God that empowers women to speak the truth of their lives. It is also the voice of God that women hear in the voices of others, a voice that enables each woman to claim her identity as a beloved child of God and empowers her to speak and act for truth-telling and justice-seeking ways. In each case, this speaking and hearing happens in a community of people.

Luther and the Living Word of God

Martin Luther was concerned with the embodiedness of the Holy Spirit's work, albeit in a different way and for different reasons, at least at first glance. He connected the Spirit's work to external means in his debate with the enthusiasts who claimed direct, unmediated, and authoritative experiences of the Spirit.[23] The traditional Lutheran emphasis here is on the word and sacrament as the "means" of grace and their presence in the worshiping assembly as the necessary means through which the Holy Spirit works in order to create faith in the believer and enlighten the believer with spiritual gifts. On the one hand, this seems to limit the work of the Spirit in an unhelpful way. Feminists would not be the only theologians who critique such a view as a sort of captivity of the Holy Spirit who, as the scriptures say, blows where it will (John 3:8). Does this tie the Spirit too closely to the written and preached Word (and by extension, to theories of verbal inspiration), in ways that are less than liberating to women and other marginalized people in the history of the church? Further, wouldn't Luther's critique of the spiritualists apply also to the idea that "women's experience" might be revelatory of God's presence? How can one claim any common ground on this point between Luther and feminist theologians?

Luther's emphasis on the "Word," of course, is first and foremost not the written Word, the holy scriptures, but the living, proclaimed Word that actualizes the promises of Christ in the event of speaking and hearing.[24] Reformation scholar Heiko Oberman called the sermon an "apocalyptic event" for Luther.[25] In the hearing of the gospel, we encounter the risen Christ who is our future, and whose promise to make all things new breaks into our present. The gospel for Luther is an "acoustical event." The Spirit "speaks" the liberating gospel through the sound of the human voice. Indeed, for Luther, the "ear" rather than the "eye" is the means by which we encounter the gospel.[26] Although theologians affirm that God acts through the spoken Word, Webb observes that "the soundfulness of that Word is rarely taken seriously."[27] We are called into a relationship with God by the Word just as we are brought into relationships with other people through words. It is in hearing the Word that we become God's children, heirs of grace, justified sinners.

On the one hand, this emphasizes the passivity of the believer in God's justifying action, as the one who receives faith by hearing. The ear is regularly accosted by sounds that it does not choose to hear. The preacher is the one who gives voice to the Word of God for a congregation as a means of encounter with Christ and his benefits.[28] This is how believers are brought to faith, as Luther famously states in the Small Catechism: "The Holy Spirit has called me through the gospel." The Holy Spirit is the person of the Trinity who enables both the speaking and the hearing of the Word.

Speaking and Hearing as the Community of the Spirit

Many feminists would be quick to criticize this traditional Lutheran view in that it leaves the hearers passive; their "job" is to sit and listen, rather than be filled with power to speak and challenge oppression in the status quo. This seems to be an especially sensitive point for marginalized persons, who are too often told to be quiet and listen; they have no space for their voices. While classic Lutheran theology holds to the necessity of an office of ministry for proclamation,[29] Luther had a richer understanding of the gospel's mediation, one that involves the community in more than passive, individually situated listening. According to Luther's teaching, it is *not* only through the pastor's proclamation in the sermon and the sacraments that the promise of new life in Christ is spoken and heard.[30] Luther's understanding of how the gospel is mediated necessarily involves a community of human bodies who speak to and hear *each other.* In the Smalcald Articles, Luther offered a list of the ways that the gospel comes to us. Not surprisingly, he began with the traditional external means of grace, word and sacraments, to which he added the office of the keys, which was sometimes considered a third sacrament by the Reformers. But then Luther named one more embodied means of grace: the mutual conversation and consolation of the brothers and sisters.[31] Although some scholars believe this phrase refers to the practice of mutual confession,[32] others propose that he meant something that includes *but goes beyond* the act of confession.[33] If you will, I imagine that this mutual conversation and consolation happens whenever we speak truth to each other and hear each other's truth by the empowerment of the Holy Spirit.

In his explanation of the Third Article of the Creed, Luther made these connections as well. The work of the Holy Spirit presupposes not only ears to hear but also a community in which to hear. Luther wrote that the Holy Spirit first "leads us into his holy community, placing us in the church's lap, where he preaches to us and brings us to Christ."[34] Thus the very same Spirit who calls individuals through the gospel and enables faithful hearing and believing simultaneously incorporates them into a community of true partnership. In both the Large Catechism and the Smalcald Articles, Luther referred to this community as a holy flock who hears the voice of its Good Shepherd.[35] The church is the people who hear the voice of their shepherd. We are made by the Spirit into a "hearing community," those who hear the promise of the gospel and, I would add, who listen for the pain in the voices of others.

According to Oberman the chief rediscovery of the Reformation was not the recovery of Scripture's authority or of the sole efficacy of grace, but the "understanding of the Holy Spirit as the dynamic presence of God."[36] In his writing, Oberman points to the "double operation" of the Spirit in enabling the voice of the preacher to speak gospel and opening the hearts of the listeners, making the sermon a "corporate action which links speaking and listening."[37] This much we have already noted. But Oberman also lists another consequence of the Spirit's embodied action, one that strongly resonates with feminist concerns. He contrasts the Reformation understanding of the church service with that of the medieval Roman Catholic tradition, which saw the church service as a place of refuge from the evils of this world, a place of respite for the pilgrim on his journey. In contrast, for the Reformers, the congregation "does not flee the world for the sanctuary, nor for that matter does it bring the world into the church, but the service takes place in the world. The world as God's creation, with its needs and promises, is not lost from sight for one moment."[38] In other words, far from taking us out of the world, the Spirit's voice draws us more deeply into world. Webb explains, "Hearing draws us out of ourselves in ways that gazing, introspecting, and looking do not. We have more control over our eyes, which we can quickly and completely close, than our ears, which are vulnerable to loud sounds even when we cover them with our hands. Words can reach deep inside us in ways we find hard to resist."[39] The New Testament also shows how the Spirit directs the church outward, constantly moving people out of their comfort zones, crossing racial, ethnic, gender, and religious boundaries.[40]

The Community Created by the Spirit

As noted above, Lutherans have tended to emphasize the work of the Holy Spirit in the life of the individual believer, creating faith and leading the believer in holiness.[41] Shults and Hollingsworth credit this individualizing tendency to medieval and early modern notions of "person."[42] However, in spite of the tendency of Western Christianity to relegate the Spirit's work to the interior life of the individual (and in the Roman Catholic tradition, also through the hierarchy),[43] the locus of the Spirit's activity is not simply the individual but *the community itself*, and it is the Spirit who enables life-giving relationships within the community, who builds it up and empowers it for mission.

The twentieth-century revival of the doctrine of the Trinity reclaimed "relatedness" as the central defining characteristic of God's being, "both intra-Trinitarian and as an outpouring of liberating and compassionate love to the world."[44] Systematic theologian Robert Jenson perhaps states it the most succinctly: "to be God is to be related."[45] The Spirit has been identified as the "bond of love that unites the Father and the Son" (Augustine), the person who frees the Father for the Son and vice versa (Jenson). Joseph Cardinal Ratzinger calls the Spirit "relation itself," and Catholic feminist Mary Grey proposes that the Spirit is "the energy of connection." Grey develops this idea in an early article on feminist pneumatology, suggesting that it is through the Spirit's "relational energy" that "mutuality is restored to the world." She continues, "For the claim of the Word to have authority must be in the originality of the drive to communicate, to connect, to relate, to respond empathically, and to utter the 'I' whose truth is at the same time interconnected with the 'Thou.'"[46]

According to Grey, as the Spirit breaks open the discourse of individualism and replaces it with connection and relationship, a new vision of the church will emerge. Not only will the church view its gathering in terms of an openness to the needs of the world by listening to those on its margins, it will also seek to embody a sense of community that is being "painfully brought to birth as part of the Shalom of God's kingdom."[47] In this same vein, theologian Nancy Victorin-Vangerud proposes a feminist maternal pneumatology of mutual recognition that draws on the "perichoretic mutuality" of the Trinity and new models of family and church practice that reflect this "'new poetics of community' where differentiation becomes the key to justice, love, and global flourishing."[48] She posits the church as a "household" gathered around a "raging hearth" that burns with the divine empowerment of life. The Spirit of this household is the liberating bonds of life that draw the members into deeper relationship with each other and the world: relationships of "dignity-in-diversity," and of "struggle and reconciliation," in which members are "freed for love as mutual recognition."[49]

Although Luther in many respects was limited by the patriarchal structures of his context, his description of the church as a "holy flock" in a general way echoes this feminist vision. Luther described the community that is created by the Holy Spirit's speaking and gathering as a community in which every believer is a "part and member, a participant and co-partner." While he did not articulate this in terms of mutual relationship and dignity-in-diversity, he did articulate the means by which such a community could be shaped: the gift of forgiveness. While feminist theologians speak of the need for reconciliation, too often this only refers to a reconciling of diversities and differences and not to relationships wounded and broken by personal and structural sin. In contrast, Luther drew a picture of the church as a community that lives by the gift of the forgiveness of sins, "both in that God forgives us and that we forgive, *bear with, and aid one another.*"[50] This requires, I would suggest, truly mutual relationships and a willingness to listen deeply to the other. Luther chastised those who would seek to merit holiness through their own works and not through the relational gift of forgiveness; such persons separate themselves from this community.[51]

The new life that the Holy Spirit brings is not only the life of a new community, but the life of new creation, as a foretaste of the future kingdom to come. This new life is received individually by faith but it also is experienced *in* community through the forgiveness of sins, in the fruits of the Spirit, and in the building up of the church so that it can be God's holy flock in the world. God's desired end is not simply the salvation of individuals, but a new community that reflects kingdom values, that is, mutual recognition and relationships made right by hearing, forgiving, and bearing one another's burdens. This mutuality is not only to be experienced within the church, but to extend out to the world, as a witness to God's promised future. According to Luther's teaching, the Holy Spirit continues to work without ceasing until the last day, and for this purpose God has appointed a community on earth, through which God continues to speak the life-giving and liberating Word to the world.[52]

Conclusion

Although feminist and Lutheran theologians are not always the most natural allies, they share similar concerns that could contribute constructively to the current theological discourse about the transforming work of the Holy Spirit in people's lives today. Both are concerned with the embodied means by which the Spirit works, particularly through the means of sound and voice, but also through the relationships within the community that the Spirit creates. Both also describe the new life given by the Holy Spirit as a sign of the in-breaking of God's eschatological promise to make all things new. As Marshall notes, "Without the Spirit, we would not have an eschatological orientation that allows us to live in hope and work toward transformation." At the same time, she adds, "The Spirit allows us to know that we are not yet finished, nor is the glory of God fully expressed in this groaning world."[53]

Suggested Reading

Grey, Mary C. "Where Does the Wild Goose Fly To? Seeking a New Theology of the Spirit for Feminist Theology." *New Blackfriars* 72 (1991): 89–96.

Hinze, Bradford E., and D. Lyle Dabney, eds. *Advents of the Spirit: An Introduction to the Current Study of Pneumatology*. Milwaukee: Marquette University Press, 2001.

Luther, Martin. Third Article of the Apostles' Creed, *Large Catechism*. In *The Book of Concord: The Confessions of the Evangelical Lutheran Church*, ed. Robert Kolb and Timothy J. Wengert, trans. Charles Arand, et. al. Minneapolis: Fortress Press, 2000.

Marshall, Molly T. *Joining the Dance: A Theology of the Spirit*. Valley Forge, Penn.: Judson, 2003.

Oberman, Heiko A. "Preaching and the Word in the Reformation." *Theology Today* 18, no. 1 (1961): 15–29.

Chapter 12

Experiencing the Spirit:
The Magnificat, Luther, and Feminists

Lois Malcolm

IN THE PAST TWO centuries, we have witnessed a gradual but unambiguous shift away from enlightenment rejection of a spiritual world. Many popular books on spirituality have appeared on the market alongside more serious studies of the spiritual practices of the world's major religious traditions. Studies of world Christianity claim that the palpable experience of the Spirit is central to many forms of Christianity practiced throughout the world.[1] There has been renewed interest in the Holy Spirit—as exemplified by the spate of books recently published on the topic.[2]

An interest in spirituality and the Holy Spirit has also been emerging in the work of feminists, womanists, and mujeristas.[3] Through spiritual awareness, many women have sought to deepen their own sense of agency and work for justice.[4] This contemporary interest in the Holy Spirit and spirituality, however, creates a difficulty for Lutheran feminists. On the one hand, Martin Luther was highly critical both of the Augustinian mystical tradition he had inherited and of the spiritual enthusiasts of his day who, in his view, carried his reforms too far. On the other hand, feminists have been highly critical of Lutheran theology for its emphasis on suffering and human passivity before God.[5]

I seek to address this difficulty through an analysis of Luther's commentary on the Magnificat (Luke 1:46-55), which treats many of his characteristic emphases from a distinctive standpoint—that of Mary's experience of God "seeing her" in the "depths," enabling her to be witness to God's raising the lowly and bringing down the mighty.[6] This standpoint opens up new vistas for a pneumatology informed by Luther's fundamental insight about the Holy Spirit: the connection he drew between the Holy Spirit's interceding for us and God's power to create "something" out of "nothing." Not only does this standpoint offer a perspective on the Spirit's work that both resonates with and yet deepens feminist spirituality, but it also broadens the scope of Lutheran spirituality in ways that are, in fact, more congruent with Paul's original use of the metaphor of childbirth to describe the Spirit's work.

Luther's Theology of the Spirit

Luther developed his theology of the Spirit in a critique of the Augustinian mystical tradition he had inherited. What he criticized was the idea that we encounter the Spirit only when we strive to follow the ideals of our "higher nature" (our highest aspirations) in contrast to our "lower nature" (our baser passions and desires).[7] Later in his life, he criticized those he called "spiritual enthusiasts" for a similar difficulty: they equated their "higher" but immediate charismatic experience of the Spirit with the totality of the Spirit's work.[8] Instead of finding the Spirit in our highest yearnings or charismatic experiences, Luther argued that it is precisely in "inner conflict" that we experience the work of the Holy Spirit, a theme he developed in his early "Lectures on the Psalms" and "Epistle to the Romans" and one that would remain central throughout his work.[9]

Luther's theology of the Spirit centered on his interpretation of Romans 8:26, "the Spirit helps us in our weakness . . . interceding with inexpressible groans," which he interpreted as describing the "inner conflict" of a sinner tortured not only by guilt and the anguish of hell and death, but also by the struggle with Satan and even with God and the whole creation. Luther wrote that seeing no escape, the sinner ultimately blasphemes God, desiring God to become someone else or wishing that God did not exist. It is precisely here that God's alien work (*opus alienum*) of wrath prepares the sinner for God's proper work (*opus proprium*) of love. In the midst of this conflict, the Spirit intercedes for us, praying to God through our laments.

In this work, the Holy Spirit is always *Spiritus creator* (the creative Spirit). Luther frequently linked Romans 8:26 with Genesis 1:2, where the Spirit moved upon the waters at the first creation and brought light and life into the darkness of the deep.[10] According to Luther, in our laments, the Spirit not only "kills" the old sinful self but also creates us anew, "making us alive" with Christ's life. In our sin and suffering, God puts on a "strange garb," appearing to us not as the victorious Christ but as Christ in his suffering and death. As we cling to God's promises in the lowly signs of the proclaimed Word and the sacraments of bread and wine, the Spirit makes the crucified and raised Christ a living reality for us in the midst of our sin and suffering. It is here, in the midst of life's struggles and not in our higher strivings and aspirations, that the Spirit works in the strange garb of sin and suffering, showing us a God who is continually turning to those lost in sin and death in order to create new life out of nothing—life out of death.[11]

The Feminist Critique of Luther

Feminist theologians have tended to be highly critical of this story of the Spirit's work.[12] In this story, as Reformed feminist theologian Serene Jones points out, God wrathfully "undoes" (crucifies) the subject. God judges as guilty the arrogant unbelief of the sinner who has defined himself not only according to his own desires, but also according to his own attempts to justify himself. The law reveals the sinner's narcissistic self-understanding—a self-understanding exhibited most vividly in his desire to save himself. The sinner's pretensions to self-definition and pride are broken by the law's harsh, judgmental force. Before God, the sinner is "fragmented" and "lost."[13]

What happens, Jones asks, to the woman who enters this tale having spent her life not in a space of narcissistic self-definition but in a space of "fragmentation" and "dissolution"? What happens to the woman who, as the feminist theorist Luce Irigaray has described, exists without much self-definition, because she has been defined by her culture to be radically "fluid," to be in a space that is always receiving—that is always *in* her relation to others, to a fault. Unlike "man," who lives in an impenetrable container of his own making, she has lived without an "envelope" to hold her.[14] Moreover, because of her lack of self-definition, she has no boundaries to define herself against the onslaught of a culture that also wishes to define her in her fluidity, according to an economy of male desire. Her few borders serve only to have value when they are used by another. In this, she is not allowed to be truly "other"—to be truly a subject in her own right.[15]

Jones points out that feminist theory helps us realize that this woman suffers from an illness different from Luther's classical male sinner. Her sin is not that of an overly rigid self-construction; her brokenness lies in her *lack* of containment, in her cultural definition *in relation* to others.[16] The source of her alienation from God is not an overabundance of self, but a lack of self-definition. She lacks the structuring boundaries that could allow her to be an other in relation to God and to others. She exists as one whose will and identity has been diluted in her many relations.[17]

What happens, Jones goes on to ask, when this woman encounters Luther's tale? She either may not relate to the story, unable to see herself in the narration, or she may identify with Luther's sinner and take upon herself a script designed for the prideful sinner. Using Luther's understanding, when God meets this woman, who already suffers from a debilitating lack of self-containment, God potentially recapitulates the dynamics of her oppression and self-loss. Rather than opening into transformation and a new beginning, this conversion story simply reenacts this woman's story of a cultural unraveling she knows only too well—more like sin than the freeing act of divine mercy.[18]

Luther's Commentary on the Magnificat

With this feminist critique in mind, we turn to Luther's commentary on the Magnificat. There he developed his characteristic themes, but from a unique standpoint: that of *Mary's experience* of God's "seeing her in the depths"—an experience that leads not only to mystical exaltation, but also to prophetic witness to God's bringing down the mighty and raising the lowly.

In the commentary, Mary speaks out of her experience, where the Holy Spirit "enlightens" and "instructs her." According to Luther, "*Experience is the school of the Spirit.*" We cannot understand God or God's Word without receiving such understanding "immediately" from the Holy Spirit—"without experiencing, proving, and feeling it" for ourselves.[19] Through her experience, Luther observed, Mary teaches us the "art" of understanding the "work, method, nature, and will of God."[20] This "art," as we will see, is related to three central insights that Luther wove together in order to interpret Mary's hymn, drawing on both mystical themes (to describe Mary's exaltation in the first part) and prophetic themes (to describe her prophetic witness in the second part).

MARY'S THREE INSIGHTS

What "deep insight and wisdom" does Mary's experience teach us about the Holy Spirit? It teaches us that the Spirit continues to act in the same way that the Spirit has acted since the beginning of time when God created the world out of a "formless void"—out of nothing (Gen. 1:2). Human beings cannot make something out of nothing (an allusion to the old axiom *Ex nihilo nihil fit*, "out of nothing, nothing is made"). By contrast, God always creates out of "nothing"[21] and God's creative power continues to be an "energetic power"—a "continuous activity"—that "works and operates without ceasing."[22]

Nonetheless, Mary's experience also teaches us that the Spirit's creative power affects us differently—depending on our circumstances: God brings down the mighty, the rich, and the proud, and God raises the lowly, the poor, and the humble. Whatever is *nothing*, God makes into something that is "precious, honorable, blessed, and living" and whatever is *something* God makes it to be "nothing, worthless, despised, wretched, and dying" (see 1 Cor. 1:28).[23] The same divine activity both "comforts" and "terrifies." Those in affliction hear words of comfort; those who are self-satisfied—and oppress others—hear words that terrify them.[24]

Moreover, Mary's experience teaches us about a fundamental difference between the Spirit's epistemology (the way God "sees" things) and human epistemology (the way human beings "see" things). Here we touch on a theme central to Luther's work—exemplified in the Heidelberg Disputation, where he described how the "theologian of the cross" says what a thing is in contrast to the "theologian of glory" who disguises self-interest by only appearing to be wise and righteous.[25] However, Mary's prophetic witness does not attend to the individual's internal conflict between reality (experiencing the cross) and appearance (using the law and wisdom to disguise self-interest); rather, her prophetic witness draws on broader patterns of relationships among people to describe the contrast between God's way of seeing and our human way of seeing. Only God, she witnessed, has that "sort of seeing that looks into the depths of need and misery;" only God is "near to all who are in the depths." Human beings, by contrast, tend to look to what is above them—to what attracts them. They strive after "honor, power, wealth, knowledge, a life of ease, and whatever is lofty and great." There are many "hangers-on" around people who have these things. The entire world gathers around them, gladly yielding in their service, wanting to be at their side to share in their exaltation. No one is willing to look into the depths—into poverty, disgrace, squalor, misery, and anguish. We avoid people afflicted with these things; we forsake them, shun them, and leave them to themselves: "No one dreams of helping them or of making something out of them."[26] Because we cannot create what we desire, as human beings we tend only to love or desire what we find attractive and appealing. By contrast, as Luther pointed out in the Heidelberg Disputation, God's love always *creates what it desires*.[27]

MARY AS AN EXEMPLAR OF FAITH

Having presented these three insights, Luther's commentary goes on to say that we are to honor Mary not because she had a miraculous birth without violating her virginity or because she is an idol to be worshiped but because she is an *exemplar of faith*. According to Luther, Mary taught through her experience and through her words, that when "God sees us in the depths" and thereby creates something out of nothing, our hearts overflow with gladness.[28] God could have chosen many other women, women of higher status, but God *chose her*, precisely in her poverty and lowliness, and because of this, she is able to leap and dance with great pleasure:

> And Mary said, "My soul magnifies the Lord,
> and my spirit rejoices in God my Savior,
> for [God] has looked with favor on the lowliness of [God's] servant.
> Surely, from now on all generations will call me blessed;

for the Mighty One has done great things for me,
and holy is [God's] name (Luke 1:46-49).

Mary's words "my soul magnifies the Lord" expressed the "the strong ardor and exuberant joy" she felt as she was "inwardly exalted in the Spirit." Her words flowed forth with "sighs and groaning," and the Spirit came seething with them. Her words live. They have hands and feet. They are fire, light, and life. Not only her words, but her whole body and life strained for utterance. It is as if she said: "My life and all my senses float in the love and praise of God and in lofty pleasures. . . . I am exalted, more than I exalt myself, to praise the Lord." She was so "saturated with divine sweetness and the Spirit" that she was given an exuberance that is not a human work, but a joyful experience that is "the work of God alone."[29]

With these words, we learn from Mary that faith is about tasting before seeing. When we experience God "seeing us in the depths," we taste a "sensible sweetness" that cannot be proven by reason or empirically verified by the senses, but can only be known by experiencing and feeling it. Such experience affects our whole lives—not only our spirit and minds, but also our bodies and the full range of human emotions including "hatred, love, delight, horror, and the like." God sees both our good parts and our bad parts, and by seeing us in our totality transforms our whole being.[30]

We also learn from Mary that we are not to put our trust in the *gifts* God gives, regardless of how great they may be (spiritual or temporal). Rather, we are to trust solely in *God's very own* self—even as we can appreciate and not despise the gifts we receive. In the gifts, we may touch God's "hand," but with God's gracious regard for us, we receive God's very own "heart, mind, spirit, and will."[31]

Here Luther's commentary uses *mystical* language, with its logic of double-negation, to describe how Mary trusted solely in "God's *bare* goodness," which at times may be "unfelt," and not in whether she either *had* or *had not* received certain gifts from God.[32] On the one hand, Mary differed from "impure and perverted lovers," who only seek the gifts that God gives them and are plunged into despair when they are taken away. Like Job, Mary is a model of faith who loved and praised God evenly, whether in want or plenty (compare with Phil. 4:12). On the other hand, she also differed from the "falsely humble," who think that they need to appear humble, affecting humble clothing, faces, gestures, and words, but with the intention of merely having others *perceive* them as being humble. When Mary rejoiced in God's having "regarded her in her low state," her stress was not on her *low estate* but on the fact that God has *regarded* her. Like Queen Esther, whom God used precisely because of her wealth and power, Mary relied solely on how God *regarded her*—not comparing what she was given to what others were given, but focusing solely on what God was calling *her* to do.[33] In sum, Mary solely loved "the *bare, unfelt goodness* that is *hidden* in God." Indeed, Luther observed, this is the only way to *"equanimity"* and an *"even mind."*[34]

MARY AS A PROPHETIC WITNESS

Nonetheless, the Magnificat is not merely a hymn about Mary's mystical exaltation. Her ecstatic sighs and groans were directly related to her sense of vocation as a *prophetic witness* to God's great transforming work of justice in history.

> [God's] mercy is for those who fear [God]
>> from generation to generation.
> [God] has shown strength with [God's] arm;
>> [God] has scattered the proud in the thoughts of their hearts.
> [God] has brought down the powerful from their thrones,
>> and lifted up the lowly;
> [God] has filled the hungry with good things,
>> and sent the rich away empty.
> [God] has helped [God's] servant Israel,
>> in remembrance of God's mercy,
> according to the promise God made to our ancestors,
>> to Abraham and to his descendants forever (Luke 1:50-55).

Here Luther's commentary uses *prophetic* themes from Jeremiah 9:23-24 to describe what Mary has to teach us in the second part of the hymn, organizing his comments around three kinds of divine works of God and three classes of people:

1. God's *kindness* shows *mercy* to those who are "poor in spirit," but *breaks the spiritual pride* of those who boast in their *wisdom* (in their spiritual possessions and all the gifts they bring—not only "popularity, fame, good report" but also "intellect, reason, wit, knowledge, piety, virtue, and a godly life");
2. God's *justice exalts* the oppressed, but *brings down* those who boast in their *might* (their "authority, nobility, friends, high station, and honor, whether pertaining to temporal or to spiritual goods or persons");
3. God's *righteousness* takes care of the poor and all who "lack life's necessities," but sends away those who boast in their *riches* (their wealth, good health, beauty, pleasure, strength, and so on).[35]

These different modes of "divine work" are intrinsically related to God's way of "seeing only in the depths." As demonstrated when Christ was powerless on the cross, God performs God's greatest work—conquering sin, death, hell, the devil, and all evil—precisely at the points where God's power appears to be most contradicted. In turn, God's strength ends precisely when human beings try to have everything under their control. "When their bubble is full-blown, and everyone supposes them to have won and overcome, and they themselves feel smug in their achievement, then God pricks the bubble, and it is all over."[36]

Luther's writing elaborates at great length on how God "breaks the spiritual pride" of those who boast in their "false wisdom." No one—whether rich or mighty—is so "puffed up and bold" as the "smart aleck" who feels and knows that "he is in the right, understands all about a matter, [and] is wiser than other people." When he finds that he ought to give way and confess himself in the wrong, he becomes "so insolent and is so utterly devoid of the fear of God" that he dares to boast of "being infallible"—declaring that "God is on his side" and the "others on the devil's side," with "the effrontery" of appealing to God's judgment. When such a person has power, he rushes "headlong, persecuting, condemning, slandering . . . all who differ with him, saying afterward he did it all to the honor and glory of God. . . . Oh, how big a bubble we have here!" Luther exclaimed. People like this *must* have their way. They cannot imagine that they could be wrong or give way. They simply assert, "We are in the right" and "that is the end of it."[37]

Ought we not to defend the truth and what is right? Are we merely to remain passive in the face of evil? Are we not to defend a righteous cause? Everything depends, Luther responded, on a "proper understanding of *being in the right*." Of course, we are to defend the truth and what is right—and even suffer for it. This is what martyrs have done throughout the ages. Nonetheless, we are not to defend righteous causes by means that negate the very things we are seeking to defend. That would be to turn "the right" into "a wrong." We need not "rage and storm" and assert our will "by force" or "sulk impatiently." Once we have made our case and "confessed" its "goodness" with "*equanimity*," we can "*let such things go*"—that is, such things as our "need to be right"—and "cleave to God alone."[38]

The Magnificat and Feminist Spirituality

We can see that Luther's commentary on the Magnificat presents us with a very different picture of the Spirit's activity than the one usually given in Luther's writings. In this commentary, we do not find God—to use the language Jones uses—"wrathfully crucifying" ("undoing") a sinner, revealing his "narcissistic self-understanding," a self-understanding most evident in his desire to save himself.[39] Rather, we find a woman seen by God in her depths, what could be described as her "fragmentation" and "dissolution." Seen precisely in her fluidity, in the lowly estate by which she had been defined by others, Mary was given a new identity. Inwardly exalted by the Spirit, she became fully alive. She experienced an ecstasy that overflowed with such exuberance that she was lifted out of her state of ignominy and empowered to become a powerful agent in her own right—a bold exemplar of faith and prophetic witness to God's bringing down the mighty and raising the lowly.

The Magnificat does not tell a tale of God meeting a prideful sinner. Rather, it tells a tale of God meeting a woman whom society had seen as insignificant and giving her a new status (as an exemplar of faith alongside Abraham, Job, and Esther) as well as a new sense of agency in God's coming reign (as a prophetic witness alongside the prophets of old). Her story of God's "seeing" her undid not her pride, but the "cultural unraveling" she knew only too well. Far from reca- pitulating the dynamics of her previous life, Mary was transformed and entered a new beginning.

Nonetheless, this tale of Mary's mystical exaltation and prophetic agency is not merely a tale about a reversal of power. Its tale of transformation is much more profound than this. Mary's experience was rooted in a divine sort of see- ing—God's regard for her—that always creates out of nothing. God's regard for Mary made her a prophetic witness to a much more fruitful potency than any- thing wealth, power, and wisdom could create. This divine epistemology, which always creates what it desires, is very different from human ways of perceiving and responding to life. In other words, this divine creative potency does not merely reverse roles in an existing finite system of relationships when it brings down the mighty and raises the lowly (even though it also does this). It does not merely shift the placeholders of who has the most power or wealth, or who is the wisest or most "in the right." Rather, it brings about a more radical trans- formation in how human beings relate to one another—one that is rooted in the Spirit's fecundity of righteousness, justice, and kindness. God's sort of seeing not only gave Mary equanimity in the face of want or plenty, it also enabled her to make her prophetic case without needing to be in the right or powerful or wealthy. Far from being a passive acquiescence to the status quo, this equanim- ity was rooted in a creative potency that has the power to change the *very terms* that define how human beings perceive and respond to one another.

In sum, Mary's experience gave witness to God's raising the lowly and bring- ing down the mighty (recall Mary's second insight about the Spirit's work). Her standpoint provides us with a fruitful context for understanding Luther's chief contribution to pneumatology: his insight into the Spirit's capacity to create out of nothing, a capacity that characterizes what lies at the heart of God's sort of seeing (recall Mary's first and third insights about the Spirit's work). The standpoint of Mary's experience enables us to appropriate this pneumatological insight in ways that not only empower many women but that perhaps also *deepen* that empowerment with a much more freeing way of being in the world. Mary's tale not only resonates with a feminist spirituality that seeks to undo all such cultural unraveling, but her tale also deepens such a spirituality with a way of perceiving and responding to life out of the Spirit's potency to create the very conditions for just, righteous and compassionate relationships in the first place.

The Magnificat and Themes in Paul's Theology

Moreover, if Mary's tale resonates with and deepens feminist spirituality, then it also *broadens* the scope of Lutheran pneumatology. Because Mary's witness encompasses both those who are high and those who are low within human scales of perception, it encompasses a much more *comprehensive* perspective for understanding the Spirit's work than simply that of the torments of an individual conscience. Furthermore, it does so in ways that are, in fact, more *congruent* with the apostle Paul's original formulation of these themes.[40]

THE SPIRIT'S GROANING THROUGH OUR WEAKNESS

In his letter to the Romans, Paul located the Spirit's "groaning" (*stenágmois*) (Rom. 8:26) not only in relation to the inward "groaning" (*stenazámen*) of those who have the "first fruits" of the Spirit (Rom. 8:23) but also in relation to the entire creation's "groaning" (*sustenázei*) in the face of its own "futility" as it awaits the full disclosure of God's purposes for history (Rom. 8:19-22).[41] For Paul, the conflict at the heart of this groaning, the conflict between the *flesh* and the *Spirit* (Rom. 8:5-8), was not simply that of a tormented conscience—although it included such torment (see Rom. 7:14-25)—but, rather, the more fundamental apocalyptic conflict between the *"old age"* of this passing world, which is enslaved by the unraveling patterns of sin and injustice, and death as a consequence, and the *"new age"* of the Spirit ushered in by Jesus' death and resurrection (1 Cor. 15:45).[42] In the language of the Magnificat, the conflict between the old age and the new age is precisely the conflict between human ways of perceiving and responding to life (based on power, wealth, and even wisdom) and God's sort of seeing that always creates "something" (a new world, a new pattern of relationships, based on God's righteousness, justice, and kindness) out of "nothing" (sin, injustice, disease, and death).

It is within this context that Paul described how faith and baptism into Christ's death and life enables one to have a foretaste, a "first fruit," of the Spirit's giving birth to a new age not only through our own "inward groaning"—our own personal cries for something better—but also through the entire creation's yearning for something beyond its seeming futility.[43] Paul used the biblical metaphor of the pangs of childbirth to describe how we live between these two ages in the interim period, the hiatus, between Christ's resurrection and his final return when all things will be created anew and God will be "all in all" (1 Cor. 15:28). As the Spirit "groans" through our "groaning," we now can, indeed, perceive that we are, in fact, a "new creation." We no longer need to view one another in the same way (2 Cor. 5:17).[44] The cultural cosmos of the ancient world—founded as it was on distinctions between male and female, Jew and Greek, slave and free—no longer exists (Gal. 3:28).[45] It has been replaced by a new age of the Spirit's fecundity of justice and mercy ushered in by the "foolishness" and "weakness" of the cross. A new people now exists, whose old selves have been crucified with Christ and whose new selves are now enacted by a shared faith in Christ (Gal. 2:20).

Nonetheless, the evidence of our lives and of the world around us presents us with a different picture. This new way of seeing things is a matter of *faith* and not of sight. Moreover, there is a difference between the way the Spirit "groans" (and thereby creates out of nothing) and the way we "groan" (yearning for something better)—a difference that serves a *critical function* in the way we perceive and respond to life.

In 1 Corinthians, Paul illustrated this critical function when he described how the Spirit discloses the "secret and hidden" *wisdom of the cross* (1 Cor. 2:7). Within the context of a congregation beset with factions and internal conflicts,[46] Paul urged the Corinthians to boast only in the wisdom of "Christ crucified" (1 Cor. 1:30-31). Echoing Jeremiah's contrast between "boasting" in wealth, power, and wisdom and "boasting" in God's righteousness, justice, and kindness (Jer. 9:24), Paul urged his readers to boast not in human wisdom and power, but in the "weakness" and "foolishness" of Christ crucified (1 Cor. 1:18-25).

He went on to say that although the Spirit's way of understanding things stands in sharp contrast to the "wisdom" of this passing age, with its strictly empirical ways of knowing (1 Cor. 2:6-16), it is not merely an ethereal perception divorced from the realities of everyday life. Indeed, it is enacted precisely amidst our very human, and often very petty, conflicts over wealth and power, and who has the most superior wisdom (and therefore is "in the right")—continually creating life anew, enabling us to discern that it is in the most weak and needy among us that God's power is most radically at work (1 Corinthians 12). In other words, it is precisely amidst our petty human conflicts that the weakness and foolishness of the cross manifests God's power and God's wisdom by creating something out of "nothing" (the lowly and despised), even as it reduces to nothing those who think they are "something" (the rich, the powerful, and the wise) (1 Cor. 1:26-28).

In the midst of these conflicts, Paul boasted (in a fashion similar to the way Mary "exalted" in her experience) in the truth he was given to proclaim. Like Mary, he did so not because he had more wealth and power or even more wisdom than his hearers, but because he had faith in the Spirit's abundant fecundity. He had an ecstatic confidence in the Spirit's capacity to bring about new life even amidst the despair and dysfunction of a community torn apart by factions and competing claims over who was most in the right. The Spirit's fecundity, which

Paul experienced the most profoundly precisely when he was the most vulnerable, enabled him to endure with equanimity the paradoxes of being an apostle: "treated as imposters, and yet are true; as unknown, and yet are well known; as dying, and see—we are alive; as punished, and yet not killed; as sorrowful, yet always rejoicing; as poor, yet making many rich; as having nothing, and yet possessing everything" (2 Cor. 6:7-10).

Conclusion

Luther's commentary on the Magnificat describes the art of understanding the Spirit's work from the distinctive stance of Mary's experience of mystical exaltation and prophetic witness to God's raising the lowly and bringing down the mighty. In light of a feminist critique, this opens up new vistas for a pneumatology informed by Luther's fundamental insight into the Spirit's creative power. Not only does this stance offer a perspective on the Spirit's work that resonates with and deepens feminist spirituality, but it also offers a perspective that *broadens* the scope of Lutheran pneumatology. This broader scope is, in fact, more congruent with Paul's original description of how—in spite of all the empirical evidence in our own lives and in the world around us that would appear to contradict the Spirit's life-giving power—the Spirit continues to transform our laments and cries for a better world into potent agency for God's new age of justice, righteousness, and mercy.

Suggested Reading

Gaventa, Beverly Roberts. *Our Mother Saint Paul*. Louisville: Westminster John Knox, 2007.

Jones, Serene. *Feminist Theory and Christian Theology: Cartographies of Grace*. Guides to Theological Inquiry. Minneapolis: Fortress Press, 2000.

Malcolm, Lois. *Holy Spirit: Creative Power in Our Lives*. Minneapolis: Fortress Press, 2009.

Prenter, Regin. *Spiritus Creator*. Philadelphia: Muhlenberg Press, 1953.

PART 6

Knowing and Living

WOMAN-IDENTIFIED THEOLOGIES SEEK TO unmask and dismantle not only gender-based oppression but multiple forms of oppression that haunt the human family and damage everyone's lives. In Part 6, Beverly Wallace and Cynthia Moe-Lobeda draw from resources of Lutheran traditions and from womanist and feminist theory for claiming moral-spiritual power to resist systemic injustice. In particular, they address the injustice of white privilege and economic injustice. In chapter 13, Wallace challenges the long-standing tendency for Lutheran theology and ethics to be defined by white voices. She proposes a Lutheran womanist ethic grounded both in Lutheran theological claims and in the lived experiences of Lutheran African American women. In chapter 14, Moe-Lobeda brings Euro-American feminist theology to bear on the problems of white racism and economic injustice as they intersect with the oppression of women. She challenges the church to recognize white privilege in its midst and to strive toward dismantling it as a dimension of proclaiming the gospel. Both authors are guided methodologically by the conviction that Lutheran theologies are most faithful to Lutheran tradition when they entail critique, retrieval, and reconstruction.

Chapter 13

Hush No More!
Constructing an African American
Lutheran Womanist Ethic

Beverly Wallace

Hush: To be quiet—often at the request of someone else.
Hush. Parents say it to children when they don't want or have time to hear
*   that which is important to the child.*
Hush. Grown folks say it to others when they don't want or have time to hear
*   that which is important to the other.*
Hush! People say it when they are focused on their own agendas and the speaking and the voice of
*   another is perceived to be annoying.*
Hush! People say it when they don't want another to share the spotlight—get out of the way.
*   Hush!*

I WRITE THIS CHAPTER from the perspective of an African American Lutheran womanist theologian. The voices of African American women are often hushed, and in the corpus of Lutheran theological perspectives, black women's voices are sorely missing. To counter this, I have utilized the perspectives of other African American Lutheran women, asking them to share their voices as we collectively begin an academic construction of a Lutheran womanist ethic.

Christian ethics is the construction of God's claim on humanity in the relationship God has with God's people: "I will be your God and you will be my people" (Jer. 7:23). It is the understanding of God's love for God's people and the concern with our participation in the collective life of the family of God in our everyday decisions and interactions.[1] Ethics also has to do with the moral evaluation of social relations as they are mediated in and through systems, particularly as some systems produce unshared power.[2] Ethics is therefore the analysis of existing practices that promote or inhibit, affirm or assault the social and spiritual well-being of God's people and the freedom for God's people to be.[3] God calls us to respond to varied situations *because* of God's love. But how do we respond? Many questions can be raised in the analysis of the condition of humanity and the ethical deliberation of our response to God's love: "What is it that we should do with and for our beloved sisters and brothers?" "Why do we do what we do?" However, according to Lutheran ethicist Reinhard Hütter,[4] the first question should *not* be "What ought I to do?" Rather, Hütter suggests the question should be, "What does the world really look like?" It is in answering this question that one can respond. But the omission of many voices and perspectives, including those of African American Lutheran women, minimizes this understanding of what the world looks like. Only in the inclusion of multiple perspectives can we know more fully the picture of humankind, the needs of God's people, and how to respond more appropriately to the brokenness within the family of God. Ethics, including Lutheran ethics, must emerge from a thorough exploration and understanding of the care of all of God's people from the voices of all of God's people.

Womanist theologian Karen Baker-Fletcher raises additional questions to consider in describing what "doing" ethics might entail. Baker-Fletcher asks, "[I]f we presuppose that God is a God of freedom and justice, how do we fully participate in God's freeing, just activity? What kind of theology can give adequate direction for such participation in God's freeing activity?"[5] I suggest a womanist ethic is one such way.

Defining Womanist

The term *womanist* was coined by Alice Walker in her book *In Search of Our Mothers' Gardens*.[6] According to Walker, "Womanist is to feminist as purple is to lavender."[7] The term has appeal because it emerges directly from black women's social, cultural, and historical contexts. African American women also resonate with the term because it gives a way to name the experience of African American women of varied social locations without depending on either the sexist views of men of any race or the racist view of the predominant culture.

For African American women, racial and gender discrimination intersect to produce economic oppression and marginalization, situating black women disproportionately within the categories of being poor and working class. Taken together, racial, gender, and economic oppression connect to place many African American women among the least advantaged groups in society.

Like other women of color, womanist theologians have found it necessary to create forms of Christian thought and practice that speak to and emerge directly from our own contexts and in our own voices.[8] Womanist theology gives an opportunity for African American women to be, to do, to write, and to proclaim our understanding of God that is often neglected. Situated as the least, black women derive hope from the focus in black Christianity on a "high" christological position that places a high value on the life and the salvific work of Jesus. We also derive hope from reinterpreting our situation in the context in which African American women struggle to experience liberation and hope.[9]

Womanist theology and other theologies proposed by women of color (for example, Latina, mujerista, and Asian women's theology) have emerged partly in response to the problematic marginalization of women of color. Our theological reflections historically have been overlooked and have not been seen as essential. However, as Mary (Joy) Philip contends in this volume, from within marginalization, gifts arise. Womanist theology is one such gift that attempts to break open this systemic bondage and reframe for ourselves what it means to be God's people in order that we can respond freely.

Defining a Womanist Ethic

A womanist ethic looks at the experiences of humanity through the lens of black women, posing a more inclusive response to moral situations. This ethical position is borne of a black woman's or womanist spirituality. Living out womanist spirituality means the integration of faith and life. As womanist theologian Emilie Townes notes, "We are called to a new awareness of our humanness and our infinite possibilities. God makes demands on us to live into our faith in a radical way out of the possibilities we have before us."[10] Possibilities are all about God's grace.

Grace is a fundamental theme in Lutheran theology and justification by grace through faith is a central principle of Lutheran ethics. An equally important theme in Lutheran theology is freedom. "You are called to freedom" was stressed by Luther.[11] Freedom for Luther was a description of the relationship between God and God's people. We are free and able to respond because we are God's children.[12] Freedom is the insistence that our performance in the moral life does not establish the nature of our relationship to God.[13] God freely loves us and because of that freedom, we are free to love in return. Freedom is granted by the Spirit in the context of the community.[14]

Like Luther, African American women also embrace this understanding of freedom. In her essay "An Irresistible Power Not Ourselves," Baker-Fletcher refers to Anna Julia Cooper, a black feminist, scholar and educator of the late nineteenth and early twentieth centuries—an early womanist. Cooper wrote, "'Humans have the capacity not only to reflect God's image, but to prophetically echo God's voice. God's speech is freeing, liberating, emancipating.'"[15] To echo God's voice, Baker-Fletcher reflects, is to participate in God's continuous movement toward freedom, which in Cooper's view is "not the cause of a race or a sect, a party or a class, but the cause of humankind, the very birthright of humanity."[16] For Cooper, humankind is ontologically and universally free. Moreover, our participation in the movement toward freedom is moved forward by a power that is greater than one's self.[17]

Contemporary African American women also hold a position similar to classical Lutheran theology because we believe that human freedom is the result of God's power and God's promise—a promise and a relation in which one can be free to be in the midst of all kinds of threats.[18] Threats do exist in the lives of African American women; racism, classism, and sexism permeate the lives of many. In spite of these threats, African American women know that by faith and because of God's grace, we are still free. It is out of this faith that African American women respond to God freely and in love.

Love is key in the ethics of African American women embracing womanist theology. According to Walker, a womanist loves. She loves other women, sexually and/or nonsexually. She sometimes loves individual men, sexually and/or nonsexually. A womanist "loves music. Loves dance. Loves the moon. Loves the Spirit. Loves love and food and roundness. Loves struggle. Loves the Folk. Loves herself. *Regardless*."[19] This principle of love is borne out of the aforementioned understanding of freedom. This womanist understanding of faith and freedom and love is also not unlike what we claim in Article 6 of the Augsburg Confession: "Our church teaches that this faith is bound to bring forth good fruits and that it is necessary to do the good works commanded by God. We must do so because it is God's will and not because we rely on such works to merit justification before God."[20]

In his preface to the Epistle of St. Paul to the Romans Martin Luther says:

> Faith is a living, daring confidence in God's grace, so sure and certain that the believer would stake his life on it a thousand times. This knowledge of and confidence in God's grace makes us glad and bold and happy in dealing with God and with all creatures. And this is the work which the Holy Spirit performs in faith. Because of it, without compulsion, Christians are ready and glad to do good to everyone, to serve everyone, to suffer everything, out of love and praise to God who has shown them this grace.[21]

Several Lutheran ethicists claim that the ethics of Martin Luther are spiritual and of God because they have such a profound notion of agape love.[22] Our faith becomes active in love and expresses itself in deeds that follow spontaneously from faith.[23] Similar to a womanist way of thinking, this Lutheran understanding of agape love is about mutual love and involves the quest for equal dignity for all persons.[24]

Equal dignity is the object of justice. If freedom violates equality, it must be adjusted to increase equality.[25] The purpose of justice-seeking is to move people to act ethically. Justice-seeking is both creative and constructive in that one might have to develop interesting and unique ways to help establish equality and seek freedom. A womanist ethic is creative and constructive in that it seeks to determine how to eradicate injustices, challenging those social structures that limit and define the freedom and agency of people.[26] And in the midst of efforts to stop such action that pose threats to survival, a womanist ethic aims to make a way to freedom and survival even when the odds of doing so look perilous. Womanist theologians, in their constructive and creative way, name this idea of justice-seeking as "making a way out of no way" for the purpose of survival.[27]

"Making a way out of no way" is also a means toward African American women's survival. Because of the reality of living in an oppressive society, African American women have regarded survival against systems of oppression as the true sphere of moral life. This understanding is based solely on the knowledge that life is God's gift, which includes freedom to flourish fully as God's people.

A womanist ethic is also communal. Racial uplift names the perspective and practices of African Americans that attend to survival in a communal manner.[28] Historically this response included the desire and striving of African Americans as a community to survive oppression, gain independence, develop self-sufficiency and well-being, fully engage in the fullness of society, and assist others in the community, leaving no one behind. Continued to be embraced and encouraged today, it is also expected that the work that one does is not solely for oneself, but to improve the condition of African Americans.

Another major theme in womanist ethics is social responsibility. Womanist ethicists, like Lutheran ethicists, understand social ethics as an ethic of responsibility.[29] As noted in Rosetta Ross's *Witnessing and Testifying: Black Women, Religion, and Civil Rights*, social responsibility includes the responsibility to work in partnership with God for community survival and positive quality of life, the responsibility to attend to the needs of the least, and the responsibility to participate in community-building and community-sustaining practices.[30] Social responsibility therefore seeks to ensure that all of humanity as full members of society are able to realize God's gift of life.[31]

While care for the African American community is important for African American womanists, there is also the understanding from a womanist perspective that the obligation of social responsibility does not stop just with the needs of the African American community. As a moral value, social responsibility includes the duty to help all those in need. Fulfilling this responsibility means determining the appropriate and necessary response to social needs and to respond ethically.

Justification for Constructing a Lutheran Womanist Ethic

Womanist ethicist Traci West in *Disruptive Christian Ethics: When Racism and Women's Lives Matters* critiqued the work of Reinhold Niebuhr and his construction of social ethics.[32] She poses this question, "[E]ducated in Harlem, how was the construction of ethics by the son of a German immigrant [Niebuhr] informed by the ideas and experiences of daughters and granddaughters of former slaves and free Black Women?"[33] I ask a similar question: "How might Lutheran ethics in the American context be informed by the ideas and experiences of daughters and granddaughters of black women of the civil rights era and beyond?" How might our thinking and ethical practices inform and reconstruct Lutheran ethics?

In the historical critique of both black theology and feminist theology, oftentimes the experiences and voices of women of color are expressed by others without actually listening to the experiences and voices of African American women.[34] Lutheran theologian Karen Bloomquist notes that a "Christian ethic in a Lutheran vein needs to take seriously the particularities that profoundly shape persons, their situations and their moral agency in the world."[35] The construction of a formal Lutheran womanist ethic therefore begins with the voices of African American Lutheran women. My approach also uses the suggestion of Lutheran ethicist Martha Stortz of being "intentionally empirical, descriptive, and concrete" rather than abstract and speculative.[36]

The voices of African American women that were used for the construction of this Lutheran womanist ethic came from a variety of women around the country. The recruitment of participants for this study consisted of sending correspondence to select women and requesting their opinion on their understanding of African American Lutheran women's ethics, their own ethical behaviors, and the sources of their particular ethical positions. African American Lutheran women of various ages, both lay and clergy, from across the country were contacted. A sample of convenience was used.[37] The following questions were asked:

1. How would you define a black women's ethic?

2. In what ways do you respond to God, to the community, and to the world?

3. Where did you learn to act and function and respond to God and your community in the manner in which you do?

Twelve African American Lutheran women from Tennessee, Chicago, New York, Pennsylvania, Florida, and Mississippi participated. Their responses using pseudonyms are reported here. An emancipatory meta-ethnographic analysis was used, which "captures the in-depth perspectives of a few individuals, validating each voice without claiming to be representative of the reality of all."[38]

The Responses of African American Women

Many of the respondents struggled to define a black women's ethic. Stevie, a young woman in her thirties from Florida, responded:

> When reading this question, I found myself for the first time in a long time without words. So to trigger me, I looked up the word "ethics" in the dictionary. Here's what I found:
>
> 1 a system of moral principles: the ethics of a culture.
> 2. the rules of conduct recognized in respect to a particular class of human actions or a particular group, culture, etc.: medical ethics; Christian ethics.
> 3. moral principles, as of an individual: His ethics forbade betrayal of a confidence.
>
> To answer the question to the best of my ability I will say that for me, black women's ethics is being whatever it is that God has called us to. We wear many hats. We are daughters, wives, mothers, lovers, care-givers, friends, business-women, pastors, lay assistants, prayer warriors and the list goes on and on. I believe that culturally we have been placed as the "head of household," the person that keeps our communities together and our families strong. We are the backbone that keeps everything functioning as it should.

The reaction of Tonya, a forty-year-old layperson from New York was, "I never thought about a black women's ethics; I only thought about a black ethic, where the value is place on hard work, education, and family." Lisa, a fifty-four-year-old clergywoman in the Northeast also admitted she had not thought of African American women's ethics:

I never thought about this. I wonder if it isn't something linked to some archetypical characteristic of being woman and procreating and protective. For me maybe it also includes knowledge of being a child of God who has been blessed with the challenges and opportunities of being a black woman. As a black woman I am a survivor, accommodator and nurturer, interested in growth (for myself and others) more than a need to trample on others who are trying to make their own way.

Several women did propose a definition of black women's ethics. Toni, a sixty-year-old woman in Nashville studying to be a Lutheran pastor responded:

For me, as a black woman my ethics are inherited and (not) learned in theory, meaning my mother did "show and tell," teaching us to take care for people who have less than we do, even if what we have is little. I learned responsibility from scripture along with the study of issues presented to us.

Nicky, a thirty-six-year-old laywoman from New York defined a black women's ethic as "the way women have to be strong yet supple, assertive yet demure, super-intelligent yet feigning ignorance as a child." According to Nicky,

It is hard, really, to put such a general definition as "code of morals" to what we are as a people, what we have had to endure, and not just through the last Diaspora, I mean throughout HISTORY! Sure, I can say as women and as the human race period, we have been through a lot and look how far we have come. True. But when I stop and think about what women of Africa have had to put up with. My soul cries out HALLELUJAH!! Our ethics were passed down from those that first knew God, maybe not in the 'traditional' Christian sense, but we always KNEW God and worshipped God.

Tina, a twenty-seven-year-old young woman from Chicago said:

I would describe black women's ethics as strong and weak. It's strong because most of us are single mothers who are the backbone of our families. We are raising children by ourselves and trying to teach boys how to be men. We do our best to give and teach our children what's right so they may grow to be productive citizens. Then the weak sides are the ones who do the opposite. Music videos etc., etc. says it all. The weak side that glamorizes all the fast cash, need a man, baby daddy drama, you know what I mean. But I'm glad to say that most women I know have the strong side.

It was apparent from the stories of the women that African American Lutheran women respond ethically in a variety of ways. They work in congregations; they give to organizations; and they simply obey God in prayer. Toni, for example, answered the second question in this way:

> I work in the house of Lord, living in faith that everything is going to be all right, working to feed the people in the community with the Word of God [and] food for the stomach [and providing] housing when available and clothes. In doing all this I feel that the world community is being taken care of—one community at a time.

Nicky's response showed the creativity of being an African American woman:

> Just like any woman I try to respond to God, the community and the world by working in the feeding ministry; always donating my slightly used clothing and helping to ensure that our clothing ministry has nice plus-sized clothes; always helping another sister or child, and helping my brothers if they need it too. . . . Because I cannot be everywhere at once like God, I tithe and give to organizations that help those most in need globally.

When asked how she responded to God, community, and the world, Tonya simply replied, "I try to listen [to] and obey God and I try to be a law-abiding citizen."

Eve is thirty-one and from New York. Eve's answer focused on prayer as her response:

> I respond to God by talking with Him in prayer, or when I feel He is urging/pushing me in a certain direction, I pursue it until I find out what it is He is showing me. Also, when I . . . feel something God's telling me in my heart, I like to just lift my head and say "I hear you Lord, I hear you."
>
> In my community, the youth tend to enjoy conversing with me from time to time on various different topics. . . . More often than not, I find myself encouraging them strongly to seek God, to pray (Very often I end up in a prayer with them.), to stay in school, and to get the best education they possibly can. [I say,] "Knowing God and a solid education are two of the greatest things you can accomplish, and the two things NO ONE can ever take from you."
>
> As for the world, well I'm still praying on that.

Tina admitted that she did not always participate in working in the community in a tangible way:

The ways I respond to God and the community and the world is I pray to God all the time. I try not to pray to ask for the things that I need, but for the people around me who need. As for the community, I'm sad to say that I don't participate in many community organizations, but I do support them all that I can. And to the world: I guess I have an optimistic view (but not always). Life and age has taught me to learn the difference between the things I can and cannot change; to me, because the world will be the world, I pray that a better tomorrow will come.

Stevie also cited prayer as an important means to respond ethically, stating, "We are continuously in conversation with God, praying for the needs of our people and empowered to action in our communities and the world." Most of the women responded that they learned to respond to God and the community from members of their families, especially mothers and grandmothers. Stevie wrote:

I would have to say that I learned mostly from my mother. It was all of the unspoken teachings, how I saw her take care of our family, how I heard her pray, how I see her exude strength, how she never complained and was always doing something to better our household, our church, and my relationship with God.

Tonya responded:

The way that I learned to act, function, and respond to God and community was through my family, by watching them react, function and respond, and behave—part of being from a southern family.

Nicky, while extending the familial influences to include the larger community, also commented on the nature of family influences. Her response suggests the need also to be critical in utilizing sources of influences:

I learned to act and function and respond to God from my great-grandmother, grandmother, mother, church mothers, aunts and women cousins that were strong women of color. I learned to do for family, church and the greater community because it was what Jesus would want and because we need each other. Lately I have also had to learn, however, what we do not talk about so much—sometimes that same family will drag you down and you got to cut them loose!!! Not everyone, but some.

Lisa, a fifty-four-year-old from Pennsylvania, answered the question of where she learned to respond by talking not only about her family but also the church as sources for her ethical development:

> [I learned to respond from] my mother, who was pretty poor when she grew up but loved me unconditionally and was the primary care-giver for my siblings and me, and [from] my grandmother (father's mother) who was also poor, but very proud. . . . I can't help but stand on their shoulders (or sit, held tightly in their laps), as their influence has contributed in large and small ways to who I am. I was also part of a family who encouraged me to be the best I could be—even to being the best garbage collector if that was my job. And I belonged to a church which always accepted my gifts and encouraged me to be a leader even when I was in elementary school. The mentoring from my pastor, even before girls acolyted in our church, stuck with me.

Two women talked about their life experiences as sources of their ethical lessons. Toni talked about her personal experience:

> My background is in child and adult abuse. I formed my ministry around my own suffering. I turned my anger upon God for letting me suffer through such darkness as a child and a failed marriage to an abuser as an adult. [However,] through the process of forgiveness—forgiving God [and] all the people who stood by and watch[ed] children being abused and women being beaten into submission; forgiving the abusers and most of all forgiving myself—God gave me a vision of service to help others to overcome the abuse and live a whole life with joy, laughter and a peace of mind [knowing] that God will always take care of them.

Tina talked about her life experience in the armed services:

> For me, it was being in the military that taught me to have an open mind. A closed mind cannot absorb anything; an open [mind] will continue to want more. Even though I see God the way I do, looking at God through different eyes . . . actually made me more aware of who God is.

Interpretation of the Responses

It is clear that many of the respondents in this study embraced a womanist ethical position, although the women did not necessarily self-identify as womanist. Interpretations of their responses indicate that they possess womanist virtues.

They define their ethical responses in their own terms, stemming from personal experiences, tradition, history, culture, scripture, or their own intuitive knowledge, and they live out their ethics in either priestly, political, prophetic, or even womanist manners.

Womanist ethicist Katie Cannon identifies cultural virtues that characterize activities through which black women determine the means to be and to survive.[39] Cultivated by African American women's life history, these virtues also inform how African American women are ethical. The virtues visible in these women's lives are: (1) invisible dignity (discerning how and to what extent to confront threats to survival, even while maintaining a feistiness[40] about life in face of such pervasive threats); (2) quiet grace (the persistent struggle for human dignity in defiance of degrading oppression); and (3) unshouted courage (the capacity to constantly confront threats to survival in the face of reprisals for one's determination to survive). It is apparent from their responses that the women in this study exhibited this kind of dignity, grace, and courage, as well as vulnerability, evidenced in their willingness to share their thoughts.

The African American Lutheran women who participated in this study defined black women's ethics both in secular terms (Stevie going to the dictionary for her definition) and in theological terms (their understanding of who they are as women of God). They understood ethics in terms of a value system—the value placed on hard work, education, and family, and on who and what black women do. Importantly, black women's ethics was defined as being whatever it is that God has called black women to be. While these descriptions may not be fully fleshed out in formal theological terms, these women are thinking about their relationship to God and are describing their understanding of ethics.

As noted earlier, sources of ethical action could come from experience, tradition, history, culture, or scripture. Not all sources were utilized by the women in this study. I have added to this list another source; ethical actions can also come from women's own innate wisdom.

For those respondents for whom *experience* was a source of ethical response, the "lived experience" of being an African American woman was particularly important. One young woman talked about her experience of being in the military. Another woman talked explicitly of her experience of being a victim of spousal abuse. These personal experiences guided their understanding of what they were to do.

The women also reported *tradition*—the legacy and the wisdom of foremothers, mothers, and grandmothers—as a source of ethical response. As one woman said, "I stand on their shoulders or sit, held tightly in their laps, as their influence has contributed to who I am."

A part of their tradition was their religiosity. African American Lutheran women's ethics included their use of traditional religious practices. Central to almost all of the women was the significance and the importance of prayer.

At least one woman mentioned the importance of *history* as a source of ethical response, especially the history of Africans in the Americas. "Our ethics," she said, "were passed down from those that first knew God, maybe not in the 'traditional' Christian sense, but we always KNEW God and worshipped God." Another also lamented, "When I stop and think about what women of Africa have had to put up with, my soul cries out."

For some, *culture* was an additional source of ethical and moral behavior. One woman described how she was part of a family that encouraged her to be the best she could be. African American women's culture in particular was another source. As one woman said, "the way women have to be strong yet supple, assertive yet demure, super intelligent yet feigning ignorance as a child when they want to show something they just learned but you have known for decades."

Scripture may have also been a source for ethical practices of the women of this study, but the use of scripture as a source was not necessarily articulated. Only one woman said that it was from scripture that she learned how to respond. Follow-up questions are needed to explore this further. However, despite this omission of scripture, the women expressed what could be considered a high christology. In this study, all of the women expressed the centrality of Jesus Christ as to why they do what they do.

Finally, the emotional, *intuitive knowledge* of African American women was another source of ethical response.[41] For example, Toni testified that her faith afforded the audacity to provide for others and to act ethically. She is "living in faith that everything is going to be all right." The intuitive knowledge to which Toni referred is connected to Nicky's reflections on black women's ancestral heritage of knowledge of God: "Our ethics were passed down from those that first knew God, maybe not in the 'traditional' Christian sense, but we always KNEW God and worshipped God." Being grounded in faith provides Toni and Nicky intuitive knowledge to live ethically.

African people, including African people within the global Lutheran communion, have established a plurality of ways of living out their Christian ethics. These ethical responses are typically priestly, political, or prophetic.[42] All three of these characteristics can be identified as ways these African American Lutheran women say they live out their ethics. In addition, some womanist principles were also identified, such as social responsibility and community uplift.

A *priestly response* is related to the care of the souls of God's people.[43] This kind of response was shown by the ways in which the women in the study responded to situations in an intercessory role. While the women reported that they fed the hungry or provided other service in and to the community, what was striking was that the initial response given by many of these women was almost always that of prayer. Prayer was extremely important to the women of this study. The women reported that their foremothers prayed them "up" and prayed other people "up." They were taught about prayer and functioned as prayer warriors to help with the healing of the brokenness of the world. As such, the women's ethical responses were primarily priestly responses.

A *political response* is an effort geared toward creating a just community. In political responses, problem-solving efforts are organized to address issues of injustice and to provide tangible assistance to the needs of God's people. This category would also include an element of protest. The respondents in this study reported that they addressed issues of social needs. Most of the women reported assisting those who had needs—for food, clothing, and shelter. In a creatively womanist way, one woman said she provided plus-sized clothing to meet the particular needs of some African American women. It seems that the women in the study are protesting, as well. There was a sense that even if they did not engage in formal political activism, they understood and felt a sense that they had to be socially responsible.

A *prophetic response* seeks a moral end in all of its activities.[44] A response in this categorical understanding views society as good yet recognizes the need to confront evil practices. The prophet, listening to God, has a vision of what church and society should be, and uses moral persuasion to bring about transformation. African American Lutheran women respondents said they listened to and tried to obey God. They understood their connection to Jesus and to God. It was God who would do what needed to be done and God would direct their response towards God's vision for the church and society.

A *womanist response* is inclusive of all of the above categories and at the same time is based on some of the womanist principles described previously. These African American Lutheran women respondents, as noted above, understood the importance of social responsibility. They understood and reported how they knew to care for other members of the community. As illustrated in the words of the youngest of the respondents, the womanist ethical principle of social responsibility and community uplift is part of one's personal ethics and behavior:

> My personal ethics are to continually strive to be the best I can be in all
> that I do; to love, honor and cherish myself; to never settle for less than
> what I feel I deserve; to respect myself as a whole; to demand the same
> respect for myself from others, not only as a female, but as a respectable
> African American woman; to do right when my peers and society around
> me pressure me to do the opposite; to lend a helping hand whenever and

however I can without compromising my integrity and my Christianity; and above all else, to keep God first and foremost in my life.

African American Lutheran women in this study therefore appear to embrace what most other African American Christian women possess—a womanist ethic.

Constructing a *Lutheran* Womanist Ethic

African American Lutherans have a long history of belonging to the Lutheran church.[45] We embrace Lutheran theology and perhaps even some of the traditional liturgy (though we often make the liturgy our own). We choose. African American Lutheran women also choose to live ethical lives. Our ethical and moral behaviors are integrated within our experiences of being black women and are inclusive of our embrace of Lutheran theology.

Findings from this preliminary study suggest that African American Lutheran women's ethics are theologically *Lutheran*. We are Lutheran because of our love of God, our understanding of who God is, and our belief in the salvific work of God. Justification is the primary tenet we embrace, whether we articulate this theoretical concept or not. We know because of our everyday experiences, our history, and our legacy, that we can do nothing to be saved because God's grace is salvific. We also know that because of this gracious gift of God's love through the life and death of Jesus and through faith given to us through the Holy Spirit, we can joyfully and freely respond in a responsible manner, bringing change in an oppressive and oftentimes unjust world.

Findings from this study also suggest that African American Lutheran women's ethics are a *womanist* ethic. Because of the social and historical context and the "lived" experience[46] of being black women, the women in this study understood the particular concerns of persons on the margin. Freedom is important for African American women, and the African American Lutheran women in this study understood that the work for freedom comes from a power not of themselves.

They understood, though mildly spoken, that it is God's power within humanity that urges them to "rise up, come to voice, and proclaim God's intention of freedom and justice."[47] They also understood they had a responsibility to care for God's people because of this freedom. Through speculations based on the writer's experiences with the African American Lutheran community (and not just from this select group of respondents), I would suggest that in the construction of a Lutheran womanist ethic, we can borrow from the works of womanist ethicist Marcia Riggs. Riggs describes in her book *Awake, Arise, & Act* a mediating ethic for black liberation:[48] "We begin a Christian ethical process of mediating intentional work to change oppressive realities with our faith in Jesus Christ who bestows grace. We also begin with our faith as the assurance that we may attempt any such change at all."[49] This mediating method is also "a process of acknowledging seemingly diametrically opposing positions and creating a response that incorporates opposing sides."[50] As such, this mediating ethic is a process that lives with tension. Using our Lutheran premises of paradox and tension and a womanist creative response, a mediating ethic also suggests creative tensions and incorporates tensions, for example, between the beliefs of those individuals who embrace individual social advancement and a belief that a just God calls persons and communities to participate in creating a just society. Specifically, within the African American community this might hold in tension the responses that mediate one's individual fulfillment of obligations (economic independence, or individual self-actualization through education) and a duty to racial uplift and a commitment to serve the entire community.

While noting the diversity of the African American Lutheran communion and the nature and demographics of those who are African American Lutherans—primarily educated, perhaps even in a higher socioeconomic status—one could speculate that economic educational advancement is important to African American Lutheran women (whether the worldview is more communal or individualistic may differ from individual to individual). At the same time, as noted by the women reported here, there is a sense of knowing that we are also to care for and work for a just society.

I also want to propose that in order to understand more fully the processes used by African American Lutheran women for ethical deliberation and response, ethicists might also want to consider an exploration of what I am calling a "moderating ethical process."[51] This process would examine the influence in the strength of the relationship between being a Lutheran and being a womanist. In other words, a moderating ethical process would ask, "What are the ethical standards that strengthen the spiritual, emotional, ethical being of African American Lutheran women?"

With the voices of the women reported here and the voices of other African American Lutheran women whose voices are not reported, we have an initial construction of a Lutheran womanist ethic. Seeing the world through the eyes of African American Lutheran women; analyzing the world with a womanist race, class, and gender analysis; and uncovering African American Lutheran women's theology and the sources of their theology and ethics leads to a picture of how African American Lutheran women think ethically. Freedom and love are important aspects of womanist ethics. These principles appear to be embraced by the women in this study. "Making a way out of no way," social responsibility, and community and racial uplift are also principles seemingly employed by the women.

The promise of Lutheran ethics "is given fully within the life, death and resurrection of Jesus Christ."[52] This assurance is also the belief and hope held by African American women, borne out of a belief in God and the teachings of Jesus passed on by our foremothers. Like traditional Lutheran thinking, African American Lutheran women recognize that our ethics lie primarily in our relationship with God and God's people, the life of family, work, and citizenship, and life in the church.

Conclusion

The lived experiences of African American Lutheran women, while diverse, show the uniqueness of being both African American and women. Social and historical context shapes understandings of why African American women do what we do. As in the words of African American theologian Dwight Hopkins, "Her funky free passion for a holistic life allows her to define herself culturally as a free black woman. Consequently she assumed the risk to define politically what to *do* in life."[53]

How might our thinking and ethical practices inform and reconstruct Lutheran ethics? What is missing from the corpus of Lutheran ethical discourse? Cynthia Moe-Lobeda and theologian Richard Perry suggest that part of our interpretation and discernment of Lutheran ethics involves welcoming to the table voices that many Lutherans simply have not yet learned to hear.[54] Since many African American Lutheran women sitting in pews have yet to have an opportunity to share their stories, the challenge is still to hear these perspectives and know these stories as we continue to pass on that legacy of ethical responsibility and moral obligations. Hütter raises a related question: How do we who are Lutherans become socially responsible in the face of social myths that distort facts in order to undergird oppressive ways of life?[55] My answer is that we cannot without restorying our understanding of contemporary Lutheran ethics and by making the theological principle grounded in freedom and love more expansive. The challenge for Lutherans is to embrace fully the ethics of freedom we claim to be central to our theology and to live out the tenet of this belief, allowing space in God's kingdom for all of God's people. African American Lutheran womanists take seriously this ethical promise of freedom and our call to understand the plight of our sisters and brothers. A Lutheran womanist ethic may challenge contemporary Lutheran ethics to reclaim the historical understanding of how Christians understand freedom and our response to that claim. A critical analysis through the lenses of racial, gender, and social position can assist in helping know more clearly how we as Lutherans are to respond. While the number of women's voices shared is small, it is still my hope that hearing African American Lutheran women's voices will contribute to a richer understanding of Lutheran ethics. Using a womanist ethical perspective gives us a theological method for doing so.

The African American phrase, "Honey, Hush," is an exclamation used among black women, especially those from the South, as a friendly encouragement, a mild suggestion of playful disbelief, or as a suggestion that one is telling truths that are prohibited.[56] Perhaps African American Lutheran women can use the "hush" as a reminder to continue to tell truths that have not been spoken in public arenas. African American Lutheran women as well as other women of color are often on the margins of theological discourse. Those of us who are of the darker hue are placed on the margin even before we open our mouths.

But open our mouths we must. In doing so, we can as Stacey Floyd-Thomas suggests, move the margin to the center—"placing the most marginalized experiences of black women at the heart of a burgeoning narrative of religious awareness and spiritual empowerment; affording the academy a moral opportunity to consider how the Divine becomes manifested in the everyday experience of African American women."[57]

Suggested Reading

Cannon, Katie G. Black Womanist Ethics. Atlanta: Scholars Press, 1988.

Grant, Jacquelyn. White Women's Christ and Black Women's Jesus: Feminist Christology and Womanist Response. Atlanta: Scholars Press, 1989. No. 64 in the American Academy of Religion Academy Series. Ed. Susan Brooks Thistlethwaite.

Riggs, Marcia. Awake, Arise & Act: A Womanist Call for Black Liberation. Cleveland: Pilgrim, 1994.

Ross, Rosetta. Witnessing and Testifying: Black Women, Religion, and Civil Rights. Minneapolis: Fortress Press, 2003.

West, Traci C. Disruptive Christian Ethics: When Racism and Women's Lives Matter. Louisville: Westminster John Knox, 2006.

Chapter 14

Being Church as, in,
and against White Privilege

Cynthia Moe-Lobeda

THE FEMINIST THEOLOGIES OF white women are multiple and diverse, even contradictory. So too are womanist theologies and mujerista, Chicana, and Latina theologies. I begin, therefore, with a central feature of my stance within the world of feminist theologies. It is a feminism that sees gender-based oppression as interlaced with ecological degradation and with oppression based on race/ethnicity, class, sexual orientation, and other markers of human difference that have been used by some groups of people to subordinate, marginalize, or otherwise violate others.

Feminist theology initially centered on gender issues and the well-being of "women." It was invaluable work that paved a way through the ominous landscape of patriarchy in its many insidious forms. To that courageous work we are indebted. Yet that path-breaking work in itself was also oppressive; it universalized and normalized the particular experiences of educated white women. The lived realities and needs of most women were obscured and hence minimized.

Feminist theology has evolved—primarily in response to the critiques of black, Latin American, and Asian sisters—to a more critical, inclusive, and complex focus. Feminist theology at its best now aims at an interstructural analysis. That is, it seeks to unmask and dismantle the multiple axes of structural violence that infect the human family and Earth's broader web of life.[1] Central among these are oppression based upon gender, race/ethnicity, class, sexual orientation, colonialism, and human dominion over the rest of creation. It is here, in a feminism committed to action based on an interstructural understanding of oppression, that I locate myself.[2]

The oppression of women, both in the United States and globally, entangles with white racism, classism, heterosexism, ecological devastation, and the militarization that requires and enables these. The same worldviews and social structures set up over millennia to favor men over women also favor people seen as white over people seen as all other colors, people with economic privilege over those without, human creatures over all others, and military resolution of human conflict.

My emphasis is on two forms of structural violence that brutalize women— white racism and economic exploitation. Those connections are intricate and insidious. Seventy percent of the world's economically impoverished people are women and their dependent children. Women who are economically poor and also are any color but white suffer trifold domination based on class, race/ethnicity, and gender. Poverty and white racism become even more dangerous in light of the ecological crisis. The "environmental refugees" produced by global climate change are and will be disproportionately people of color other than white who are economically impoverished; so too are the victims of toxic dumping and other forms of environmental degradation. For the church to serve the well-being of women, it must seek to dismantle the white racism and economic exploitation that damage the lives of women the world over.

Two central presuppositions undergird my argument here. First, structural violence is a form of sin. To renounce sin is to renounce sin in all of its forms, including social structural sin.[3] The second is grounded in Martin Luther's theology of justification by grace through faith. As a "fruit and consequence"[4] of having been made right with God by God's free gift of grace alone, Christians are given by God a "second kind of righteousness."[5] It is a change toward love in our relationships with other people. The second kind of righteousness is a "whole way of living" that includes living "justly with neighbor,"[6] in every dimension of life, including the political-economic dimensions. Many Lutherans know this as faith active in love.

So what would it mean for the Lutheran church in the United States to be a church that actively promotes racial and economic justice, a church that sees evangelical defiance to white racism and economic violence as central to proclaiming the gospel? That is the question of this inquiry. First, being such a church would entail seeing and telling the truth about reality. Second, it would entail claiming the moral-spiritual power offered by the great mystery that Jewish, Christian, and Muslim traditions so inadequately call God. In this chapter I seek to unfold these two dimensions of the church's contribution to the task of building racially and economically just ways of being human and being Christian in the world today. Before doing so, it is important to note that many people and offices of the Evangelical Lutheran Church in America (ELCA)—in its churchwide, synodical, and congregational expressions and in its parachurch organizations—have been working with courage and insight for decades to build economic and racial justice in the church and the broader society.[7]

Truth-Telling or Seeing What Is

Evil exists as an intricate web of injustice in many forms (including white racism) that remain largely invisible to people advantaged by them. This injustice is concealed by uncritically assumed notions of what is natural, normal, inevitable, or God's will. People "privileged" by white skin or by economic status do not see and utter truth about white dominance or economic exploitation because our perception of reality is socially constructed to ignore it. A crucial step in dismantling the structural dynamics that give white people access to power and resources and enable relatively wealthy citizens to benefit materially from policies and practices that exploit others and the Earth is realizing that these structures of injustice exist.

The failure of white people to recognize white dominance and its derivative white privilege fosters moral inertia in the face of these dynamics. Likewise, failure of economically privileged people in this world to see the links between our material wealth and others' poverty fosters complicity with economic structures that buy our relative material wealth at the cost of life for many others, most of whom are colors other than white. Said differently, dearth of truth-telling is one of the reasons why white people fail to resist racism and why people of economic privilege fail to resist the deadly economic injustice and ecological degradation woven into our lives.

Therefore, a primary task of Christian faith is truth-telling—seeing clearly "what is going on." I refer to this as moral vision. The church as locus of moral vision or truth-telling will unmask what Dietrich Bonhoeffer called the "huge masquerade of evil" disguised as good "in the form of light, good deeds, historical necessity, social justice"[8] for the sake of uprooting it. That is, we will seek to reveal where social structural injustice damages life, but goes largely unrecognized by those who have a vested interest in maintaining "the way things are." This commitment to moral vision is a faithful effort to perceive and live toward the in-breaking reign of God on Earth.

Note the links here to theologies of repentance. Christians claim that the first step in renouncing sin is confession and repentance. That is, the call to renounce sin—including structural sin—is a call to confess it and repent of it. However, sin unrecognized cannot be confessed or repented. Renouncing or uprooting racism and other forms of structural sin, then, demands the truth-telling that enables the sin to be recognized by those once made oblivious to it by their own privilege. If we do not tell and hear truth about the structural sin in which we live and breathe, we cannot confess it or repent of it, and thus we remain captive to it.

Moral vision, or truth-telling, complicates the question with which we began: What would it mean for the Lutheran church in the United States to be a church of racial and economic justice, a church that holds evangelical defiance to white racism and economic violence as central to proclaiming the gospel? The question deepens dangerously, for we must consider what it means to be antiracist for a church composed of both colonizers and colonized, especially when the colonizers still in some senses dominate. We must grapple with what constitutes economic justice-making for a church that includes people whose ways of living depend upon the exploited labor of others in the same body. To illustrate: What if the ELCA includes both a company's custodians—whose wages are not enough to keep a roof over their heads—and its corporate executives, who are paid 400 times as much as are those custodians? Or what if some white ELCA members own houses that African American members were prohibited from owning by policies of red-lining?

Finally, what is the proclamation of the gospel by U.S. Lutherans of all colors when our way of life depends on global economic systems that impoverish and even kill people in other lands whom we call brothers and sisters and to whom or with whom we may claim to proclaim the gospel? Many people with whom I have worked voice the pathos of that reality:

> A small World Council of Churches team at a United Nations project gathered around a table to introduce ourselves to one another. When the time came for one man to do so, he said—with a voice of quiet power—only one sentence: "I am Bishop Bernardino Mandlate, Methodist bishop of Mozambique, and I am a debt warrior." Later that week, when asked to address a United Nations meeting concerning the causes of poverty in Africa, Bishop Mandlate identified the external debt as a primary cause. The debt, he declared, is "covered with the blood of African children. African children die so that North American children may overeat."[9]

The bishop was speaking of the millions of dollars in capital and interest transferred yearly from the world's poorest nations to foreign banks and international finance institutions controlled largely by the world's leading industrialized nations. The money spent in debt servicing is then not available for health care, education, or food and water security. According to an Oxfam Education Report, "Each year sub-Saharan Africa pays more in debt servicing (capital and interest) to the World Bank, other multilateral institutions, and corporate banks than the total of all health and education budgets of the entire region."[10] Hold this together with the fact that "four million children under the age of five will die this year of preventable diseases—for lack of clean water and sanitation."[11]

The examples are literally countless. Some years ago, a Mexican strawberry picker spoke with a delegation of local elected officials from around the United States. They were part of a fact-finding delegation to Mexico and Central America that I was leading. In a clear and steady voice she declared to us: "Our children die of hunger because our land which ought to grow food for them, is used by international companies to produce strawberries for your tables."

What are implications of the Lutheran proclamation of forgiveness by God's grace alone where there is no repentance of the deadly collective sin illustrated by these voices? Make no mistake: I do believe that we are forgiven regardless of the magnitude of sin, be it corporate or individual. Likewise, nothing we do—not even the noblest of deeds—can win God's forgiveness. Hence, we are utterly free from striving toward any form of the good *for the purpose of gaining God's forgiveness or favor*. This claim is a profound and life-giving contribution of Lutheran traditions to the world community. In my life, this claim has been life-saving. However, there is great danger in making this claim—which, as Lutherans, we know by faith to be true—without daring also to excavate its unsettling meanings and radical practical implications in the context of structural sin.

The practical implications of moral vision and of these questions for the church are endless, although far from the radar screen of much white Lutheranism. To illustrate: in the context of structural sin, church as truth-teller will dare to uncover the manifestations and reinforcement of white dominance in the rituals of Sunday morning—liturgical, educational, and social—in order that we might repent and renounce that sin. While the following mechanisms of dominance may be very clear to people of most colors, they are hidden behind layers of denial and entitlement for those of us who are white. Consider these examples:

- One congregation in Seattle recently finished a series of videos in which highly respected theologians discussed important theological and moral issues. As far as I could tell, no one watching the films seemed concerned that nearly all of the theologians were white.
- The portrayals of Jesus in many churches would have a newcomer assume that Jesus came from some village in Norway. If a black Christ, an indigenous Christ, or an Asian or Latino Christ appears, he is identified as "black" or by his ethnicity, while his brother the Norwegian Christ is never called "the white Christ."
- Youth are taught to help the victims of Hurricane Katrina, but are they taught to seek help for themselves and other white people to overcome

the racism that made those victims largely people of color or poor people?[12]

- A quick trip through a Lutheran worship book and use of the word "white" in the church reveals a veritable indoctrination in the goodness of white in contrast to black.
- Gratitude is good. Yet to what extent do our prayers of gratitude for our many material blessings conceal the extent to which those blessings are stolen goods, taken primarily from the world's peoples of color? To conceal that theft is to perpetuate it.[13]
- Constant claims to being "one in the Spirit" or "one great people of God" do not often encourage Euro-American congregants to question what it means to be one in the Spirit with peoples who suffered near-genocide at our ancestors' hands in recent history.

To what extent do our joyful declarations of Christian unity hide the disunity of socioeconomic arrangements that buy wealth for some Christians with the lifeblood of others who are disproportionately people of color? Where do our celebrations of "unity" insulate dominant culture Christians from the lived reality of disunity in a world that privileges and universalizes their expressions of Christianity? I will never forget a representative of the Sami people at the Lutheran World Federation General Assembly in Winnipeg. "Our legacy with the church," the man declared, "has been one of having to adopt the ways of the colonizers. . . . They consider their ways as universal. Therefore we have often experienced how dangerous it can be to welcome a well-intentioned invitation by the majority to 'celebrate' our unity. We have experienced so many times that this meant to enter the fellowship on the premises of the majority. We had to leave ourselves behind."[14]

In short, church as truth-teller will risk recognizing where expressions of Christian faith conceal structural sin or are fused with expressions of whiteness, thus reinscribing white superiority. And church as truth-teller will construct practices of worship that enact and nurture evangelical defiance of injustice.

It is my growing conviction that neighbor-love in this sense, the path to the future if we are to have one, requires moral courage and power beyond what is humanly possible, for we are according to Martin Luther selves curved in on self. However, I refuse to believe that God calls us to love neighbor as self without also empowering us to do so. Quite the contrary, trust in God's unconditional forgiveness provides, I believe, the moral-spiritual fortitude to see our implication in structural sin and, by virtue of seeing it, to repent of it and turn the other way. Said differently, assurance of God's forgiveness opens the door to lives of resistance to social structural sin, including the sins of white racism and economic oppression.

Claiming Moral-Spiritual Power: Clues in Lutheran Traditions

The church's moral vision, or truth-telling, reveals the unthinkable about white U.S. Christians' heritage and our lives built upon it: lives built on near-genocide of this continent's peoples and confiscation of their homeland, on chattel slavery theologically rationalized, and on the exploited labor of this land and continents to the south and east. I would not be here had my grandparents not taken over the land of people in the Dakotas who were killed or forced into exile. Many white Lutherans own houses that black people were prevented from owning by gentrification or red-lining. This is the horror of structural sin: that simply by being white, I participate in white privilege.

In a similar vein, most of us reading these words, just by housing, feeding, clothing, and transporting ourselves, are destroying or using up the very necessities for life of countless others who are disproportionately people of colors other than white and are economically impoverished. Consider the tribal people from the state of Orissa in India who were forced off the land that had sustained them for centuries into urban destitution by transnational companies mining the rich deposits of bauxite in that area. The people lost their homes, community, livelihoods, and means of maintaining culture. Some even lost their lives to the repression that met their efforts to organize opposition to the mining operations. How many products in our North American homes depend upon that bauxite?

Or what of the countless families in Mexico who lost their land and livelihoods and were forced north into sweatshop labor because the North American Free Trade Agreement (NAFTA) destroyed the corn industry that had sustained them for generations? It allowed U.S. corn to be sold very inexpensively in Mexico, devastating much of the small-scale Mexican farms. The reality is that many of us have mutual funds that benefit from free-trade agreements allowing U.S. corn, textiles, and other products to be "dumped" in nations of the global South, essentially destroying the small industries or microbusinesses that had provided livelihoods. Many of us enjoy purchasing goods made inexpensive by cheap sweatshop labor and the "efficiency" it enables corporate owners to achieve. Even the computer on which I write this may have cost less because it was produced in a "free-trade zone" in which "freedom" from environmental and labor protections raised corporate profits while costing many people their lives.

And what of the lives lost to maintain our addiction to oil: the Iraqi children, young U.S. women and men from impoverished families serving in the armed forces, and resisters to oil drilling in their homelands on the Niger Delta and elsewhere? The realities of structural sin are soul shattering. People of privilege (be it white privilege, national privilege, or economic privilege) flee from truth-telling of that kind. Moral oblivion is far more bearable. Where the truth sinks in, denial lurks. We shrink from it, our moral agency dulled by a sense of despair and powerlessness. We seek refuge from the torment of structural sin in the safe haven of virtue in private life.

Wherein lies the moral-spiritual wisdom and courage for white people and the world's overconsuming minority of all colors to see, unmask, and dismantle white privilege and economic violence in church and society? Here Lutheran traditions offer life-giving resources. I touch on three: a theology of the cross critically appropriated, a paradoxical moral anthropology, and Luther's sense of God indwelling all of creation. Finally, I note a fourth resource that runs through the Christian story, but is largely unrecognized: our heritage of resistance.

THE CROSS

There is good reason to distrust many theologies of the cross. I do. To others, I owe my hope and therefore, perhaps, my life.[15] The question, of course, is, "Which cross and whose cross?" A dual hermeneutic is the obligation of Christian faith—a hermeneutic of trust and of suspicion working together. Led by our forebears and by Jesus himself, we are a critical tradition, testing our claims and convictions to see whether they pass on or betray the splendid mystery of God's unbounded and undefeatable love for this good creation and presence with and within it.[16] So it is with theologies of the cross. To evoke for life-giving purposes a symbol that also has betrayed God's love requires pointing out that betrayal. Whose cross and which cross? False crosses have been with us since at least the year 313 C.E. when Christianity became the religion of the "known world's" reigning imperial power. The cross of Constantine for 1,700 years justified war in the name of God. It was not and is not the cross of the God revealed in Jesus of Nazareth. The cross of the "white Christ," known most horrifically in the American slaveholders' religion, betrayed and betrays the cross of Jesus Christ.[17] It is present today in well-intentioned pictures of the Northern European Jesus, subtly linking whiteness with goodness and saving power. The cross of "bear your suffering meekly, like a lamb" drives abused women and others back into the hands of their abusers. It also is not the cross of Jesus. Nor is the cross of Christian religious supremacy, raised in towns and cities where the faith of Jews, Muslims, or people of other religious traditions is denigrated. The medieval cross that retains Jesus nailed to it, forever dead or dying, bears other dangers; the risen Christ, alive and breathing in and through creation, is lost. The Incarnate One revealed today in a grain of wheat, in the touch of wind or sun on bare skin, and in human goodness—this Christ with us and within us—may be pushed aside when the cross holds Christ dead and captive on it.[18] Indeed, false crosses abound, historically and currently. At worst, they have justified domination, exploitation, and dehumanization. The responsibility of "faithful disbelief" includes recognizing and exposing these falsehoods. Yet, this part of the life-giving story remains central: the cross and resurrection.

My own experience convinces me that clear vision of our corruption into systemic sin is indeed too dangerous. It is a realization too horrible to bear without descent into shame or even the torment of self-hatred, unless we see that precisely there, in the furthest reaches of brokenness and in bondage to evil, the saving Christ is present, healing, and liberating. The only force that truly can heal creation is drawn instinctively to our brokenness, and there draws forth power that we did not know we had. This truth enables us to see the structural brutality of which we are a part without being destroyed by that knowledge. This truth beckons us out of the denial and avoidance that render moral complacency. In Luther's words, when reality seems "distorted and sinful, and seemingly God-forsaken . . . a theologian of the cross is not afraid to recognize reality for what it is."[19] "A theologian of glory calls evil good and good evil. A theologian of the cross calls the thing what it actually is."[20]

However, the message of the cross of Jesus Christ does not and cannot stop there. As expressed by Canadian theologian Douglas John Hall, the central message of the cross "is not to reveal that our condition is one of darkness and death; it is to reveal to us the One who meets us in our darkness and death. It is a theology of the cross not because it wants to put forth this ghastly spectacle as a final statement . . . but because it insists that God . . . meets, loves, and redeems us precisely where we are: in the valley of the shadow of death."[21]

This claim is stranger than it seems. It is not unusual to realize that in illness, death, despair, destitution, and other forms of suffering, our saving God is present. Many of us have experienced this grace. However, God's presence in the depths of our brokenness means that God is present with grace even where "I" am perpetrator of economic or ecological violence against others. God is present even if I continue with that violence and even if I have no awareness of God's presence and have no faith that God is present. A central message of what became known as Luther's theology of the cross and continued in Bonhoeffer's writing is that where God seems absent, there God is. God is hidden in God's apparent absence. The saving power of God is hidden in the form of its opposite (*sub contrario suo abscondita sunt*). And no force in heaven or on Earth, including our own bondage to structural sin, can stop God's saving presence (see Rom. 8:39). The God present with us even as perpetrators of structural sin is the God whose liberating and healing power ultimately overwhelms the powers of death and destruction.

The power of this claim is immeasurable for those who have glimpsed even momentarily the horror of being an extravagantly wealthy Christian in a world filled with hungry people, especially when their hunger is connected to our wealth, or of being a white Christian where white privilege pushes others into poverty, exploitation, or death. The cross and resurrection proclaim that, while my social location always will be white, I can change my social stance, moving—however haltingly—toward a justice that reflects the God whom Jesus loved. White people can actively resist white privilege and white dominance, even while not fully escaping them. This saving claim makes it possible to see rather than deny these realities. Therein lies one seed of moral-spiritual power to repent of them and other forms of structural sin.

A PARADOXICAL MORAL ANTHROPOLOGY

Closely related to this theology of the cross and resurrection is yet another seed of moral power offered by Lutheran traditions: our participation in and acquiescence to structural sin is a manifestation of the ubiquitous presence of sin in human life. Lutheran insistence on facing sin's pernicious presence may seduce us toward the dangerous conclusion that God's forgiveness even for structural sin means that one may decline to fight it. Luther's paradoxical moral anthropology and theology of the Holy Spirit utterly negate that conclusion. While we are in bondage to sin, we *also are* the very dwelling place of God. The God who was born as earthling and was executed for allegiance to the ways of God and whose love proved stronger than any force in heaven or earth including death— *this* God is *breathed into* us. Thus speaks the Holy Spirit. Said differently, Christic, justice-making love indwells believing communities.

The human habitation of God is collective, ecclesial. Bonhoeffer elaborated on this moral anthropology wed to ecclesiology. "The church," he insisted, "is nothing but a section of humanity in which Christ has really taken form."[22] The church is "the place where Jesus Christ's taking form is proclaimed and accomplished."[23] This is the paradox: While we are implicated in cruel forms of oppression, we also are the body of Christ on Earth. The living Christ and the Spirit of God abide within and among the people of God, becoming their power to resist structural evil, including white racism. Bonhoeffer was adamant that the love of Christ—revealed most fully in the cross—has chosen to "abide in" the church (he was using Luther's words here), although not only in the church. For Bonhoeffer, as for Luther, the finite bears the infinite (*finitum capax infiniti*). The "finite" is all of creation. Yet, in a particular way, "the finite" is the church. "Christ's relationship with the church is two-fold; he is the creator of its entire life . . . and he is also really present at all times in his church, for the church is his body," Bonhoeffer wrote. "In the community, Christ is at work as with an instrument. He is present in it."[24] That Christ-presence engenders power to uproot and disassemble the bondage of white dominance and economic exploitation. That power, the cross and resurrection promise, is stronger than death itself.

In Bonhoeffer's terms, Christ dwelling in the church "conforms" it to "the form of Jesus Christ." God's overflowing love incarnate becomes a believing community that acts responsibly in the world on behalf of abundant life for all and against what thwarts it. This action requires recognizing social evil, naming it, and "putting a spoke in the wheel" of earthly powers that demand disobedience to God. In fact, Bonhoeffer's use of the word *gestaltung* for "conformation" with the form of Christ (in his last two works) was a play on the same word used by Hitler to mean conformation to fascism. Thus Bonhoeffer implied a refusal to conform with ways of life that betray Christ.[25]

This power to serve others and resist social structural evil, even when so doing is terribly costly, is the actual love of God as Christ taking form in the community of faith.[26] For Bonhoeffer, as for Luther, the wellspring of the church's power for "participating in God's mission" in the world was the crucified and living Christ abiding in and gradually, but never fully, transforming the community of believers.[27] Christians as objects of Christ's love become subjects of that love. Faith is both "faith in Christ" and "faith of Christ."[28] Such love faithfully *subverts* racial, economic, and ecological violence and faithfully creates alternatives.

This was not, for Bonhoeffer, a matter of effort to "become like Jesus." Rather, it was a matter of the Spirit working to unite human beings (individually and collectively) with God in Christ. This God, in whom the church has its being and who abides in it, is a God utterly active in history and in every dimension of life. As revealed in the cross and resurrection, this is a God whose life-serving love is indomitable, even when it appears to be defeated. Thus speaks the incarnation today.

GOD INDWELLING CREATION

Consider now a third wellspring of moral agency inherent in Lutheran traditions, yet widely under-recognized by many of them. Like multiple streams of Christianity from its earliest centuries, Luther affirmed the *mysterium tremendum* that God dwells not only within human beings, but within all creatures and elements: "[T]he power of God," he insisted, "must be essentially present in all places even in the tiniest leaf."[29] God is "present in every single creature in its innermost and outermost being,"[30] wrote Luther. God is "in and through all creatures, in all their parts and places, so that the world is full of God and He fills all."[31] According to Luther, "[E]verything is full of Christ through and through. . . . [A]ll creatures are . . . permeable and present to [Christ]. . . . Christ . . . fills all things. . . . Christ is around us and in us in all places. . . . [H]e is present in all creatures, and I might find him in stone, in fire, in water."[32]

Said differently, creation is filled with the life-giving, life-saving, life-sustaining, and life-savoring power of a God whose love for this world cannot be thwarted by any force in heaven or on earth. God as boundless, justice-seeking love, living and loving not only in human beings but also in the rest of creation, implies that *other-than-human creatures and elements may embody divine agency toward creation's flourishing*. Earth embodies God, not only as creative and revelatory presence, but also as teaching, saving, sustaining, empowering presence— as agency to serve the widespread good. The question for us then is how might moral agency—as power to resist racism, economic and gender injustice, and ecological destruction and to move toward just, sustainable lifeways—be fed and watered in human beings by this God-presence and God-power coursing through "all created things"?[33]

Furthermore, if indeed Christ fills Earth's creatures and elements, then the Earth now being "crucified" by human ignorance, greed, and arrogance is, in some sense, also the body of Christ. Followers of Jesus the Christ in every age are charged with asking Bonhoeffer's lasting question: Who is Christ for us today? Where is the cross today? Where are we lured into denying Christ crucified? If believers took seriously this christological claim that Earth, as habitation of God and body of Christ, is cruciform, might we be motivated to treat this Earth differently?

God's love in Christ "flowing and pouring into [all creatures], filling all things" is an ancient faith claim that offers creative, saving, and sustaining power for the healing of a broken world.[34] Two notions stemming from this claim— God's saving presence at work within the created world, and Christ crucified in a crucified Earth—indeed may render moral motivation and moral agency for the long, uncharted journey toward a world in which humankind is not toxic to our planetary home and in which none amass wealth at the cost of others' impoverishment. Pursuing the theological possibilities at the intersection of cross and indwelling presence may be key to enabling moral agency in the face of white racism, economic violence, and ecological degradation today.

DESCENDENTS OF RESISTERS

Increasingly, I sense another source of moral spiritual agency for resistance to structural sin: Christians' heritage as descendents of resisters. Contemporary Christians all around the globe are working toward a world where all may have life with abundance. They are part of an age-old "cloud of witnesses" that seeks to live according to love for God, self, and neighbor, despite all forces that stand in opposition. We join a long line of courageous resisters who refused to comply with structural evil, despite the cost:

- We are descendents of Shipra and Puah, the two gutsy midwives who defied the Pharaoh's demand that all male babies be killed, thus giving life to Moses who brought Israel out of slavery.
- We are children of second-century Christians who defied Imperial Rome even at the cost of death by the most brutal means.

- We stand in the heritage of the French Huguenots, including the woman who, during seventeen years imprisoned in a tower, carved into the stone with her fingernails one word: Resist.
- Our brothers and sisters in Christ include Africans enslaved in North America who dared risk death by torture to free their people. And we are kin to abolitionists who dared to realize that their wealth was bought with the blood of those African people and who then dared to fight for their freedom.
- Our faith forebears include the nameless Christians who risked their lives to save Jews from the hands of fascism and the church of the poor in Latin America who defied even the U.S. military.

We are an integral part of this community. In baptism, the Holy Spirit wove us into it. What liberative power would grow in the church if we helped each other—young and old alike—to see ourselves as descendents of resisters! I propose that we retell, reread, and reclaim our heritage of resistance to systemic injustice, recalling our subversive ancestry in liturgy, preaching, and teaching. Let us tell and sing to one another the stories of "bold undaunted courage"[35] that define the community of communities spanning the millennia, of which the contemporary church is a part. To reclaim that identity is to reclaim the moral-spiritual power inherent in it.

Conclusion

White feminist theologians are indebted to sisters of other colors for calling us to recognize the moral blinders of white privilege and economic privilege and to see the intricate connections between these forms of injustice and gender-based injustice. The roots of oppression are linked. By chipping away at one, we chip away at others.

In light of these connections, we have asked what it would mean for the Lutheran church in the United States to be a church that actively promotes racial and economic justice, a church that sees evangelical defiance to white racism and economic violence as central to proclaiming the gospel. In response, we have identified two ingredients of that stance. It would entail:

1. a commitment to seeing and telling the truth about forms of injustice structured into the lives of white people and economically privileged people but easily obscured from their vision by the experience of privilege, and
2. a willingness to claim the moral-spiritual power offered by the great mystery we call God. Despite the complexities of our existence, God

liberates us to resist privilege and dominance in the very "moment" of deepest alienation or sin.

Lutheran traditions offer priceless theological gifts to the ecumenical work of building racially and economically just ways of being human and being Christian in the world. We bring a morally empowering trust that God's unconditional forgiveness and love is at work in a world that is hungering for and hastening toward abundant life for all. God's unconditional love is manifest in a theology of cross and resurrection, a paradoxical moral anthropology, and a theology of God indwelling all of creation. Lutherans also share with other Christian traditions other wellsprings of moral-spiritual power. One of these is a heritage of faithful resistance grounded in the love of God.

A central task of the church in the twenty-first century is to build ways of being Christian and being human that nurture sustainable Earth-human relations and social justice. Here we have focused on the latter. It includes recognizing and then countering injustice grounded in gender, economic status, race/ethnicity, and other markers. Feminist, womanist, and mujerista theologies are gracious gifts of God for pursing this evangelical work in the name of She Who Is.

Suggested Reading

Fernandez, Eleazar S. *Reimagining the Human: Theological Anthropology in Response to Systemic Evil*. St. Louis: Chalice, 2003.

Moe-Lobeda, Cynthia. *Healing a Broken World: Globalization and God*. Minneapolis: Fortress Press, 2002.

Moe-Lobeda, Cynthia. *Public Church: For the Life of the World*. Minneapolis: Augsburg Fortress, 2004.

West, Traci C. *Disruptive Christian Ethics: When Racism and Women's Lives Matter*. Louisville: Westminster John Knox, 2006.

PART 7

Hope and the Future

KRISTA HUGHES AND DEANNA Thompson close this volume with two distinct yet centrally related feminist visions of hope. Hughes focuses in chapter 15 on the practice of naming our real fears, over the distractions of virtual fears or an overly disembodied future hope. A theology of the cross is once again centrally important in these chapters, for Hughes turns to it for a clear vision of our true fears in order to turn to the shape of real hope in real bodies, here and now. A strong tendency in feminist theology to remove eschatology from death compels Thompson to outline the inadequacy of this thinking to the christocentric promise Lutherans hold. In the closing chapter, Thompson lays out a fulsome feminist Lutheran vision of the shape of real hope in the future God promises beyond death and the ways in which this future indeed shapes the present.

Chapter 15

In the Flesh:
A Feminist Vision of Hope

Krista E. Hughes

FEAR IS ABROAD IN the land in this first decade of the third millennium. From the terrorist attacks of September 11, 2001, to the global economic crisis at decade's end, U.S. citizens are facing a deep-seated vulnerability to which many are unaccustomed. Simply to live in the world—inescapably vulnerable to suffering, sin, and death—involves fear. It is thus understandable that as a nation we might feel fearful and anxious in the wake of these breaches to our sense of security, be they the threat of physical violence or the inability to put food on the table. How we as a society have responded to the events of the decade, however, has seemed not to allay our fears but to stoke them. The rhetoric of fear that has dominated the airwaves and the e-waves has cultivated what we might call "virtual" fears. These are fears that are rooted in a very real sense of threat but that have become grossly distorted and amplified, drifting further and further from their authentic source. As they grow, these virtual fears seem to take on a disproportionate life of their own, provoking our anxieties while paradoxically alienating us from our true emotions, along with any wisdom they might harbor. This displacement of the genuine by the virtual, I suggest, poses a triple danger: distracting us from real threats to livelihood and health that do deserve our attention; fostering a sense of our own helplessness; and projecting our fears onto others in the form of anger, hatred, and violence.[1] In all these we become alienated from ourselves and from one another. Fear, real yet also dangerously imagined, is abroad in the land.

Hope, of course, is the Christian response to fear. Indeed, "Be not afraid" is one of the most frequent counsels in the Christian scriptures, for God's promise to God's people is, in the words of medieval mystic Julian of Norwich, that "all shall be well; and all shall be well; and all manner of thing shall be well."[2] Thus, for Christians, hope is classically understood as a faithful attitude of expectation for the future fulfillment of God's promises. Because Christians understand this promise to be breaking into the world always already, here and now, hope bears the power to sustain and encourage human spirits in the present. In sum, hope both bridges and transcends time itself. Yet many feminist theologians—as Deanna Thompson unfolds in the next chapter—have criticized the tendency in predominant eschatologies to emphasize a spiritualized, other-worldly future at the expense of the embodied, earthly present. Proverbs 13:12 does indeed caution that "hope deferred makes the heart sick." In other words, when hope is projected exclusively onto a radical eschatological future, it too risks becoming "virtual." As such, it actually may function conjointly *with* fear, by further reinforcing the message that we are fundamentally helpless in the face of the world's overwhelming complexities and perceived threats. In this sense hope also can *dis*empower rather than inspire and encourage. Laying claim to such critical feminist insights about eschatology, I am concerned that Christian hope for the third millennium not trade in virtualities, which function outside of both time and bodies. Because we embody our vulnerabilities, anxieties, and fears, any Christian response to them must not, in theologian Sharon Betcher's words, "evacuate corporeality."[3] Hope must attend to the flesh, here and now.

The work of feminist Lutheran theologians Thompson and Mary Solberg suggests that attending to the flesh does not stray as far from Martin Luther's theological vision as conventional wisdom might suspect.[4] With them, I find in Luther's theology of the cross a powerful complement to feminist concerns about the enfleshed and very present realities of sin and suffering[5]—particularly his admonition that a theologian of the cross "names a thing what it really is."[6] For Luther this meant, in a word, *sin*—specifically the sinful self-delusion that we are in control of our own salvation. As Solberg notes, the first step of the liberating conversion we experience in God's justifying grace is a salutary (though decidedly uncomfortable) disillusionment in which we come to see "what is the case"—an awakening.[7] This, moreover, is not a passive seeing but an acknowledgment that names our own implication in sin, both systemic and personal. Such naming seems precisely the antidote for the harmful virtualities of present society. We need an honest, clear-eyed vision that sees what truly deserves our fears and that for which we might faithfully hope, inextricably coupled with the courage to name those fears and hopes as they emerge in people's lives.

In commending this Lutheran practice of seeing–naming, already claimed by feminists, I offer two supplements to earlier feminist reconstructions. First, I suggest that to be a feminist theologian of the cross, Thompson's ground-breaking proposal presupposes that one is also a theologian of the flesh, if we indeed take seriously the incarnation—our confession that the Word became flesh and dwelled among us. Jesus' suffering was not merely psychological; it registered on and in his body. Even in resurrection, he bore his wounds, no mere virtualities but in the flesh. His invitation to Thomas to look at them, acknowledge them, and even touch them—to see and to name them—was the beginning of Thomas's faith. So, too, I suggest with hope. Second, I offer that the prophetic naming to which Luther calls us ought not to be limited to (dis)illusions of grandeur. Rather, to acknowledge "what is the case" also means to name anything that impedes our flourishing and in turn to identify the hopeful possibilities for countering those strictures. Thus, it is to identify not only sin and suffering but also grace and hope. A clear-eyed seeing and a courageous naming constitute a feminist Lutheran practice of hope, in sum, ever attentive to the flesh, that serves to counter the triple danger to which virtual fear disposes us.

I explore how this seeing and naming in the flesh might constitute a practice of hope by appealing to two contemporary theological discourses: womanist theology and theology from the perspective of disablement. Each in its own way performs the naming I am proposing, both the realities of fear and the possibilities of hope here and now. In offering compelling portraits of what a clear-eyed, honest, and discerning vision for hope might look like, these discourses reveal what Betcher calls "the wisdom of an abject authority."[8] An "abject authority"—specifically a person who is visibly physically disabled—is a potential source of wisdom, Betcher offers, because in "admitting [her] mortality, [she] can teach us to traverse the tragic tears of sentient existence with some measure of equanimity."[9] I want to borrow this insight for the present vision of hope. The traditional marginalizing of persons with disablties and of black women does more than simply challenge virtual versions of fear and hope by revealing our own implication in the sinful structures, behaviors, and theologies that marginalize others. These marginalized groups—whose very bodies have historically served as grounds for the fearful projections of privileged groups—also bear the potential to teach us how to face and accept our own very real fears of mortality and suffering by naming these things for what they really are.[10] This, I offer, is the beginning of hope.

Fears, both real and virtual, are abroad in the land. What message of hope might the gospel have to offer such a fearful world? What are the contours of such a hope in this new millennium? I suggest we can find a promising answer at the intersection of feminist and Lutheran theologies, both of which caution against putting our faith in "virtualities"—be they abstractions that displace embodied needs and joys or theologies of glory that ignore suffering and sin. These complementary wisdoms of attending to real bodies and their very real

limitations nurture the present vision of hope. I see them come together especially cogently in Betcher's notion of the "wisdom of an abject authority," which
can teach us a bit about facing our vulnerabilities and limitations, our own mortality "with some measure of equanimity" rather than reactionary fear.[11] What I
propose, then, is that the first crucial step toward addressing fear with hope is
recognizing and naming those fears that are virtual and those that are genuine.
For only in acknowledging our real fears, vulnerabilities, and limitations will
we be able to truly discern the hopeful possibilities that might allow us to step
forward into our future with confidence as well as compassion.

Vulnerabilities and Virtualities

Several weeks following September 11, 2001, a friend of mine related to me
that she was having dreams about Osama bin Laden trying to hunt her down
and kill her. Many in the United States experienced a terrifying vulnerability at
that time. None of us knew if other attacks were to come. Yet I found while I
listened to her that my compassion for what was clearly a genuine and gripping
fear was mingled with something far less empathetic and far more judgmental,
namely, a sense that such dreams were utterly absurd. For my friend lived not in
the metropolitan New York City area or in any other major urban center likely
to be a terrorist target, and she knew no one personally who died or was harmed
in the attacks. Because she was genuinely gripped by anxiety, maybe even terror,
I regretted my feelings of judgment. However, I could not help but hear in my
friend some misplaced fears, especially as it came to light that she had been continuously watching television news. It was clear that the government's rhetoric
of fear and the media's accompanying images had deeply penetrated her psyche.
What was so striking to me was that in her dreams bin Laden had transformed
into a direct, personal danger; he was not threatening to bring down the West
but quite specifically to harm her.

I offer this story not to suggest that my friend is gullible. Rather, I think her
story illustrates the slippery nature of fear, how its impetus, its object, and its
aim easily shift when fear grips us. This is, I think, one key reason the rhetoric
of fear is so pernicious; it amplifies the very real anxieties of our lives—ranging
from daily worries to deep-seated fears—yet does so precisely by displacing
and occluding our genuine anxieties. What I am naming *virtual* fear takes their
place. In other words, what takes hold is a virtual fear that simultaneously stirs
the emotions, sometimes to a fever pitch, *and* functions to disempower and even
paralyze us. We can come to feel like helpless victims of the world's overwhelmingly complex threats, which is especially notable when politicians deploy a
rhetoric of fear. Legitimate fear is thereby further transformed into virtual fear,
which is used as a tool of power and manipulation. But we need to ask: Who is

defining what is to be feared? How are they defining it? Does it fully correspond to the enfleshed realities of our own communities, cities, families, and lives? What does it amplify and what does it leave out? I take the time to explore this dynamic of fear because I think a key component of the practice of Christian hope is to identify and openly articulate the distinction between *genuine* fears and threats and *virtual* fears and threats—while recognizing the potential difficulty of such a task. Like all prophetic work, this is necessarily a process of careful, continuous, and evolving discernment.

What about hope? Ideally, our hope in God's promises serves as both a comfort and a lure, empowering us in the midst of our daily lives. However, the promise of hope, as classically articulated, also risks immobilizing us if we project it into an indefinitely deferred eschatological future, so far away and so disembodied that hope too takes on qualities of the virtual. Instead of passively waiting, therefore, we must be attentive to the divine hope as it arrives to us in the present, thereby altering the present. As liberation theologies have demonstrated from the beginning, hope in the promised heavenly banquet quickly becomes bankrupt if it dismisses those whose bodies hunger and thirst right now. In this light we recognize that the practice of naming fear and hope for what they really are, with clear eyes and courageous hearts, is more than a strategy for assurance in hard times. It is equally a matter of justice, and those who count ourselves amongst privileged groups perhaps need this practice most. As the story of my friend illustrates, there is an ironic twist to the disempowerment engendered by virtual fear and hope: only those whose lives are at a fairly safe remove from *real* threats to life and health have the luxury to engage in virtualities. This is not to say that any person can be free of fear at all times, for to live involves risk and therefore fear. But fear means something dramatically different to someone who lives in a war zone or in a gang-dominated inner city or in an unsafe home where even family cannot be trusted not to abuse you. Virtual fear and hope therefore are not only misguided, but they foreclose possibilities for justice and compassion by eliding genuine threats to life and livelihood. That is, privileged groups are able simultaneously to ignore those who live in real contexts of fear and to project onto them their own fears of suffering and mortality. To shift how we think about and engage in hope, therefore, is about more than simply faith in God: it is about faithfulness to a world hungering for justice.[12]

What, then, might this practice of hope look like? The locus of my reflections is the question of where we look for and discern hope, and how we name it. To be a feminist theologian of the cross is also to be a feminist theologian of the flesh. For God whom we know through the incarnate Word lives and moves also in the bodies of the world—in human bodies and in all the various bodies that surround us and constitute our context. Two contemporary theological discourses—womanist theology and theology from the perspective of disablement—now help us trace a feminist vision of hope "in the flesh." Each in its own way offers the "wisdom of an abject authority" and in so doing names things for what they really are: not only suffering and sin, but also the possibilities of hope.

Making a Way Out of No Way: Womanist Wisdom

"Making a way out of no way," says womanist theologian Monica Coleman, is "a summarizing concept for black women's experience of struggle and God's assistance in helping them overcome oppression."[13] Drawing from the work of five womanist theologians, Coleman adopts this phrase, a common one in the traditional vernacular of black women, to describe a uniquely womanist vision of salvation. It is a phrase that Delores Williams in particular has explored for its power to describe and illuminate how black women have understood God's salvific work in their lives. It is a fruitful concept for considering a feminist vision of hope because it speaks of both the clear, courageous discernment to face one's circumstances and an active hope that moves forward, even when it seems all paths are closed.

Williams illustrates making a way out of no way with the story of Hagar, the handmaid impregnated by Abram who subsequently draws Sarai's jealous rage and is sent away into the desert wilderness. Soon after her departure, however, God sends Hagar back to their home. While this is not what Hagar especially wants (or perhaps what we would want for her)—for it seems to work directly against any liberation from her oppressors—Williams notes that the alternative certainly would have meant death, if not immediately for her, then certainly for the child she was carrying. As Williams reads the story, although Hagar is confronted by "no liberator God," Yahweh does demonstrate clear "concern for the survival and future quality of life for Hagar and Ishmael."[14] From this story, Williams and Coleman in her wake are thus able to identify "survival" and "positive quality of life" as important guiding principles for womanist theology and ethics. While full liberation is the ideal aim, meaningful salvation, more often than not, must be less ambitious and more subtle. Or as Coleman puts it, "Survival is often inadequate in terms of full liberation, but it is one of the ways in which God saves."[15] In her reading of Hagar's tale, Williams also stresses the active human agency at work in salvation, noting that God does not force Hagar to return. God's gift, rather, is the vision to see the resources that will help her survive. Coleman thus clarifies that making a way out of no way should not be interpreted as suggesting that "the way appears from nowhere, out of nothing." Rather, it is the trust, the hope that "acknowledges God's presence in providing options that do not appear to exist in the experiences of the past."[16] According to this vision of hope, God in one sense opens for us a new way by gracing us with the vision to see clearly what our various possibilities are. In this process, relations with self, world, and God shift, reoriented by the power of a here–now hope.

I lift out of the notion of making a way out of no way two elements that might nurture our own reflections on a feminist vision of hope. The first is that the sense of salvation in this vision is unremittingly concrete, embodied, and particular—necessarily more modest than Christianity's grand eschatological vision, yet also perhaps less virtual and definitely much more real. While full liberation always remains the outside aim, survival and quality of life are the focus here and now. Second, flowing from the first, hope comes alive precisely through clarified vision—God opens our eyes to see and to assess our concrete circumstances, to discern both our limiting factors and our real possibilities as well as reorient our relations to world, self, and God. In other words, the womanist wisdom of making a way out of no way potentially radicalizes the Lutheran practice of naming things for what they really are, including our fears as well as our hopes.

Attending to Our Corporeal Contours: Crip Wisdom

Feminist theologian Sharon Betcher likewise radicalizes this practice commended by Luther to theologians of the cross. If Williams, Coleman, and other womanists insist on a hope that attends to our concrete circumstances, Betcher wants to ensure that we attend to our very bodies, what she calls our "corporeal contours." Betcher may in fact be a feminist theologian of the flesh *par excellence*. In an incisive reading of the fall, Betcher deepens one of the earliest feminist theological critiques—that classic Christian doctrines, so powerfully shaped by Greek thought, have denigrated embodiment. She observes, as many feminists have, that the doctrine of the fall problematically casts suffering as unnatural: had Adam and Eve not misbehaved, we would not toil for our food or suffer labor pangs. Betcher adds something further. Using a postcolonial optic, she observes that in this traditional vision corporeality itself becomes oppression. Bodies—source of our mortality—are precisely the bondage from which we are promised escape when we die. Therefore, liberation and embodiment can never go hand in hand, despite, inexplicably, the Christian confession that God became incarnate, the Word became flesh.

Such classic theologies that denigrate embodiment and implicitly identify bodies as a form of oppression are a particular problem for those who are disabled because their physical limitations reveal them as so clearly embodied. The result, moreover, is that "normates," as Betcher calls them, project onto the so-called disabled their own fears about mortality and suffering, which Christian doctrine has tended to interpret as the price, perhaps even the punishment, of embodiment. "Disability," Betcher observes, "acts . . . as the unprocessable stigmata of mortality. . . . The catastrophic crease of disability does not allow those of us so marked to pass as anything but mortal."[17] In possessing "bodies that admit suffering,"[18] Betcher argues, those who are disabled nevertheless have a certain positive power to offer. She sees them as a resource of deep wisdom for the postmodern world. The discontinuities and fragmentations that seem newly threatening to postmodern culture are qualities of life that persons with disablilities have always negotiated. Thus, precisely those persons on whom "normates" traditionally have projected their fears of suffering and mortality may now serve as the very guides needed to negotiate the postmodern milieu and its seeming threats.

Betcher insists that any Christian message of hope absolutely cannot, in her words, "evacuate corporeality." Rather, she says, "we need a discourse that holds corporeal contours—finitude, limits, transience, and mortality, as well as the suffering and pain associated with [them]—in cultural consciousness."[19] Her aim, she continues, is

> writing religious hope, that is, love of the world (John 3:16), of a "world without end," even "resurrection of the body," without evacuating corporeality. I am interested in tracing out a religious hope that recognizes that finitude and mortality and transience are conditions for the everlastingness of the world—are conditions that "permit an infinite becoming within the finite."[20]

What Betcher is describing, what she is longing for, is not mere survival; it is about the possibility of flourishing with joy, even amidst our limitations—of, I think she would agree, "majesty at the margins," where resistance and celebration are not always distinguishable.[21] In considering not only disabled bodies but also diseased bodies (one of Thompson's points of departure in the next chapter), we must acknowledge that such flourishing does not necessarily signify restoration to full physical health. It does mean that God is lovingly, vivifyingly present even amidst pain and limitation.

To claim, to unflinchingly attend to, our corporeal contours means then for Betcher acknowledging and fearlessly accepting our shared vulnerability as mortals, those who suffer in body, mind, and spirit, regardless of whether society views us as a "cripple" or a "normate." If we have not "evacuated corporeality," relegating hope exclusively to a disembodied future and rendering it virtual, we will possess a much clearer vision of what exactly we are and to what we are not vulnerable. This can be precisely our ground for connection: "Out of a more honest acquaintance with our sentient situation," Betcher affirms, "we can reinstitute subjective economies that recognize that bodies have needs, that communities are woven together among people who need each other, that everyone has needs—not just the community of the disabled."[22] We see clearly and we name honestly our shared vulnerability, and our shared joys. Out of this may arise a palpable, embodied hope.

Hope in the Flesh

Womanists Williams and Coleman focus on our concrete circumstances while Betcher trains her gaze on the body itself. Collectively they offer resonant insights about where hope in and for this world resides: in the here–now, enfleshed present—with its hungers and thirsts, its limitations and frustrations, its sufferings—and with its concrete possibilities for a different way of being.[23] They show, in other words, how a feminist vision of hope must presume the incarnation along with the cross and resurrection. This hope sees God hidden in the flesh—of the earth, of our neighbors, of ourselves. And it names the Holy Divine's movement, ever arriving again and again, offering the best possibilities for where we are in the here–now, each moment a gift of new beginnings, of hope for making a way out of no way without denying our corporeal contours.

Yes, a feminist vision of hope in the flesh attends unapologetically to actual bodies and actual circumstances, with their limits and wounds and sufferings, yet also their possibilities and their joys. "Trust [in the Holy Spirit]," says Betcher—which, I suggest, is a practice of hope—"is a way of abiding with our mortality, where sentience not only confirms the registration of pain, but bedews the body, baptizes it unto life."[24] To be feminist theologians of the cross and the flesh is to confess boldly the incarnation and its significance for us as embodied beings. This means, in part, refusing to exclusively transcendentalize hope. A feminist vision of hope in the flesh courageously asks what we can do within the circumstances of life and among the fragmentations and discontinuities and the threats perceived and real of this postmodern world. It is to be open to the vision offered by God of what resources are available here and now, to notice where we might be able to make a way out of no way. My proposals are in no way meant to limit hope or its possibilities but, rather, to ensure that our hope is meaningful and pertinent to embodied lives and not an illusion that distracts us from attending to works of compassion, justice, and healing. Indeed, what I am proposing is that we attend more faithfully to the incarnation itself. In witnessing to the hope that already has come to earth, into our midst, into our bodies, we actually open ourselves more fully to its possibilities—for only in this way does it become *for us*, as Luther emphasized in his pastoral theology.[25]

In the next chapter, Deanna Thompson will push against a certain feminist theological overemphasis on the present, that is, a tendency to dismiss or downplay the Christian confession that God promises "more" than simply the here—now. If she and I appear to be working at cross-purposes, we are, but only—witty wordplay permitted—in a theological sense. Hope in the light of the cross is precisely our shared concern! Thompson rightly identifies a theology of glory in the conviction of certain contemporary theologians that hope rests primarily in the present. Meanwhile, I have sought to show that a theology of the cross becomes a theology of glory when the promise of transformation remains too remote to matter for those who suffer in the present. In these cases hope is grounded not in God, but in human illusions of either excessive self-reliance or passive helplessness. Together we are examining, if unintentionally, the two dangerous chasms abutting the "narrow road" identified by Dietrich Bonhoeffer in *Discipleship*: trusting in our own capacities to save ourselves on the one hand or relying on God's grace to the point of human passivity on the other.[26] One looks too much to the present, the other too much to the future. But the very word *hope* contains within itself both the present and the future. Together we are asking, with distinctive emphases, *What is a cross-centered hope that attends to the now yet does not forsake the divine promise of the more?*[27] My aim has been to ask where we might discern, and lay claim to, the holy "more" in our very midst.

In fall 2008 a *New York Times* journalist tracked down a group of young women to follow up on a story she had done twenty years earlier. In 1988, the women were the Jump Rope Girls of Parkside Avenue in Brooklyn.[28] At the height of the city's crack epidemic, with violence and homicide rates soaring, this group of girls, ranging in age from eight to eleven, claimed a space of sidewalk every single afternoon to jump rope, cheer, and dance together. Despite the violence and the very nonvirtual fear that permeated every aspect of these girls' lives—or better, precisely because of it[29]—they gathered daily to move their bodies and sing out with steady, clear voices. Today many of the women still live in the same homes in which they grew up, and even as some of them have also achieved a measure of professional success, most have not escaped the challenges they faced as girls. One had a child when she herself was only thirteen, another is dealing with several ill family members who do not have adequate health care, while another solely supports an intergenerational family of seven. In other words, these girls-now-women have not miraculously escaped their circumstances. But who can doubt the witness to hope that they offered their strife-ridden neighborhood, and themselves, over the years of their youth? My intention in telling their story is not to romanticize their situation, either then or now. Quite the opposite, for it is clear that the Jump Rope Girls were not figures of childlike innocence; their context, sadly, did not permit such freedom of care. However, I wonder if their having a very clear sense of what was to be feared granted them a certain freedom nonetheless to embrace their childlike joy at the same time that many of their mothers were obviously making a way out of no way. In their pre-adolescent youthfulness, these girls were able to claim a playful spirit that was expressed in a deeply embodied way. And this, I would offer, may be another central element of a feminist vision for hope in the flesh: not simply a clear-eyed attention to the frustrations and sufferings of real bodies but, as Betcher points out, the cultivation of joy, particularly joy that deeply involves our corporeal contours. Living more deeply into our bodies, both in their needs and in their pleasures, is a way to live hope here and now.

Isaiah 54 is a lyrical litany of God's future promises, while the subsequent chapter invites us to open our eyes to the possibilities before us, giving us a vision for survival resonant with what Williams describes—God's abundant offering of water and bread, milk and wine, without money or price. Isaiah 55 also speaks of song and dance. The prophet promises, "For you shall go out in joy, and be led back in peace; the mountains and the hills before you shall burst into song, and all the trees of the field shall clap their hands" (Isa. 55:12). For Isaiah, this too is perhaps a future promise of how God will redeem her people. But one senses that this holy promise, this vision of hope, is also very close and at certain moments already here. Dare we, as feminist theologians of the flesh, have the vision to see and to name that we already are being led with joy and peace, that the mountains already are singing, the trees already clapping, that the world is already turning. Let us join in! Virtual fear is, after all, no match for singing voices, clapping hands, and dancing feet. Hope lives—in the flesh.

Suggested Reading

Betcher, Sharon V. Spirit and the Politics of Disablement. Minneapolis: Fortress Press, 2007.

Coleman, Monica A. Making a Way Out of No Way: A Womanist Theology. Minneapolis: Fortress Press, 2008.

Solberg, Mary M. Compelling Knowledge: A Feminist Proposal for an Epistemology of the Cross. Albany: State University of New York Press, 1997.

Thompson, Deanna A. Crossing the Divide: Luther, Feminism, and the Cross. Minneapolis: Fortress Press, 2004.

Williams, Delores S. Sisters in the Wilderness: The Challenge of Womanist God-Talk. Maryknoll, N.Y.: Orbis, 1993.

Chapter 16

Hoping for More:
How Eschatology Matters for
Lutheran Feminist Theologies

Deanna A. Thompson

IT TOOK SEVERAL WEEKS for the news to sink in. My broken back was caused by metastatic breast cancer spreading through my bones. I thought I understood breast cancer—my mom has dealt with this disease twice—but I didn't quite get how it related to my two broken vertebrae. After weeks of hospitalization, radiation, and oncology visits, I began processing what having stage IV breast cancer means. In addition to being incurable, survival rates aren't good. Five years out from diagnosis, only 20 percent of patients are still alive.

Perhaps in unconscious preparation for this cancer journey, over the past year I've become increasingly interested in the subject of hope. My travels to South Africa in summer 2008 brought theological challenges of hope to the surface in a new way. Both the grand scale of suffering and the grand scale of hope I witnessed there demanded attention. My liberationist/feminist sensibilities draw me to focus on where hope lives in this world, today. And theologians like myself, I believe, are called on to reflect upon, articulate, and contribute to practices of hope in the here and now.[1]

But part of me has grown uneasy with contemporary theological preoccupations of hope as confined to the present or immediate future. Assuredly much of Christian tradition has overemphasized hope in an unrealized, heavenly future, often to the detriment of embodied life in the present. And yet, from the townships of South Africa to the chemo rooms I now frequent, I'm convinced contemporary theology needs an eschatology that not only envisions a new world for the present but also attends to the hope beyond all sorrow and suffering, a central commitment of the Christian gospel to which Martin Luther and so many others have held fast. What follows is an attempt at such eschatological thinking in a Lutheran feminist key.

Eschatology Threatened

"Always be ready to make . . . an accounting for the hope that is in you," the writer of 1 Peter proclaims (3:15). This hope testified to in scripture points Christians to God's promised future where God will wipe away every tear, and "a new heaven and a new earth" will someday be reality (Rev. 21:1; see also Isaiah 25). And yet, eschatology—theological reflection on hope in the context of God's promised future—seems threatened with extinction in certain forms of Christianity. While some corners of Christianity have maintained passionate interest in end-times discussions, such as is found in the *Left Behind* series, more liberal-leaning theologians keep their distance from eschatological musings. For instance, I participate in a constructive theology workgroup, a group of scholars who work together on issues of contemporary significance in theology. Recently almost fifty of us collaborated on a constructive/systematic textbook. When conversations turned to the loci the book would cover, eschatology barely registered on the interest index. The strength of this text is anchored in its passionate wedding of Christian thought and practice to the transformation of injustices threatening to overrun the present.[2] Thinking specifically about eschatology, however, was left for another day.

Feminist theologians also keep eschatology at arm's length. In defense of feminist disinterest in the doctrine, process theologian Catherine Keller insists that eschatological reflection too often remains "dualistic, deterministic, and other-worldly."[3] These tendencies, feminist theologians have worked hard to explain, run counter to their commitment to promote the full humanity of women in theological discourse and ecclesiological life. While feminists seek to affirm the value of earthbound bodies, particularly those in female form, Christian thought often relegates female bodies—both symbolically and literally—to the role of negative dualistic counterpart to male bodies. Feminist scholar Rosemary Radford Ruether's helpful study on eschatology and feminism points out that "opposition between female flesh and eternal life led to a discussion in early Christianity as to whether women's bodies could be redeemed at all in the resurrection of the dead."[4] Ruether exposes a strong dualistic tendency in Christian eschatology, which helps explain why feminists gravitate toward other doctrinal pursuits.

Keller and Ruether also critique eschatological thinking for its deterministic and other-worldly character. When the eschatological lens focuses on the next world, the state of bodies in the here and now often suffers from neglect. If a future world matters most, little impetus can exist for change in current conditions of earthly living. Not only do feminists seek to improve conditions for women's bodies, but, as Greek Orthodox theologian Valerie Karras notes, many feminist theologians also reach beyond human concerns alone toward a focus on all of creation.[5] Highly critical of Christian preoccupation with personal immortality, some "ecofeminists" call for movement away from questions of personal life after death to the pressing issues of ecological sustainability. Ruether acknowledges, however, that even though an anthropological focus must be displaced, women as well as men still harbor questions and concerns about the afterlife. Her response? Approach all these questions with an honest agnosticism.[6]

But when it comes to life in this world, a growing number of theologians insist that the realities of ecological degradation lead not to agnosticism, but to the conviction that "our home is dying."[7] Focus on the afterlife, then, is set aside in favor of a theology that prompts action on behalf of God's world here and now. In their most recent book, *Saving Paradise*, theologians Rita Nakashima Brock and Rebecca Parker devote almost 500 pages to this argument. Rather than viewing a new earth as promised future reality, Brock and Parker suggest that in ancient Judaism and Christianity, paradise was understood as a present rather than a future possibility. From Israelite visions of the Garden of Eden to Jesus' words to the repentant criminal hanging next to him on the cross ("*today* you shall be with me in paradise"), Judaism and Christianity affirmed the present as paradise's location. Brock and Parker conclude their argument by saying, "Having hope *may* be important, but it is more important to arrive fully at 'this present paradise before us' and respond to it with lives devoted to justice and care for the world."[8] Here Brock and Parker take feminist disinterest in all things eschatological to a new level: not only does eschatological thinking breed determinism, but hope in anything beyond today might divert us from reclaiming the paradise possible right now.

Clearly Brock and Parker want to swing the pendulum back toward attending to this life. They offer powerful arguments about how Christianity's vision of eternal life was used to justify crusading and colonizing mentalities in the medieval and modern periods. They also attend to the ecological dimensions of this neglect. The heavy emphasis on sin, they insist, led countless theologians, Martin Luther included, to argue against any present form of paradise.[9] What is desperately needed, they claim, is a passionate embrace of paradise now: "We recommit ourselves to this world as holy ground when we remember the fullness of life that is possible through our communities, our life-affirming rituals, and our love of beauty."[10]

On the one hand, this passionate view of the beauty of life and the earth we inhabit rightly challenges Christian conceptions of sin, salvation, and the after-life that promote disengagement with present-day human and nonhuman lives. On the other hand, Brock and Parker's utterly this-worldly vision runs the risk of neglecting hope in God's promised future in favor of an optimism about human capacity to embrace a paradisical existence in the present. As a theologian with Lutheran sensibilities, I worry such a view might promote a kind of theology of glory, that is, a vision of reality that neglects the extent to which human sin pervades global human and nonhuman communities. Does talk of a present-day paradise fully appreciate the daily agonies of HIV-infected families in Kyleitscha township, South Africa? Or the particular realities of women and men who sit, week after week, in chemo rooms, struggling to come to terms with what their disease has taken from them? Maintaining a starkly realistic assessment about such conditions might be a contribution a Lutheran theology of the cross can make to contemporary eschatological thinking. The world suffers and groans— that reality must inform any theological talk of hope. But as feminist critiques suggest, theologies like Luther's could benefit from contemporary visions for transformation in the here and now, both for human and nonhuman creatures. Is it possible for hope—for an eschatology—to be both fervently committed to all forms of life in this world and to articulating the hope put forth in scripture, that "mourning and crying and pain will be no more" (Rev. 21:4)? This chapter will be a first step toward a positive response to the question.

Luther: Living from Lament

For Luther, Christ's death on the cross not only testified to a God who goes to any lengths to redeem humanity, but also said something crucial about our world. Christ's dying was the result of a loving God entering a world governed by sin. A theology of the cross, which Luther strove to embody, emerges from the foot of this cross, where the groans and the cries of human despair are clearly seen and heard. And while we can and should work for justice and love in the world, the present is not nor will it ever be a paradise. Luther understood this reality all too well. At times he dwelt too long and too wistfully on suffering, but it is important to acknowledge that death sur-rounded Luther, just as it surrounded all medieval Europeans. He lived during the plague, watched helplessly as two of his daughters died before his eyes, and witnessed senseless suffering on a daily basis, similar to millions of per-sons worldwide today.

Luther also focused on the spiritual dimension of suffering, an *Anfechtung* that pointed to the "dereliction of the absence of God which for the Christian is the ultimate hell."[11] Some spiritual suffering Luther found necessary—to be brought low by our own self-presumptions, or to suffer in defense of the gospel (as he did). But the kind of spiritual suffering he experienced due to the loss of his daughters was the experience of the hell of God's absence. It is in the midst of these experiences that Luther sought out the psalmist's words. Luther gravitated toward those verses that spoke to his experience of alienation from God. When the psalmist cries out, "How long?," Luther resonates with that voice of a soul deeply troubled by "the feeling of being forsaken and rejected by God."[12] In response to the inevitable suffering in our lives, Luther—with deep reliance on the psalms—insists that crying out to God—the practice of lament—plays a vital role in Christian living *coram deo*, before God.

Crying out to God. Lamentation. Asking "Why, Lord?" from the depths of the soul. Writing recently in their provocative book, *Rachel's Cry: Prayer of Lament and Rebirth of Hope*, theologians Kathleen Billman and Daniel Migliore wonder what happened to lament, protest, and contention in contemporary Christian liturgy, prayer, and practice.[13] Billman and Migliore have no interest in denying thanksgiving and praise in Christian practice. But especially when many of us live in a culture "reluctant to grieve failures, especially corporate and public failures, limitations, and losses,"[14] we need permission to—and guidance in—lament. Billman and Migliore's title refers to Rachel's cry in Jeremiah 31:15, where her inconsolable grief at the loss of her children takes center stage. Her refusal to accept easy consolation, her cries and her protests serve as expressions of faithfulness. The authors point out that in Jewish thought and practice, Rachel's lament before God is revered, while in Christian liturgy and practice, her posture of lament receives scant attention.[15] But as Roman Catholic theologian David Tracy proclaims, "It is destructively sentimental for Christians to allow their understanding of the God who is love to be separate from the Hidden God."[16] Talk of God in a world where suffering and crucifixion predominate means talking of a God often hidden from view. The hiddenness of God and its relationship to lament are also central to Luther's theology of the cross.

At times Luther's reflections on the hiddenness of God amount to what Lutheran theologian Jacqueline Bussie, has called a "snappy theodicy," where God is hidden not only *within* the revelation of Christ on the cross, but behind it as well.[17] Even though Luther often argued that we should refrain from inquiring after the God *behind* the cross—for the will of this hidden God is "no business of ours"[18]—at times he could not resist speculating, suggesting that God's temporary withdrawal from our lives is a "sport" for God, or that God "plays" with us by testing us.[19] At these points Luther came face-to-face with that most unnerving reality: there have always been—and likely will continue to be—innocent, faithful persons beset with cruel, undeserved suffering. When this occurs, Luther's theology turns to talk of God's hidden work in an effort to answer the haunting question "Why, Lord?"

230 Transformative Lutheran Theologies

Especially when speaking pastorally, however, Luther found in scripture comfort that comes to those who lament. In his lectures on Genesis, when commenting on the story of Hagar and Ishmael, Luther reassured his hearers that "God
hears the cries of Ishmael. This is a very great comfort for those who feel they
have been cast out. . . . For [God] does not want to cast people aside. . . . And
God cannot disregard the voices and the groaning of the afflicted."[20] Luther continued by saying that we might "conclude with certainty that God has regard for
us, especially when he seems to have forgotten us, when we think we have been
forsaken by him."[21] To persons in the grip of *Anfechtung*, for those convinced of
God's absence, this message carries immense power. When all is stripped away,
these stories of God's response to lament offer "very great comfort for those who
feel cast out."[22]

Embodied Lament

As co-contributor Krista Hughes explains in her chapter in this volume, theologies of hope need to take seriously feminist concerns about "evacuating
corporeality" and relegating hope to a virtual, disembodied future.[23] Feminist
attention to embodiment, particularly to the suffering bodies of women and
others, also means that the practice of lament is never far away. Starting where
many feminists do, with the experience of bodies, leads us to turn to the bodies
highlighted in my introduction to this chapter: the bodies of marginalized black
South Africans and those living with terminal illness (understanding that these
groups also interact). South African theologian Simon Maimela, writing in the
early 1990s, cried out that "Black people experience an almost-unending Good
Friday under apartheid."[24] Another South African theologian, Denise Ackerman,
calls on Christian communities in that context to embrace more public forms of
lament. Writing during the time of the Truth and Reconciliation Commission
(1995–1998), Ackerman discovered that in addition to the profound need for
lament by victims of apartheid—crying out to God and their countrymen and
women over their wounds of torture and the defilement they endured—white
South Africans as well needed public forms of lament for both the victims of
apartheid and those whose lack of awareness or lack of moral courage allowed
the evils of apartheid to go unresisted.[25] Today in South Africa, evidence exists
that lament has turned to hope. The post-apartheid constitution staunchly supports basic rights of all kinds; thousands of new homes are being built for those
who live in township shacks; and South Africans of all races vote in elections.
Yet this country stands atop all others with the highest rates of HIV infections in
the world; xenophobic attacks still occur; and levels of education for the majority black population are appallingly low.[26] When faced with such realities, the
possibility of paradise often seems elusive.

"I am utterly bowed down and prostrate; all day long I go around mourning . . . and there is no soundness in my flesh. I am utterly spent and crushed," writes the psalmist (Ps. 38:6-8). These are the cries of lament, the "Why, Lord's?" of many of us who live with serious illness. To live with a body pulsing with cancer cells, to endure the treatments that make living with the body virtually unbearable, can shut off hope for the future, not to mention any talk of a present paradise. Many days since my diagnosis, I have been lodged in lament. The "Why, oh, why, Lord?" comes in knowing that I can't go back; I can't will it, or wish it, or give it away. In an eschatology that attends to the embodied suffering and lament of those far and near, the question becomes: How does one embrace hope in the midst of life so far from paradise?

From Lament to Hope: Embodiment, Eschatology, and the Church

A theology of the cross understands Christ's death as witnessing to our earthly reality of sin and suffering. At the same time, a Lutheran cross-centered view does not neglect the resurrection of Christ; in fact, it is this movement from cross to resurrection that forms the basis of Christian hope in the promised future of God. As Jürgen Moltmann suggests, Christians see in the resurrection "not the eternity of heaven, but the future of the very earth on which the cross stands."[27] To envision a future of this world where suffering will end may be a fine thought experiment, but how does such a promised future make a difference in the lives of those who suffer today? Luther's understanding of the link between Christ's crucifixion and resurrection and our lived reality might be helpful here. As co-contributor Mary Lowe explains, Luther's view that humanity is simultaneously sinful yet justified because of Christ's death and resurrection can be appreciated fully only when its eschatological orientation is brought to the fore. Lowe writes: that we are "saint and sinner means that [we] are being drawn into [our] future in Christ, and this hope constitutes [our] present."[28] Furthermore, as Mary (Joy) Philip suggests, the eschatological promise of freedom in the future is also part of our everyday experience, especially, for Christians, in the embodied reality of the church.[29]

Even though both Luther and feminists understand the church as a flawed and ambiguous institution, the gospel vision of the church is one where the future is proleptically embodied in the present. Moltmann writes, "The church serves the world not so the world may be preserved in the state it is in, but in order that it may transform itself and become what it's promised to be."[30] Rather than taking the gaze off the concrete experiences of bodies, this eschatological orientation redirects the members of the body of Christ to be with those who suffer and live in pain. Indeed, as South African theologian Denise Ackerman suggests, probing more deeply into the lament of those who suffer has the potential to contribute to both individual and social transformation. "In finding a common language [of lament], the isolation of suffering is broken by an experience of solidarity that is essential if change is to occur."[31] Pain isolates, creating worlds that cut us off from one another. Church is one vital context for claiming common language for Christians—a practice that can break through the isolation that pain creates.

Luther's image of Christian community, the "priesthood of all believers," gives the church a communitarian shape, emphasizing the vocation each member of the body of Christ is summoned to take up. One concrete embodiment of Luther's "priesthood of all" came when Germans were taken ill by the plague. Lifting up the model of ministry set forth in Matthew 25, Luther insisted, "We are bound to each other that no one may forsake the other in distress." Knowing the temptation of the healthy to keep their distance from the sick, Luther admonished them to understand such temptations as "the devil's doing." In the midst of a pandemic that took one-third of Europe's population,[32] Luther's admonition was quite remarkable. While Christians might rush to the side of "Christ or their mother" should they need care, Luther hammered the command of Matthew 25, proclaiming that care for the sickest is care for Christ.[33] In our day, theologian and ethicist Stanley Hauerwas echoes Luther's call, intoning that when the church lives out—or literally, embodies—its call to be the body of Christ in the world, it is present with those who suffer, cutting through the isolation that lurks there. But Hauerwas observes with frankness how the temptation to flee remains ever present:

> [I]t is no easy matter to be with the ill, especially when we cannot do much for them other than simply be present. Our very helplessness too often turns to hate, both toward the one in pain and ourselves, as we despise them for reminding us of our helplessness. Only when we remember that our presence is our doing . . . can we be saved from our fevered and hopeless attempt to control others' and our own existence. Our willingness to be ill and to ask for help as well as our willingness to be present with the ill is no special or extraordinary activity, but a form of the Christian obligation to be present to one another in and out of pain.[34]

Members of the body of Christ are called to embody the hope in the promised future of God, where suffering and death shall be no more. This is the eschatological horizon opened up by God's gift of justification and the resurrection promise of new life given in the midst of our current sinful existence. Freedom from self-preoccupation opens us to be present with others, especially those who suffer.

Since my diagnosis, my family and I have been overwhelmed by the ministries of presence Hauerwas describes; by simply showing up, loved ones and strangers alike have broken through the isolation that suffering brings. Even though some friends and loved ones remain on the other side of the "isolation brought by illness" barrier, communion within the body of Christ—in its conventional forms and beyond—has helped turn our lament into hope. Hearing my name in the corporate prayers of worship and being prayed over during our monthly healing services, I know in new ways, as my pastor recently wrote, that "worshipping with the same people Sunday after Sunday . . . [means] bearing each others burdens isn't just a concept." It is something we Christians are called on to embody in tangible ways.[35] At their best, communities of faith, in anticipation of the promised reality of God's new future, can help transform the very conditions that rob those who suffer of any hope for a better future.

As important as embodied reality of the human community is, contemporary feminists call for an expansion of theological focus beyond the anthropological to include and embrace the cosmological. Brazilian Lutheran theologian Wanda Deifelt insists that the contemporary church is called to "promote a wider and deeper sense of what community itself is all about: a reflection of the body of Christ concerned with the well being of [all] bodies."[36] Feminist theologian Sallie McFague suggests that eschatological thinking in the context of Christian claims of incarnation suggests that all bodies matter. From the agrarian images Jesus employs to his many acts of healing, McFague insists, Christians see we are called to face the deep sickness of many bodies, including nonhuman bodies.[37]

It is true that for Luther, nonhuman bodies did not rank as highly as feminists insist they should. Luther believed that he lived in the last days. He wrote, "If I didn't see the tumults, I should say that the Word of God was not in the world. The whole world is shaken and shattered on account of the Word of God."[38] Clearly Luther saw tumults more than he saw paradise in the world around him. Moltmann observes that Luther's preoccupation with "knowledge of God and self" leaves little room for any consideration of the wider scope of creation.[39] At the same time, Luther was no eschatological enthusiast. He stood resolutely against Thomas Müntzer and others who "used the power of the future not to care for the world, but as an excuse to ignore it, or blast it to hell."[40] Luther even suggested, "Even if I knew the world would end tomorrow, I still would go out and plant an apple tree today."[41] While such a statement can sound trivial in the face of global ecological challenges, it nevertheless opens—albeit narrowly—a pathway to the larger affirmation that this world, God's creation, should not be neglected.

Nevertheless, feminists rightly demand more from traditional theologies like Luther's. As McFague argues, "creation is not one thing and salvation something else; they are related as scope and shape, as shape and form, and as place and pattern."[42] Increased attention is needed to further unpack biblical claims about the eschatological future of all creation. Both 2 Peter 3:13 and Revelation 21:1

proclaim that God's promised future includes "a new heaven and a *new earth.*" In any proleptic participation in God's promised future, then, tending to God's good creation becomes integral to the daily practices of those of us who live in that future today.

Hoping for More: Death Is Not the End

While some versions of Christian eschatology contain elaborate visions of what lies beyond, Luther stood more in line with feminist claims about how little we know about God's future reign. Luther imagined that just as *in utero* we know nothing about life outside the womb, we in this life can scarcely imagine what lies ahead.[43] He also believed it foolish and a waste of time to try to determine what God's plans are for people beyond this life. "Let God be God!" Luther insisted.[44] Luther also had scant interest in the book of Revelation, expressing doubt that it preached Christ. Our task as Christians, he claimed, is to live in grateful response to God's work and promises. Despite this reticence to speak of life after this one, he would nevertheless insist that Christian faith offers more than agnosticism when it comes to life after death.

Luther believed the promise of scripture is clear: Christ drew sin, death, and hell in to himself so that we might live without fear of any of them. "Death has lost its sting," he wrote.[45] But we also know that in Luther's life living fully in that joyous reality proved elusive. He understood human beings to be at once justified, set free, righteous, and simultaneously living in a fallen, finite world, where suffering and death still hold sway. He wrote after the death of his beloved thirteen-year-old daughter, Magdalene: "The separation troubles me beyond measure. . . . It's strange to know that she is surely at peace and she is well off there, very well off, and yet to grieve so much!"[46] But his writings testify repeatedly to trust in the promise that life with God is ours, now and beyond the grave.

I have thought much about death in recent months. My biggest fear of dying is no longer being with those I love most in this world. And while a call to agnosticism about what might lie beyond death has rational appeal,[47] I find the response theologically and pastorally insufficient, particularly for those staring death in the face. While I can't claim certainty, I can, as Luther did, claim faith in God's promises, that as Paul wrote even death cannot separate us from the love of God (Rom. 8:38).

What might that mean in death? The author C. S. Lewis, who struggled with the early death of his wife, spoke of how discomforting it was to face death knowing so little about what lies beyond: "[T]here is no good applying to Heaven for earthly comfort. Heaven can give heavenly comfort; no other kind. And earth cannot give earthly comfort either. There is no earthly comfort in the long run."[48] Lewis captured well the anxiety that comes with imagining life beyond death. But in light of the promise that we were created by God and will return to God, Lewis suggested,

> [I]t is not that we shall be asked to turn from them, so dearly familiar, to a Stranger. When we see the face of God we shall know that we have always known it. He [sic] has been a party to, has made, sustained and moved moment by moment within all our earthly experiences of . . . love. . . . In heaven there will be no anguish and no duty of turning away from our earthly Beloveds. First, because we shall have turned already . . . from the creatures He made lovable to Love Himself. But secondly, because we shall find them all in Him. By loving Him more than them we shall love them more than we do now.[49]

What Lewis envisioned, and what scripture repeatedly emphasizes, is that life with God beyond death is not an individualized reality. Rather, it is profoundly communal, extending beyond humanity to the entire creation. Rosemary Radford Ruether's strongly ecological vision might be seen as complementary to Lewis's in this respect. She writes that our "[a]cceptance of death is acceptance of the finitude of individuated centers of being, but also our identification with the large Matrix as our total self which contains all."[50] Hoping in the promise of more than this life—while understanding that we cannot know precisely what shape that "more" will take—prompts the turn back toward the here and now, toward the hope lived in light of the promises of the future. In other words, the future God promises compels us to be here, live here, love here.

Living in Hope Today

Though this earth was no paradise for Luther, his faith in God's future reign was inextricably bound to the importance of life in this world. Death was an ever-present reality, yet much of Luther's work addressed the immediate needs of the least in God's creation. Take his commentary on the Lord's Prayer. In his explanation of "thy kingdom come," Luther wrote, "pray for earthly peace, because in times of war we cannot have bread; likewise, pray for the government, for sustenance and peace, without which you cannot eat." Elaborating on the this-worldly, justice-oriented focus, Luther continued, "Few know that this is included in the Lord's Prayer. . . . The petition is directed at everything that hinders bread."[51] Indeed, to understand eschatology as integral to the gospel, as Luther did, we must see that the gospel "maintains a continuity between this world and the next; otherwise, the gospel would be sheer dismissal of this world."[52] Such focus on the embodied reality of those who hunger for bread reinforces the link that exists between eschatology and ethics. Praying for—and identifying with—the presence of the future reign in proleptic form offers real participation in its life in the here and now, generating a vision of hope and courage for action to change the present in the direction of the eschatological future.[53] The motivation for such action in the world was not, for Luther, a concern for how one might fare in the last judgment.[54] Indeed, Luther insisted that motivation for such prayers and calls to action against worldly injustice comes instead from the freedom offered all of us through God's activity in Christ.

"These days, I'm spending more time talking about sewage than I am talking about the gospel," lamented Methodist Bishop Paul Verryn of Johannesburg, during a forum in Cape Town, South Africa, in June 2008. Bishop Verryn and his church had taken in over 600 Zimbabweans, housing them in their church building for months at a time, until they might find work or the situation in their country stabilized enough for them to return. Bishop Verryn's lament offered within it a testimony of hope to those of us who heard him speak. For if the gospel maintains continuity between this world and the next, then talking about sewage in service of mitigating the suffering of the neighbor is as eschatologically significant as talking about the future reign of God. I wager it is possible to hope for more than there is in this life while working to transform the present condition of all creation into a richer embodiment of the promised future of God, where all crying and suffering will cease.

Suggested Reading

Billman, Kathleen, and Daniel Migliore. *Rachel's Cry: Prayer of Lament and Rebirth of Hope*. Cleveland: United Church of Christ, 1999.

Braaten, Carl E. *Eschatology and Ethics: Essays on the Theology and Ethics of the Kingdom of God*. Minneapolis: Augsburg, 1974.

Deifelt, Wanda. "Globalization, Religion and Embodiment: Latin American Feminist Perspectives." In *Shaping a Global Theological Mind*, ed. Darren C. Marks. Burlington, Vt.: Ashgate, 2008.

Luther, Martin. "A Sermon on Preparing to Die." In *Martin Luther's Basic Theological Writings*, ed. Timothy Lull, 638–54. Minneapolis: Fortress Press, 1989.

Luther, Martin. "The Large Catechism: The Lord's Prayer," http://www.bookof concord.org/lc-5-ourfather.php., accessed May 13, 2010.

Ruether, Rosemary Radford. "Eschatology and Feminism." In *Lift Every Voice: Constructing Christian Theologies from the Underside*, ed. Susan Brooks Thistlethwaite and Mary Potter Engel, 111–24. San Francisco: HarperSanFrancisco, 1990.

Notes

Abbreviations

BoC   *The Book of Concord: The Confessions of the Evangelical Lutheran Church.* Trans. Charles Arand, et al. Ed. Robert Kolb and Timothy J. Wengert. Minneapolis: Fortress Press, 2000.

LW   Luther's Works—American Edition. 55 Vols. Ed. Jaroslav Pelikan and Helmut T. Lehmann. St. Louis: Concordia; Philadelphia: Fortress Press, 1955–1986.

WA   D. Martin Luthers Werke: Kritische Gesamtausgabe. 67 Vols. Ed. J. K. F. Knaake, et al. Weimar: H. Böhlau, 1883–1997.

INTRODUCTION

1. The Rev. Dr. Beverly Wallace, "No Idle Talk" (sermon, Carondelet Center, St. Paul, Minn., delivered July 12, 2009).

2. See Hans Küng, "Paradigm Change in Theology: A Proposal for Discussion" and "What Does a Change of Paradigm Mean?" in *Paradigm Change in Theology*, ed. Hans Küng and David Tracy, trans. Margaret Köhl (New York: Crossroad, 1989), 3–33, 212–19.

3. See Küng, "What Does a Change of Paradigm Mean?" 219.

4. For examples of women's roles and voices in scripture and church history, see Barbara J. MacHaffie, *Her Story*, 2nd ed. (Minneapolis: Fortress Press, 2006), and Elisabeth Schüssler Fiorenza, *In Memory of Her: A Feminist Theological Reconstruction of Christian Origins*, 2nd ed. (New York: Crossroad, 1994).

5. Mary Pellauer, *Towards a Tradition of Feminist Theology: The Religious Social Thought of Elizabeth Cady Stanton, Susan B. Anthony, and Anna Howard Shaw* (Brooklyn, N.Y.: Carlson, 1991).

6. Küng, "Paradigm Change in Theology," 21, 29.

7. For a tight summary of the notable feminist theological discussion on the dangers of a universalized definition of "woman" or "women's experience," see Serene Jones, "'Women's Experience' Between a Rock and a Hard Place: Feminist, Womanist and *Mujerista* Theologies in North America," in *Religious Studies Review* 21 (July 1995): 171–78. For a concrete argument against universalized definitions, see, for example, Delores S. Williams, *Sisters in the Wilderness: The Challenge of Womanist God-Talk* (Maryknoll, N.Y.: Orbis, 1993).

8. Ursula King, "Feminist Theologies in Contemporary Contexts: A Provisional Assessment," in *Is There a Future for Feminist Theology?* Studies in Theology and Sexuality, ed.

Deborah F. Sawyer and Diane M. Collier (Sheffield, England: Sheffield Academic, 1999), 101. Referring to the entire field of theology done with an overt commitment to the well-being of females as "feminist" is problematic, for it linguistically universalizes the variety of perspectives of women theologians by organizing them under a title more often claimed by white women and less often claimed by African Americans, for example. I continue to struggle with how to communicate in a way that does not mask difference.

9. For more on the discussion among Latina theologians on the self-identifying terms *mujerista* and *Latina feminist*, see Ada María Isasi-Díaz, *En la Lucha/In the Struggle: Elaborating a Mujerista Theology* (Minneapolis: Fortress Press, 2004) and María Pilar Aquino, Daisy L. Machado, and Jeanette Rodríguez, eds., *A Reader in Latina Feminist Theology: Religion and Justice* (Austin: University of Texas Press, 2002).

10. Kwok, Pui-Lan, "Fishing the Asia Pacific: Transnationalism and Feminist Theology," in *Off the Menu: Asian and Asian North American Women's Religion and Theology*, ed. Rita Nakashima Brock, Jung Ha Kim, Kwok Pui-Lan, and Seung Ai Yang (Louisville: Westminster John Knox, 2007), 16, 7.

11. See Brigitte Kahl, "Gender Trouble in Galatia? Paul and the Rethinking of Difference," in Sawyer and Collier, *Is There a Future for Feminist Theology?*, 57–73, esp. 57–60. Kahl traces out Paul's thinking on difference in the body of Christ through the deeply social, religious, and physical meanings and differences accentuated by the inclusion of circumcised males and those with foreskin alike in the body of Christ. Kahl further extrapolates an intriguing gender analysis through her textual exegesis, yet my point here concerns the meta-discourse on difference that she mines. In other words, neither the physical nor the social meanings of the different physical bodies were cancelled out in Galatia.

12. Ibid., 60, emphasis added.

13. Anne E. Carr, "Feminist Theology in a New Paradigm," in Küng and Tracy, *Paradigm Change in Theology*, 397–407, and Rosemary Radford Ruether, "The Task of Feminist Theology," in *Doing Theology in Today's World: Essays in Honor of Kenneth F. Kantzer*, ed. John D. Woodbridge and Thomas Edward McComiskey (Grand Rapids: Zondervan, 1991), 359–76.

14. Joy Ann McDougall, "Women's Work: Feminist Theology for a New Generation," *The Christian Century* (July 26, 2005): 20–25.

15. Gloria L. Schaab, SSJ, "Feminist Theological Methodology: Toward a Kaleidoscopic Model," *Theological Studies* 62 (2001): 341–65.

16. Michael Kinnamon, General Secretary, National Council of Churches in Christ (address to the General Assembly, November 13, 2009).

17. See Ruether, "The Task of Feminist Theology," 372–75.

18. Albert Pero and Ambrose Moyo, eds., *Theology and the Black Experience: The Lutheran Heritage Interpreted by African and African-American Theologians* (Minneapolis: Augsburg, 1988).

19. St. Augustine, *On Christian Doctrine* (Upper Saddle River, N.J.: Prentice-Hall, 1958).

20. See Caryn Riswold's contribution to chapter 1 in this volume. For more on the important effect of third-wave feminism on theology and the intersectional analysis upon which it insists, see Caryn D. Riswold, *Feminism and Christianity* (Eugene, Ore.: Cascade, 2009) and Nakashima Brock, et al., eds., *Off the Menu*.

21. For an accessible introduction to each of these theologies from a Lutheran perspective, see interviews with some of this volume's contributors at http://www.elca.org/Our-Faith-In-Action/Justice/Justice-for-Women/Resources/Transformative-Lutheran-Theologies-video.aspx, accessed May 13, 2010.

22. See, for example, Ted Peters, *God—The World's Future*, 2nd ed. (Minneapolis: Fortress Press, 2000), 55–67.

23. David P. Scaer, "How Do Lutheran Theologians Approach the Doing of Theology Today?" in Woodbridge and McComiskey, eds., *Doing Theology in Today's World*, 197–225, 223 n.37.

24. Carl E. Braaten, *Principles of Lutheran Theoogy*, 2nd ed. (Minneapolis: Fortress Press, 2007), 2.

25. Ibid., 4.

26. Wanda Deifelt, "Feminist Theology: A Key for Women's Citizenship in the Church," in *Toward a New Heaven and a New Earth*, ed. Fernando F. Segovia (Maryknoll, N.Y.: Orbis, 2003), 237–48, 241.

27. Lois Malcolm, "The Gospel and Feminist Theology: A Proposal for Lutheran Dogmatics," *Word & World* 15, no. 3 (Summer 1995): 290–98, and Deanna A. Thompson, *Crossing the Divide: Luther, Feminism, and the Cross* (Minneapolis: Fortress Press, 2004).

28. Mary M. Solberg, *Compelling Knowledge: A Feminist Proposal for an Epistemology of the Cross* (Albany: State University of New York Press, 1997).

29. Thompson, *Crossing the Divide*.

30. Linda Woodhead, "Feminist Theology—Out of the Ghetto," in Sawyer and Collier, *Is There a Future for Feminist Theology?*, 206.

31. Ibid., 198–206.

CHAPTER ONE

1. Vida Dutton Scudder, *On Journey* (New York: Dutton, 1937), quoted in Richard H. Schmidt, ed., *Glorious Companions: Five Centuries of Anglican Spirituality* (Grand Rapids: Eerdmans, 2002), 228.

2. Valerie Saiving Goldstein, "The Human Situation: A Feminine View," *Journal of Religion* 40, no. 2 (April 1960): 100–112.

3. Early work on women's involvement in the Reformation included Roland Bainton's three volumes, *Women of the Reformation: In Germany and Italy* (1971); *In France and England* (1973); and *From Spain to Scandinavia* (1977) (Minneapolis: Augsburg). For more recent scholarship see Kirsi Irmeli Stjerna's, *Women and the Reformation* (Malden, Mass.: Blackwell, 2009).

4. Betty A. DeBerg, "Lutheran Family Devotions," in *Religions of the United States in Practice*, ed. Collen McDannell (Princeton: Princeton University Press, 2001), 23–31.

5. Betty A. DeBerg, "The Spirituality of Lutheran Women's Missionary Societies, 1880–1930," *Lutheran Historical Conference Essays and Reports* 15 (1994): 142–60; Diane Jacobson, Carol Schersten LaHurd, and Susan Wilds McArver, "Luther's Legacy in American Lutheran Women's Bible Study," *Dialog* 45, no. 1 (Spring 2006): 29–35; and L. DeAne Lagerquist, *From Our Mothers' Arms: A History of Women in the American Lutheran Church* (Minneapolis: Augsburg, 1987).

6. Ingeborg Sponland, *My Reasonable Service* (Minneapolis: Augsburg, 1938), 69.

7. Mary E. Markley, "Women in Education," *Christian Education* 22 (February 1939): 21.

8. Lagerquist, *From Our Mothers' Arms*, 184–89. The charge to the Commission for Women from *Progress Report 6: Commission for A New Lutheran Church*, 20–21.

9. Le Roy Guntzelle, "Women's Week Speaker Applies Christian Perspective," *Manitou Messenger* 89, no. 17 (1976): 3.

10. Gracia Grindal, "Getting Women Ordained," in *Called and Ordained: Lutheran Perspectives on the Office of the Ministry*, ed. Todd Nichol and Marc Kolden (Minneapolis: Fortress Press, 1990), 161–79.

11. In an exchange of letters published in *God's Fierce Whimsy* (New York: Pilgrim, 1985), Pellauer and Delores S. Williams reflect upon the intersection of feminist concerns with their own experiences of race and class.

12. Prior to these appointments women taught in other capacities. These included Jennie Bloom Summers in the 1910s at the predecessor to PLTS and Bertha Paulson at Gettysburg from 1945 to 1963. See Phyllis Anderson, "Lutheran Women in Theological Studies: Headway, Hard Work, Hurt, and Hope" in *Lutheran Women in Ordained Ministry, 1970–1995*, ed. Gloria E. Bengtson (Minneapolis: Augsburg, 1995), 129–36.

13. "Speaking of God: Feminism and the Church," *Dialog* 24, no. 1 (Winter 1985); "Feminism," *Word & World* 8 (Fall 1988); "The Ministry of Women," *Word & World* 15 (Summer 1995); and "Martin Luther in Feminist Focus," *Currents in Theology and Mission* 24, no. 1 (February 1997).

14. Karen L. Bloomquist and Mary M. Knutsen, "Given Feminism, Does Theology Need a New Starting Point?" *Word and World*, 8, no. 4 (1988): 374–77.

15. Lois Malcolm, "The Gospel and Feminism: A Proposal for Lutheran Dogmatics," *Word & World* 15, no. 3 (Summer 1995): 297.

16. Gustaf Wingren, *Luther on Vocation*, trans. Carl C. Rasmussen (Philadelphia: Muhlenberg, 1957), 123–24. See Anna Mercedes in this volume for more on the self as subject.

17. Ibid., 124.

18. Wingren reflected a lack of real understanding of actual human bondage and complex systems of privilege and oppression wherein a slave cannot be said to be a fellow worker with his or her master in any meaningful way.

19. Ibid., 130.

20. Philip J. Hefner, *The Human Factor: Evolution, Culture, and Religion*, Theology and the Sciences (Minneapolis: Fortress Press, 1993), 36.

21. Ibid., 38.

22. Saiving Goldstein, "The Human Situation," 100–12.

23. "The Freedom of a Christian, 1520," LW 31:355–56.

24. Amina Wadud, *Inside the Gender Jihad: Women's Reform in Islam* (Oxford: Oneworld, 2006), 28–30.

25. Wingren, *Luther on Vocation*, 139.

26. The Heidelberg Disputation, 1518, LW 31:52.

27. "The Babylonian Captivity of the Church, 1520," LW 36:62.

28. Ann Milliken Pederson, "Christmas and the Reality of the Incarnation: *Finitum capax infiniti*," *Word & World* 27, no. 4 (Fall 2007): 382.

29. Bloomquist and Knutsen, "Given Feminism, Does Theology Need a New Starting Point?" 374.

CHAPTER TWO

1. Vítor Westhelle, *The Church Event: Call and Challenge of a Church Protestant* (Minneapolis: Fortress Press, 2009), 7.

2. See R. S. Sugirtharajah, *Voices from the Margin: Interpreting the Bible in the Third World* (Maryknoll, N. Y.: Orbis, 1991).

3. Gayatri Chakravorty Spivak, "Can the Subaltern Speak?" in *Marxism and the Interpretation of Culture*, Cary Nelson and L. Grossberg, eds. (Chicago: Illinois University Press, 1988), 271–313.

4. Vítor Westhelle, Christian Theology III (lecture, Lutheran School of Theology at Chicago, 2002).

5. The concept of skin as the margin and its function in bringing about mechanisms not operational before is gleaned from Vítor Westhelle, "Christian Theology III" (lectures, Lutheran School of Theology at Chicago, 2000).

6. Mary Douglas, *Purity and Danger* (New York: Routledge, 2002), 150.

7. Ibid.

8. After Johann Gregor Mendel, "the father of genetics.

9. Douglas, *Purity and Danger*, 149.

10. June Jordan, "Poem for South African Women," *Passion: New Poems*, 1977–80 (Boston: Beacon, 1980), 43.

11. Walter Benjamin, *Illuminations: Essays and Reflections* (New York: Schocken 1968), 17.

12. Ibid., 254.

13. Ibid., 60.

14. Jacques Derrida, *The Gift of Death*, trans. David Wills (Chicago: University of Chicago Press, 1995), 97.

15. Michael Taussig, *Walter Benjamin's Grave* (Chicago: University of Chicago Press, 2006), 8.

16. Westhelle, *The Church Event*, 155.

17. Based on a quote by the nineteenth-century novelist Marie-Henri Beyle, better known by the pseudonym Stendhal, who said: "Politics in a work of literature is like a pistol-shot in the middle of a concert, something loud and vulgar, and yet a thing to which it is not possible to refuse one's attention."

CHAPTER THREE

1. Patriarchy is a way of organizing the world that privileges the male and things associated with men over the female and things associated with women.

2. Anna Julia Cooper, *A Voice from the South* (New York: Oxford University Press, 1988), 28.

3. Joy Ann McDougall, "Feminist Theology for a New Generation," *The Christian Century* (July 26, 2005): 20–25.

4. I discuss Luther as political theologian at more length in *Two Reformers: Martin Luther and Mary Daly as Political Theologians* (Eugene, Ore.: Cascade, 2007), 179–96.

5. The Heidelberg Disputation, 1518, LW 31:52.

6. In his Small Catechism, Luther states that that "the Word of God . . . is with and alongside the water" of baptism, and that the "the true body and blood of our Lord Jesus Christ [is] under the bread and wine." This is one key source for the Lutheran description of God's presence in, with, and under. "The Small Catechism," "The Sacrament of Holy Baptism," and "The Sacrament of the Altar," BoC (Minneapolis: Fortress Press, 2000), 359:9-10; 362:1-2.

7. "Commentary on Galatians, 1535," LW 26:401.

8. David Ratke, "Preaching Christ Crucified: Luther and the Revelation of God," 43, no. 4 (Winter 2004): 272.

9. Other philosophers and theologians like Ludwig Feuerbach and G. W. F. Hegel reflect parts of the social construction theory described here; Peter Berger's work most clearly describes the entire process, and is specifically invoked by feminist theologians.

10. Peter Berger, *The Sacred Canopy: Elements of a Sociological Theory of Religion* (New York: Anchor, 1990), 8.

11. Ibid., 9.

12. Ibid., 15.

13. Mary Daly, *Beyond God the Father: Toward a Philosophy of Women's Liberation* (Boston: Beacon, 1973), 135–36.

14. Elizabeth A. Johnson, *She Who Is: The Mystery of God in Feminist Discourse* (New York: Crossroad, 1992), 4.

15. Ibid., 15.

16. The Heidelberg Disputation, 1518, LW 31:39.

17. Paul Althaus, *The Theology of Martin Luther*, trans. R. C. Schultz (Philadelphia: Fortress Press, 1966), 34.

18. Ibid., 21.

19. Martin Luther, *The Bondage of the Will: The Masterwork of the Great Reformer*, trans. James I. Packer and O. R. Johnston (Tarrytown, N.Y.: Revell, 1957), 100–104.

20. "Luther's Last Observation Left in a Note, 1546," LW 54:476.

21. "Disputation against Scholastic Theology, 1517," LW 31:9.

22. "The Freedom of a Christian, 1520," LW 31:354.

23. Valerie Saiving Goldstein, "The Human Situation: A Feminine View," *Journal of Religion* 40, no. 2 (April 1960): 100–12.

24. See further discussion of feminist interpretation of Luther and the notion of sin in Deanna A. Thompson, *Crossing the Divide: Luther, Feminism, and the Cross* (Minneapolis: Fortress Press, 2004), 105–16.

25. Philip J. Hefner, *The Human Factor: Evolution, Culture, Religion*, Theology and the Sciences (Minneapolis: Fortress Press, 1993), 35.

26. Stefan Lovgren, "Nobel Peace Prize Goes to Micro-Loan Pioneers," *National Geographic News* (10/13/06), http://news.nationalgeographic.com/news/2006/10/061013-nobel-peace.html, accessed May 14, 2010

27. Ebenezer/herchurch ELCA, http://www.herchurch.org, accessed May 14, 2010

28. President Barack Obama's Inaugural Address, http://www.whitehouse.gov/blog/inaugural-address, accessed May 14, 2010

CHAPTER FOUR

1. "Lectures on Genesis, 1535: Chapters 1–5," LW 1:191.

2. Ibid., LW 1:183.

3. Serene Jones is a fine example of a theologian influenced by narrative theology. See her *Feminist Theory and Christian Theology: Cartographies of Grace*, Guides to Theological Inquiry (Minneapolis: Fortress Press, 2000), particularly the ways each chapter opens with story.

4. George A. Lindbeck, *The Nature of Doctrine: Religion and Theology in a Postliberal Age* (Philadelphia: Westminster, 1984), 121.

5. Theresa Sanders, *Approaching Eden: Adam and Eve in Popular Culture* (Lanham, Md.: Rowman & Littlefield, 2009), 1.

6. *The New Oxford Annotated Bible with the Apocryphal/Deuterocanonical Books*, ed. Bruce M. Metzger and Roland E. Murphy (New York: Oxford University Press, 1991), 5.

7. "Lectures on Genesis, 1535: Chapters 1–5," LW 1:180 and 183, respectively.

8. Ibid., LW 1:191.

9. Phyllis Trible, *God and the Rhetoric of Sexuality*, Overtures to Biblical Theology (Philadelphia: Fortress Press, 1978), 4.

10. "Lectures on Genesis, 1535: Chapters 1-5," LW 1:189 and 103, respectively.

11. Ibid., LW 1:190.

12. Ibid., LW 1:196.

13. Ibid.,LW 1:180.

14. Ibid.,LW 1:178.

15. Ibid., LW 1:179.

16. Ibid., LW 1:193.

17. Ibid., LW 1:242.

18. Ibid.

19. Ibid.

20. Ibid.

21. Ibid.

22. "Lectures on Genesis, 1535" LW 1:242

23. Ibid., LW 1:325. I hesitate to use this quotation because of the way it characterizes the Roman Catholic Church. Yet Luther's vitriolic remarks about the Roman Catholic Church are well known; they may be quoted without being endorsed.

24. Ibid., LW 1:190.

25. Ibid.

26. Need source for quoted material.

CHAPTER FIVE

1. "The term [transgender] has been extended to include intersexuals, transsexuals, cross-dressers, drag queens and kings, androgynes, and anyone else who feels 'otherwise' from society's gender assumptions." Virginia Ramey Mollenkott, *Omnigender: A Trans-Religious Approach* (Cleveland: Pilgrim, 2001), 43. For an introduction to intersex issues see http://www.isna.org, accessed May 14, 2010.

2. "Patristic theology assumed women's subordination to man in the order of nature, and her special 'carnality' in the disorder of sin. . . . This double definition of woman . . . allows the Fathers to . . . attribute women's inferiority first to sin and then to nature." Rosemary Radford Ruether, "Misogynism and Virginal Feminism in the Fathers of the Church," in *Religion and Sexism: Images of Women in the Jewish and Christian Traditions* (New York: Touchstone, 1974), 157. See my article "Woman Oriented Hamartiologies: A Survey of the Shift from Powerlessness to Right Relationship," *Dialog* 39, no. 2 (Summer 2000): 119–39. For a mujerista interpretation of sin, see Ada María Isasi-Díaz, *En la Lucha / In the Struggle: Elaborating a Mujerista Theology* (Minneapolis: Fortress Press, 1993).

3. See Rosemary Radford Ruether, *Womanguides: Readings Towards a Feminist Theology* (Boston: Beacon, 1985); Delores S. Williams, "A Womanist Perspective on Sin," in *A Troubling in My Soul*, ed. Emilie M. Townes (Maryknoll, N.Y.: Orbis, 1997); Wolfhart Pannenberg, *An Introduction to Systematic Theology* (Grand Rapids: Eerdmans, 1991).

4. Lois Tyson, *Critical Theory: A User Friendly Guide*, 2nd ed. (New York: Routledge, 2006), 335.

5. Early gay/lesbian theology often assumed that persons were born gay. Queer theologians reject this essentialist view and suggest instead that sexual identity is fluid.

6. Daniel A. Helminiak, *What the Bible Really Says About Homosexuality* (San Francisco: Alamo Square, 1994).

7. "Lectures on Genesis 1535," LW 3:255. "[F]or the cardinals and the Sodomists and hermaphrodites of your court lead such horrible lives that heaven and earth quake and tremble before them" ("Against the Roman Papacy, An Institution of the Devil 1545," LW 41:287–88). Sodomy is not easy to define. It has been broadly defined as homoerotic acts between males. However, numerous biblical scholars and theologians view the threatened male rape in Genesis 19:5 as a violent act of inhospitality to the stranger. See Christopher Elwood, "A Singular Example of the Wrath of God: The Use of Sodom in 16th Century Exegesis," *Harvard Theological Review* 98, no. 1 (2005): 67–93.

8. St. John Chrysostom, "Commentary on Romans, Homily 4," quoted in John Boswell, *Christianity, Social Tolerance, and Abuse* (Chicago: University of Chicago Press, 1980), 361.

9. "Lectures on Romans, 1515," LW 25:164.

10. Desire should be understood in two contexts. In the Augustinian sense, desire for anything other than God is an expression of concupiscence and pride. (See *City of God* XIV. xiii.) Queer theorists argue that discourses have regulated desires to comply with the rules of discourse.

11. "We ought not therefore to conclude that everyone has always considered sexuality a basic and irreducible element in . . . human life." David M. Halperin, "Is There a History of Sexuality?" in *The Lesbian and Gay Studies Reader*, ed. Henry Abelove, Michèle Aina Barale, and David M. Halperin (New York: Routledge, 1993), 424.

12. Mark D. Jordan, *The Invention of Sodomy in Christian Theology* (Chicago: University of Chicago Press, 1997), 42.

13. "Considerations Regarding Proposals to Give Legal Recognition to Unions Between Homosexual Persons," Congregation for the Doctrine of the Faith (July 2003): I.4.

14. Reinhold Niebuhr described individual sin as pride and sensuality, and social sin as group egoism. Although he emphasized the social character of humans, he employed a traditional, isolated portrait of an enduring human subject who possesses a will, an ego, self-transcendence, and exists in anxiety and freedom. See Reinhold Niebuhr, *Nature and Destiny of Man*, vol. 1 (New York: Scribner's, 1964), 75, 192, 251, 260.

15. For further reading on social structures, see Cynthia Moe-Lobeda in this volume. For more on subject position, see Anna Mercedes in this volume.

16. Chris Weedon, *Feminist Practice and Poststructuralist Theory*, 2nd ed. (Malden, Mass: Blackwell, 1997), 105.

17. Michel Foucault, *Madness and Civilization: A History of Insanity in the Age of Reason*, trans. Richard Howard (New York: Vintage, 1988).

18. Wolfhart Pannenberg, *Systematic Theology*, vol. 2, trans. Geoffrey W. Bromily (Grand Rapids: Eerdmans, 1994), 252–65.

19. "Lectures on Romans, 1515," LW 25:260.

20. Ibid., 299; 319–20.

21. On sin as ingratitude see "Selected Psalms III: Psalm 118," in LW 14:51; on sin as *curvatus en se* see "Lectures on Romans, 1515," LW 25:291; on sin as unbelief see "Lectures on Romans, 1515," LW 25:319.

22. "The Private Mass and the Consecration of Priests," LW 38:158.

23. "Lectures on Romans, 1515," LW 25:474.

24. "The Catholic Epistles," LW 30:264.

25. "Lectures on Galatians, 1535," LW 26:387.

26. Daphne Hampson, *Christian Contradictions: The Structure of Lutheran and Catholic Thought* (Cambridge: Cambridge University Press, 2001), 27. See also James Arne Nestingen, "The Catechism's Simul," *Word & World* 3, no. 4 (Fall 1983): 364–72.

27. Martin Luther, *The Freedom of a Christian*, trans. Mark Tranvik (Minneapolis: Fortress Press, 2008), 63.

28. "The Bondage of the Will, 1537," LW 33:70.

29. The Small Catechism, BoC, 360.

30. Martin Luther, "Disputation on the Power and Efficacy of Indulgences," in *Works of Martin Luther* vol. 1, trans. and ed. Adolph Spaeth and Henry Eyster Jacobs (Philadelphia: A. J. Holman, 1915), 40–41.

31. "Lectures on Romans, 1515," LW 25:258.

32. http://www.census.gov/dmd/www/pdf/d02p.pdf

33. Mary McClintock Fulkerson, "Changing the Subject: Feminist Theology and Discourse," *Literature and Theology* 10, no. 2 (1996): 139. See also Caryn Riswold in this volume, on third-wave feminism.

34. "First Lectures on the Psalms: Psalm 73," LW 10:418. See also "First Lectures on the Psalms: Psalm 95," LW 11:252; "The Bondage of the Will, 1525," LW 33:240; "Lectures on Romans, 1515," LW 25:219.

35. Caryn D. Riswold, *Coram Deo: Human Life in the Vision of God* (Eugene, Ore.: Pickwick, 2006), 150.

36. Gordon Rupp, *The Righteousness of God: Luther Studies* (New York: Philosophical Library, 1953), 106.

37. Deanna A. Thompson, *Crossing the Divide: Luther, Feminism, and the Cross* (Minneapolis: Fortress Press, 2004), 19.

38. Caryn D. Riswold, "*Coram Mundo*: A Lutheran Feminist Theological Anthropology of Hope," *Dialog* 48, no. 2 (Summer 2009): 129.

39. Gerhard Ebeling, *Luther: An Introduction to His Thought*, trans. R. A. Wilson (Philadelphia: Fortress Press, 1977), 195.

40. Martin Luther, *Lecture on Romans*, Library of Christian Classics, trans. and ed. Wilhelm Pauck (Philadelphia: Westminster, 1961), 322.

41. Luther, *The Freedom of a Christian*, 82.

42. Ibid., 50.

43. "Two Kinds of Righteousness, 1519," LW 31:300.

44. The Large Catechism BoC, 452. "We still stumble daily and transgress because we live in the world among people who sorely vex us. . . . Besides, the devil is after us, besieging us on every side."

CHAPTER SIX

1. Some biblical scholars suspect that Paul added his own lines of emphasis to the preexistent hymn, including "the form of a slave" and "death on a cross," thus increasing the gravity of the hymn's message in a characteristically Pauline emphasis on the power of Christ's cross. See Ralph Martin, *A Hymn of Christ: Philippians 2:5-11 in Recent Interpretation and in the Setting of Early Christian Worship* (Downers Grove, Ill.: InterVarsity, 1997), lix–lx.

2. See the translation of Luther's statements about the theology of the cross in Mary M. Solberg, *Compelling Knowledge: A Feminist Proposal for an Epistemology of the Cross* (Albany: State University of New York Press, 1997), 55–56.

3. Feminists have, even in the midst of their theological critique, vigorously taken up the prodigal and vulnerable generosity "that was in Christ Jesus." Already at the time of the first woman's movement, those we would come to call "feminists" were willingly embodying self-sacrifice in the course of their activism. Feminists of the twentieth century have also served others and risked their security as they advocated for human dignity and planetary health. Feminist theology's criticism of the rhetoric of self-sacrifice does not come from a generation of self-indulgent or individualistic women. To the contrary, feminism's deepest currents connect us to the generous and vulnerable lifeways that also characterize Christianity.

4. Mary Lowe in this volume explores the ways that sin as discourse hinders the fullness of life and the ways that our position as both saint and sinner enables our resistance to sin.

5. "Epiftel aff den Palmtag. Philippen 2" WA 17:237–45. I am very grateful to my friend Jakob K. Rinderkneckt for his help with the translation of Luther's commentary on Philippians.

6. The word for "form" or "likeness" in Greek transliterates as morphe, and this same term is used to describe Christ in the "form of a slave" later in the passage. Thus μορφη θεου is contrasted to μορφη δουλου. The Philippians text itself far precedes doctrinal arguments about Christ's divine and human natures, but with the language of the "form of God" and the "form of a slave," it does inspire such thinking, as it did for Luther.

7. "Epiftel aff den Palmtag. Philippen 2" WA 17.2.239.25-30.

8. Ibid., 239.18.

9. Ibid., 239.5-18.

10. Ibid., 239.24-25.

11. Ibid., 239.22-24.

12. For a discussion of the proper and alien works of God, see chapter 14, "Man Under the Wrath of God," in Paul Althaus, The Theology of Martin Luther (Philadelphia: Fortress Press, 1966).

13. "Epiftel aff den Palmtag. Philippen 2" WA 17.2.239.25-36.

14. Ibid., 240.24-40 and 241.27-32. Feminist hermeneutics emphasize that this is not the truth about all human selves. See Deanna A. Thompson, Crossing the Divide: Luther, Feminism, and the Cross (Minneapolis: Fortress Press, 2004), 105-108.

15. In his 1535 Galatians commentary, Luther writes, "Now what good does it do you to know that God exists if you do not know what God's will is toward you?" LW 26:399–401. Gender language emended.

16. "Epiftel aff den Palmtag. Philippen 2" WA 17.2.241.11–242.9.

17. Luther did not have an adequate awareness of the way in which social class affects understandings of service and empowerment. See Joan M. Martin, "Between Vocation and Work: A Womanist Notion of a Work Ethic," in Feminist and Womanist Essays in Reformed Dogmatics, eds. Amy Plantinga Pauw and Serene Jones (Louisville: Westminster John Knox, 2006), 180.

18. "Epiftel aff den Palmtag. Philippen 2" WA 17.2.241.15–242.9.

19. Luther, The Freedom of a Christian, 82.

20. See note 2, above.

21. Valerie Saiving, "The Human Situation: A Feminine View," in WomanSpirit Rising: A Feminist Reader in Religion, eds. Carol Christ and Judith Plaskow (San Francisco: HarperSan Francisco, 1979), 25–42.

22. "Epiftel aff den Palmtag. Philippen 2" WA 17.2.244.19-21.

23. Ibid., 17.2.244.23–24.

24. Luther has already explained the form of God that is Christ's according to his being, and has then envisioned a "three-fold manner of slavish form or likeness." See WA 17.2.239.31–240.7.

25. Mary Lowe's work in this volume on sin as subject position helps to shift sin into a relational framework, such that one form of sin does not comprise the enduring nature of an individual. In my reading of Christ in the "no-form," one might draw on Lowe's work to imagine the "no-form" as a subject position, just as the egotistically stolen "form of God" would also be a subject position. Thus, the pride-filled individual, whether male or female, inhabits a sinful subject position to which he or she has been conditioned and through which he or she both benefits and suffers. But this subject position is temporary and mutable, socially constructed and individually and socially perpetuated; it is not reflective of

some enduring essences of this person, as would be the case in the false claim, "Because you are a man, you are fundamentally egotistical."

26. Neither the "no-form" of diffusion nor the "no-form" of feigning God is a form of service, and thus neither is part of the three listed by Luther. The latter is the sin discussed throughout Luther's theology: the sin of the "old creature." Feminist theology looks for a word for the former, the sin of women and men hiding away from the full life of the new creature, those seeking invisibility rather than godliness.

27. Lisa Dahill has emphasized the contrast between Bonhoeffer's egotistical predicament and the struggle that survivors of abuse may face, writing that "Bonhoeffer's lifelong illusion, from which he aches to be freed, is that of the self's omnipotence and others' unreality. For the victim of abuse, however, it is that the self is 'nullipotent,' unreal, effaced: the abuser is omnipotent." For abused persons, "what is revolutionary, breath-taking, truly illumative of reality would be a spirituality which . . . invites them to 'be there for themselves.'" Lisa Dahill, *Reading from the Underside of Selfhood: Bonhoeffer and Spiritual Formation* (Eugene, Ore.: Pickwick, 2009), 176.

28. Dietrich Bonhoeffer, "Lectures on Christology," in Berlin 1932–1933, ed. Larry L. Rasmussen, trans. Isabel Best et al. Dietrich Bonhoeffer Works, vol. 12 (Minneapolis: Fortress Press, 2009), 349–350. The objective distance attempted by a person arrogantly seeking to understand the "how" of Christ parallels the state of Luther's sinner who is busy feigning the form of God.

29. Ibid., 314. See also Clifford Green, *Bonhoeffer: A Theology of Sociality*, rev. ed. (Grand Rapids: Eerdmans, 1999), 225: "As the representation or 'personification' of true humanity, Christ encounters the self. Person confronts person." Bonhoeffer does not present Christ's mediatory role in the sense of traditional atonement theology, as in Christ standing before the angry god and taking the beating for us. Rather, Christ is standing in the truly human spot, and standing there not in front of God but in front of the beloved human person, signaling a location of fullness of life, fullness of self. See Bonhoeffer, "Lectures on Christology," 324.

30. Bonhoeffer, "Lectures on Christology," 303.

31. Ibid., 307.

32. Ibid., 308.

33. Ibid., 324.

34. Dahill, *Reading from the Underside of Selfhood*, 187. Dahill gives a different interpretation of the application of law and grace for abuse survivors than I do.

35. Acknowledging the simultaneous realities of victimization and resistance, Traci C. West uses the phrase "victim-survivor" in her *Wounds of the Spirit: Black Women, Violence, and Resistance Ethics* (New York: New York University Press, 1999).

36. Bonhoeffer, "Lectures on Christology," 322.

37. Ibid., 324.

38. L. J. Tessier studies the spirituality of abuse-survivors and finds guttural strength in the images they seek out: "Survivors are rarely drawn to images of pretty buds opening or sweet little butterflies emerging from cocoons. . . . Theirs is Tiamat, silenced, skewered, and split asunder" (189). Though Tessier does find that many survivors have trouble appropriating dominant religious symbols, I offer that the tradition of Christ crucified does offer a "silenced, skewered, and split" re-creation story with which some abuse survivors can identify. See Tessier's *Dancing After the Whirlwind: Feminist Reflections on Sex, Denial, and Spiritual Transformation* (Boston: Beacon, 1997).

39. Epiftel aff den Palmtag. Philippen 2" WA 17.2.245.29-30.

CHAPTER SEVEN

1. The Spanish word *mujer* means "woman" in English. Mujerista theology is a theological praxis with the goal of the liberation of U.S. Latinas. As a diverse body of women from multiple ethnic communities, U.S. Latinas are joined together by our rich diversity and our common experiences of marginalization and oppression. It is primarily through the communal historical project of telling these types of stories that we theologize, thereby providing social analysis, our witness of faith, and hope-filled empowerment for our lives of dignity in God's love.

2. Marit Trelstad argues in this volume that Jesus Christ, God incarnate, was sent to love. In a similar manner, this pastor was not sent by God to suffer, but to love.

3. For more on the simultaneity of being oppressed and oppressor, see Anna Mercedes, Mary Lowe, and Cynthia Moe-Lobeda in this volume.

4. For more on the links between racism and classism, see Beverly Wallace and Moe-Lobeda in this volume.

5. See Ada María Isasi-Díaz, *En la Lucha / In the Struggle: Elaborating a Mujerista Theology* (Minneapolis: Fortress Press, 2004).

CHAPTER EIGHT

1. Edna St. Vincent Millay, "Conscientious Objector" in *Edna St. Vincent Millay: Selected Poems*, ed. Colin Falck (New York: HarperCollins, 1999) 103.

2. Carl Braaten and other theologians have also argued that Jesus' death is not the sole key to atonement but, rather, that God's promises are known through the life, death, and resurrection of Jesus Christ seen together. While my argument comes from a different angle, I am clearly not alone in saying that the cross be understood in a wider theological context. See Braaten, *Principles of Lutheran Theology*, 2nd ed. (Minneapolis: Fortress Press, 2007), 103–104.

3. See Anna Mercedes's chapter in this volume for an explication of Philippians 2.

4. For further exploration of the suffering of Christ, see Kathryn Kleinhans in this volume.

5. For example, see Joanne Carlson Brown and Rebecca Parker, "For God So Loved the World?" in *Christianity, Patriarchy and Abuse: A Feminist Critique*, ed. Joanne Carlson Brown and Carole R. Bohn (Cleveland: Pilgrim, 1989).

6. For more on intersubjective ontology, see Mary Lowe in this volume.

7. Rita Nakashima Brock and Rebecca Ann Parker, *Saving Paradise: How Christianity Traded Love of this World for Crucifixion and Empire* (Boston: Beacon, 2008).

8. Julian of Norwich, *Showings* in *Mystics, Visionaries, and Prophets: A Historical Anthropology of Women's Spiritual Writings*, ed. Shawn Madigan, C.S.J. (Minneapolis: Fortress Press, 1998) 198.

9. See "Salvation: the Path of Theosis," in Donald Fairbairn, *Eastern Orthodoxy Through Western Eyes* (Philadelphia: Westminster John Knox, 2002), 79–95.

10. For supporting data concerning domestic violence in the United States see the Domestic Violence Resource Center Web site: http://www.dvrc-or.org/domestic/violence/resources/C61, accessed May 14, 2010

11. Joann M. Garma, "A Cry of Anguish: The Battered Woman," in *Women in Travail and Transition: A New Pastoral Care*, ed. Maxine Glaz and Jeanne Stevenson Moessner (Minneapolis: Fortress Press, 1991), 133–34.

12. Rita Nakashima Brock and Rebecca Ann Parker, *Proverbs of Ashes: Violence, Redemptive Suffering, and the Search for What Saves Us* (Boston: Beacon, 2001).

13. Ibid., 25.

14. Delores S. Williams, "Black Women's Surrogacy Experience and the Christian Notion of Redemption," in *Cross Examinations: Readings on the Meaning of the Cross Today*, ed. Marit Trelstad (Minneapolis: Fortress Press, 2006).

15. Geerhardus Vos, "The Doctrine of the Covenant in Reformed Theology," in *The Covenant in Reformed Theology*, trans. S. Voorwinde and W. Van Gemeren (Philadelphia: K. M. Campbell, 1971).

16. Following this tradition, Wesleyan theologian R. Larry Shelton argues in his book *Cross and Covenant* (Tyrone, Ga.: Paternoster, 2006) that covenant is a grounding theological concept for atonement, albeit for different reasons than I am advancing here.

17. Found in the writing of Thomas Blake, John Ball, and Francis Roberts as well as the work of the Westminster Assembly, such as the Westminster Confession.

18. Eberhard Jüngel, *The Doctrine of the Trinity: God's Being Is in Becoming* (Edinburgh: Scottish Academic Press, 1976), 2. For further explanation from Barth concerning election, grace and the doctrine of God, see Karl Barth, *Church Dogmatics, II.2: The Doctrine of God: The Election and Command of God*, ed. G. W. Bromiley and T. F. Torrence, trans. G. W. Bromiley and R. J. Ehrlich (Edinburgh: T & T Clark, 1960).

19. "Weekdays with Steve Scher," conversation with entomologist Don Ehlen, KUOW Seattle, National Public Radio, June 16, 2008.

20. Catherine Keller, *From a Broken Web: Separation, Sexism, and Self* (Boston: Beacon, 1986).

21. See Alfred North Whitehead, *Process and Reality: An Essay in Cosmology*, ed. David Ray Griffin and Donald W. Sherburne (New York: Free Press, 1978 [1929]).

22. Gabriel Marcel, *Being and Having*, trans. Katherine Farrer (Glasgow: University Press, 1949), 167.

23. For example, see R. Larry Shelton's discussion of covenant in *Cross and Covenant*.

24. Moltmann states, "Freedom as it truly is, is by no means a matter of power and domination over a piece of property. So total power is by no means identical with absolute freedom. Freedom arrives at its divine truth through love. . . . We have to understand true freedom as being the self-communication of the good." Jürgen Moltmann, *The Trinity and the Kingdom: The Doctrine of God*, trans. Margaret Kohl (Minneapolis: Fortress Press, 1993 [1981]), 55.

25. Ibid., 56.

26. Charles Chase, unpublished poem. Available at http://www.swer.net/english .chase_rememb.html, accessed October 15, 2009.

27. For more on the slave of Christ, see Anna Mercedes in this volume. For more on the bride of Christ, see Kathryn Kleinhans in this volume.

28. Martin Luther, "The Freedom of a Christian" in *Martin Luther's Basic Theological Writings*, 2nd ed., ed. Timothy F. Lull (Minneapolis: Fortress Press, 2005), 396.

29. Ibid.

30. Ibid., 393.

31. In an article of this length, it is not possible to develop this idea further but a covenantal ontology, along with Luther's own affirmation of the primacy of grace, and feminist analysis of domestic violence patterns may suggest that Lutheran theologians consider a reversal of the traditional ordering of law and gospel.

32. Whitehead, *Process and Reality*, 346.

33. Catherine Keller, *On the Mystery: Discerning God in Process* (Minneapolis: Fortress Press, 2008), 113.

34. For more on this idea, see Christine M. Smith, *Risking the Terror: Resurrection in This Life* (Cleveland: Pilgrim, 2001).

CHAPTER NINE

1. Mary Daly, *Beyond God the Father: Toward a Philosophy of Women's Liberation* (Boston: Beacon, 1973), 19.

2. Rosemary Radford Ruether, *Sexism and God-Talk: Toward a Feminist Theology* (Boston: Beacon, 1983), 116.

3. Joanne Carlson Brown and Rebecca Parker, "For God So Loved the World?" in *Christianity, Patriarchy, and Abuse: A Feminist Critique*, ed. Joanne Carlson Brown and Carole R. Bohn (New York: Pilgrim, 1989), 26.

4. Ibid., 27.

5. Carter Heyward, *Speaking of Christ: A Lesbian Feminist Voice* (New York: Pilgrim, 1989), 18.

6. Rita Nakashima Brock, *Journeys by Heart: A Christology of Erotic Power* (New York: Crossroad, 1988), 51.

7. Daphne Hampson, *After Christianity* (Valley Forge, Penn.: Trinity Press International, 1996), chaps. 1–2.

8. Because of the interrelationship of christology and soteriology, I prefer to use the phrase *personal work of Christ* rather than the classic distinction between "the person of Christ" and "the work of Christ."

9. "A Brief Instruction on What to Look for and Expect in the Gospels," LW 35:123.

10. "The Freedom of a Christian, 1520," LW 31:351.

11. Rita Nakashima Brock, "And a Little Child Will Lead Us: Christology and Child Abuse," in *Christianity, Patriarchy, and Abuse*, 51.

12. See Joy Ann McDougall, "Women's Work: Feminist Theology for a New Generation," *The Christian Century* (July 26, 2005): 20–25.

13. "Selected Psalms I: Psalm 45," LW 12:279.

14. "Two Kinds of Righteousness, 1519," LW 31:300.

15. "Lectures on Titus, 1527," LW 29:18.

16. "Sermons on the Gospel of St. John: The Fortieth Sermon," LW 22:440.

17. "Sermons on the Gospel of St. John: The Forty-second Sermon," LW 22:450.

18. See Kristen E. Kvam, "Luther, Eve, and Theological Anthropology: Reassessing the Reformer's Response to the *Frauenfrage*" (Ph.D. diss., Emory University, 1992), on "Luther's waverings between hierarchical and egalitarian understandings" of gender relationships.

19. "To Mrs. Martin Luther, October 4, 1529," LW 49:238.

20. "Sermons on the Gospel of St. John: The Forty-third Sermon," LW 22:460.

21. "*So ist sie dan nicht schlecht ein weibsbildt, sondern eine mennin, die des mannes gutter und leibes mechtig ist*," WA 47:172.

22. "Lectures on Genesis, 1535," LW 1:137.

23. "Lectures on Isaiah, 1528: Chapter 61," LW 17:342.

24. "Lectures on Isaiah, 1528: Chapter 66," LW 17:406.

CHAPTER TEN

1. By 1808, Sitka was the Russian capital of Alaska. The Russian Bishop's House was completed in 1842 and officially closed in 1969, yet the Chapel of the Annunciation is still a consecrated site. Visitors are therefore not allowed directly into the chapel. See the

National Park Service, U.S. Department of the Interior, at http://www.nps.gov/sitk/history culture/russian-bishops-house.htm.

2. See, for example, Anne Fausto-Sterling, *Sexing the Body: Gender Politics and the Construction of Sexuality* (New York: Basic Books, 2000), 1–3, 51–54, and 257 n.4.

3. My gratitude goes to Schleiermacher scholar Jack Verheyden, Professor Emeritus of Theology at Claremont School of Theology, and Lutheran feminist scholar Caryn Riswold, Associate Professor of Religion at Illinois College, for their comments on a previous draft of this paper, which was first presented at a Lutheran World Federation consultation, "Theology in the Life of Lutheran Churches: Transformative Perspectives and Practices Today," March 25–31, 2009, Augsburg, Germany. All errors and omissions are fully mine.

4. See Doris Strahm, "Christianity: Feminist Christology," in *Routledge International Encyclopedia of Women*, ed. Cheris Kramarae and Dale Spender (New York: Routledge, 2000), 172.

5. Janet Martin Soskice, "Blood and Defilement: Reflections on Jesus and the Symbolics of Sex," in *The Convergence of Theology: A Festschrift Honoring Gerald O'Collins, S.J.*, ed. Gerald O'Collins, Daniel Kendall, and Stephen T. Davis (New York: Paulist, 2001), 287–88.

6. Mary Daly, *Beyond God the Father: Toward a Philosophy of Women's Liberation* (Boston: Beacon, 1973), 19.

7. See Lisa Isherwood in Marcella Maria Althaus-Reid and Lisa Isherwood, *Controversies in Feminist Theology* (London: SCM, 2007), 81–05.

8. See Serene Jones, *Feminist Theory and Christian Theology: Cartographies of Grace*, Guides to Theological Inquiry (Minneapolis: Fortress Press, 2000).

9. See the other chapters on christology in this volume and my essay "Maternal Sacrifice as a Hermeneutics of the Cross," in *Cross Examinations: Readings on the Meaning of the Cross Today*, ed. Marit Trelstad (Minneapolis: Fortress Press, 2006), 63–75; 283–85.

10. See Rosemary Radford Ruether, *To Change the World: Christology and Cultural Criticism* (New York: Crossroad, 1983), and Delores S. Williams, *Sisters in the Wilderness: The Challenge of Womanist God-talk* (Maryknoll, N.Y.: Orbis, 1993) for views on Jesus as an ethical model. See Karen Baker-Fletcher, *Dancing with God: The Trinity from a Womanist Perspective* (St. Louis: Chalice, 2007), and Elizabeth A. Johnson, *She Who Is: The Mystery of God in Feminist Theological Discourse* (New York: Crossroad, 1994) for discussions of Jesus Christ's divine nature.

11. See Ada María Isasi-Díaz, *Mujerista Theology: A Theology for the Twenty-first Century* (Maryknoll, N.Y.: Orbis, 1996), and Ivone Gebara, *Out of the Depths: Women's Experience of Evil and Salvation* (Minneapolis: Fortress Press, 2002). For a different interpretation of suffering and the work of Christ, see Alicia Vargas's contribution in this volume.

12. See Adolf von Harnack, *What Is Christianity?*, trans. Thomas Bailey Saunders (Minneapolis: Fortress Press, 1986) [1900].

13. The operative meanings of "sex" and "gender" I employ are: "sex" refers to biology; "gender" refers to the meanings given to particular biology. Some scholars argue that the idea that there are "only" two sexes is a social construction. See Judith Butler, *Gender Trouble: Feminism and the Subversion of Identity* (New York: Routledge, 1990), 8–10.

14. Alister McGrath, *Christian Theology: An Introduction*, 3rd ed. (Oxford: Blackwell, 2001), 367.

15. Frances Young, *The Making of the Creeds* (London: SCM, 1991), 80.

16. Ibid., 79–80.

17. Ibid., 81.

18. Catherine L. Kelsey, *Thinking about Christ with Schleiermacher* (Louisville: Westminster John Knox, 2003), 59.

19. Ibid., 63. See Friedrich Schleiermacher, *The Christian Faith: English Translation of the Second German Edition*, 1822, trans. H. R. Mackintosh and J. S. Stewart (Edinburgh: T & T Clark, 1989), §100.

20. See Kelsey, *Thinking about Christ with Schleiermacher*, 51–52. See Schleiermacher, *The Christian Faith*, §14.1 and §93.

21. Schleiermacher, *The Christian Faith*, §93 and §94.

22. Kelsey, *Thinking about Christ with Schleiermacher*, 72.

23. Schleiermacher, *The Christian Faith*, §3 and §4.

24. See Kelsey, *Thinking about Christ with Schleiermacher*, 73.

25. See ibid., 75. Kelsey states that Jesus is different in degree, but not in kind, which I think misleads readers from Schleiermacher's subtle explication of divinity. See Schleiermacher, *The Christian Faith*, §96.3, wherein he argues that the existence of God in Jesus Christ is "true exclusively of Him." See also §94.

26. Eleanor McLaughlin, "Feminist Christologies: Re-Dressing the Tradition," in *Reconstructing the Christ Symbol: Essays in Feminist Christology*, ed. Maryanne Stevens (New York: Paulist, 1994), 121.

27. Ibid., 127–28.

28. See ibid., 128.

29. Understanding "person" as "countenance, condition, or status," as per Jeffrey Hopper, *Understanding Modern Theology II: Reinterpreting Christian Faith for Changing Worlds* (Philadelphia: Fortress Press, 1987), 10–11.

30. McLaughlin, "Feminist Christologies," 129.

31. Lois Malcolm, "The Gospel and Feminist Theology: A Proposal for Lutheran Dogmatics," *Word & World* 15 (1995): 293.

32. Ibid., 293.

33. McLaughlin, "Feminist Christologies," 130.

34. Ibid.

35. Deanna A. Thompson, *Crossing the Divide: Luther, Feminism, and the Cross* (Minneapolis: Fortress Press, 2004), 140; see also 178 n.3. Thompson is here relying as well on the work of Lutheran ethicist and theologian Ann Milliken Pederson.

36. Ibid., 125.

37. Ibid. See also Thompson's theological critique of injustice, 140.

38. For more on the false binaries of sex and gender, see Butler, *Gender Trouble*, 8–10.

39. See Carolyn Bynum, *Fragmentation and Redemption: Essays on Gender and the Human Body in Medieval Religion* (New York: Zone Books, 1991), 108–109.

40. See ibid., 114.

41. Ibid.

42. Ibid., 109.

43. See Beverly Roberts Gaventa, *Our Mother Saint Paul* (Louisville: Westminster John Knox, 2007) and Bynum, *Fragmentation and Redemption*, 109.

44. See Bynum, *Fragmentation and Redemption*, 85–86.

45. Ibid., 116.

46. Ibid., 90.

47. What medieval iconography and theology offers for contemporary christology raises several important questions for feminist christology. Namely, is there a danger of including "female" bodies in christological interpretation especially because of biology? Is the medieval birth imagery associated with the crucifixion a positive way to understand the female in Christ and in christology? Or is this a negative appropriation of biological

female experience that leaves real female bodies once more in the margin? See what may be gender essentialism in Janet Martin Soskice, *The Kindness of God: Metaphor, Gender, and Religious Language* (Oxford: Oxford University Press, 2007).

48. Fausto-Sterling, *Sexing the Body*, 31.

49. Ibid., 33.

50. Ibid., 51–54. It is important to note that her study is "an order-of-magnitude estimate rather than a precise account" (51). Fausto-Sterling also notes in her study that there are varieties across different populations.

51. Ibid., 45.

52. Ibid., 76.

53. Brigitte Kahl, "Gender Trouble in Galatia? Paul and the Rethinking of Difference," in *Is There a Future for Feminist Theology?*, ed. Deborah F. Sawyer and Diane M. Collier (Sheffield: Sheffield Academic Press, 1999), 59.

54. Ibid., 70.

55. Ibid.

56. Ibid., 67–68.

57. Ibid., 71.

58. See ibid., 71–72.

59. Ibid., 72.

60. See ibid., 71.

61. Sandra Hack Polaski, *A Feminist Introduction to Paul* (St. Louis: Chalice, 2005), 70.

62. Ibid., 70–71. Kahl also refers to the pluriformity in unity that Paul extols as a central message of Galatians. This was an intra-"Christian" question, as Kahl makes clear. My intentions are to stay focused on this internal conversation, not to support anti-Jewish rhetoric in contemporary theology.

63. Thompson, *Crossing the Divide*, 125.

CHAPTER ELEVEN

1. F. LeRon Shults and Andrea Hollingsworth, *The Holy Spirit: Guides to Theology* (Grand Rapids: Eerdmans, 2008), 9.

2. For overviews, see Shults and Hollingsworth, and also Veli-Matti Kärkkäinen, *The Holy Spirit in Ecumenical, International, and Contextual Perspective* (Grand Rapids: Baker Academic, 2002). Some of the most significant works in pneumatology in the last fifty years have come from Roman Catholic and Reformed theologians: Yves M. J. Congar, *I Believe in the Holy Spirit*, 3 vols., trans. David Smith (New York: Seabury, 1983); Jürgen Moltmann, *The Spirit of Life: A Universal Affirmation*, trans. Margaret Kohl (Minneapolis: Fortress Press, 1992); Michael Welker, *God the Spirit*, trans. John Hoffmeyer (Minneapolis: Fortress Press, 1994). Feminist and Lutheran theologians have tended to address the person and work of the Holy Spirit in a larger work on the Trinity. See Robert W. Jenson's *Systematic Theology*, Vol. 1: *The Triune God* (Oxford: Oxford University Press, 2001), and Elizabeth A. Johnson, *She Who Is: The Mystery of God in Feminist Theological Discourse* (New York: Crossroad, 1991).

3. In spite of the prominence the topic of pneumatology gained in Chung Hyun Kyung's famous speech at the 1991 Assembly of the World Council of Churches in Canberra, there have only been a handful of full-length manuscripts on pneumatology written by feminist theologians.

4. Shults and Hollingsworth, *The Holy Spirit*, 77.

5. Molly T. Marshall, *Joining the Dance: A Theology of the Spirit* (Valley Forge: Judson, 2003), 5.

6. For example, Eilert Herms, *Luthers Auslegung des Dritten Artikels* (Tübingen: J.C.B. Mohr (Paul Siebeck), 1987); and Jeffrey Mann, "Luther and the Holy Spirit: Why Pneumatology Still Matters," *Currents in Theology and Mission* 34 no.2 (2007). To date, the only full-length work on Luther's pneumatology remains Regin Prenter, *Spiritus Creator: Luther's Concept of the Holy Spirit*, trans. John M. Jensen (Philadelphia: Muhlenberg Press, 1953).

7. D. Lyle Dabney, "Naming the Spirit: Toward a Pneumatology of the Cross," in *Starting with the Spirit: Task of Theology Today II*, ed. Stephen Pickard and Gordon Preece (Australian Theological Forum, 2001), 32–33.

8. Mary C. Grey, *Sacred Longings: The Ecological Spirit and Global Culture* (Minneapolis: Fortress Press, 2005), 109.

9. D. Lyle Dabney, "Why Should the First Be Last? The Priority of Pneumatology in Recent Theological Discussion," in *Advents of the Spirit: An Introduction to the Current Study of Pneumatology*, ed. Bradford E. Hinze and D. Lyle Dabney (Milwaukee: Marquette University Press, 2001), 254.

10. ELCA Constitution, Confession of Faith, Chapter 2.06. In particular, I draw on Luther's exposition on the Third Article of the Apostle's Creed in his Large Catechism (which sets the work of the Spirit within a Trinitarian framework). This work has been woefully neglected as a source for pneumatological reflection in American Lutheranism.

11. Rebecca Button Prichard, *Sensing the Spirit: The Holy Spirit in Feminist Perspective* (St. Louis: Chalice, 1999), 3.

12. Elizabeth A. Johnson, *Women, Earth, and Creator Spirit*, 1993 Madeleva Lecture in Spirituality (New York: Paulist, 1993), 10–11.

13. David H. Jensen, "Introduction," in *The Lord and Giver of Life: Perspectives on Constructive Pneumatology*, ed. David H. Jensen (Louisville: Westminister John Knox, 2008), xiv.

14. David H. Jensen, "Discerning the Spirit: A Historical Introduction," in ibid., 1.

15. Moltmann, *The Spirit of Life*, 95, cited in Marshall, *Joining the Dance*, 146.

16. Prichard, *Sensing the Spirit*, 123.

17. Ibid., 20.

18. Ibid., 25.

19. Ibid., 29.

20. Stephen H. Webb, *The Divine Voice: Christian Proclamation and the Theology of Sound* (Grand Rapids: Brazos, 2004), 60.

21. Prichard, *Sensing the Spirit*, 126.

22. Nelle Morton, *The Journey is Home* (Boston: Beacon, 1985), 202–11.

23. An example of Luther's insistence on God's working through the external means of word and sacrament is found in Part III:8 of the Smalcald Articles: "In these matters, which concern the spoken, eternal Word, it must be firmly maintained that God gives no one his Spirit or grace apart from the external Word which goes before. We say this to protect ourselves from the enthusiasts, that is, the 'spirits,' who boast that they have the Spirit apart from and before contact with the Word. On this basis, they judge, interpret, and twist the Scripture or oral Word according to their pleasure." BoC, 322.

24. Webb, *The Divine Voice*, 144–45. Webb recognizes that the Jewish and Christian emphasis on the Word that is both spoken and heard could easily be used to discriminate against the deaf. However, he claims that the structural similarities between sign language and spoken language are such that most of what he says about the proclamation of the Word can be applied equally to either style of communication. He writes that "When St. Paul argued that Christians receive God's grace through hearing, he meant that literally, but we know today that the deaf can receive the good news through their

other senses as well. While the history of Christianity cannot be told outside the history of sound, preaching can take place in complete silence. Hearing is the gift from God that makes faith possible, whether it is a matter of listening to voices or looking at hands." See Webb, 51–54.

25. Heiko A. Oberman, "Preaching and the Word in the Reformation," *Theology Today* 18, no. 1 (1961): 16.

26. Robert W. Jenson, *Systematic Theology, Vol. II: The Works of God* (Oxford: Oxford University Press, 1999), 295.

27. Webb, *The Divine Voice*, 36.

28. It follows from this understanding of the office of ministry (that privileges the preaching of the Word) that women should be ordained alongside of men. Simply put, women have voices as well as men to speak God's Word. See Paul Hinlicky, "Whose Ministry? Whose Church?" *Lutheran Forum* (2008): 48–53.

29. As Article V of the Augsburg Confession (English translation of the German Text) states, "To obtain such faith God instituted the office of preaching, giving the gospel and the sacrament. Through these means, he gives the Holy Spirit who produces faith, where and when he wills, in those who hear the gospel." BoC, 40.

30. I am grateful to Amy Carr for directing me to Luther's Genesis commentary, where he discusses the three stations or estates (family, church, and state) as places where people hear one another speaking the Word. These reflect a definite hierarchical dimension for Luther that feminist Lutherans will want to redefine in more mutual ways. See Amy Carr, "Questioning Idols: Divine Countenance in Trauma and Conversion" (Ph.D. diss., University of Chicago, 2004), 266–71.

31. The Smalcald Articles, BoC, 319.

32. Paul Althaus recognizes that Luther distinguishes the office of the keys from "mutual conversation and consolation" but goes on to argue that the latter cannot be separated from absolution because according to the Wittenberg Concordia, the goal of conversation is absolution and the consolation of the sinner consists in the forgiveness of sins." Althaus, *The Theology of Martin Luther*, trans. Robert C. Schultz (Philadelphia: Fortress Press, 1979), 318 n.110.

33. For example, J. Köstlin interprets mutual conversation with others as the "total association of the Christian who is in need of comfort and advice with his brethren." J. Köstlin, *Theology of Luther in its Historical Development and Inner Harmony*, vol. 2, trans. Charles E. Hay (Philadelphia: Lutheran Publication Society, 1897), 582–84.

34. The Large Catechism, BoC, 435–36.

35. Ibid., 324–25, 437.

36. Oberman, "Preaching and the Word in the Reformation," 21.

37. Ibid., 22.

38. Ibid.

39. Webb, *The Divine Voice*, 42.

40. This is very much the movement of the narrative in the Acts of the Apostles. See Mary (Joy) Philip in this volume for further reflection on the church's call.

41. Mann, "Luther and the Holy Spirit: Why Pneumatology Still Matters," 111.

42. Shults and Hollingsworth, *The Holy Spirit*, 13.

43. For a discussion of the Protestant appropriation of pneumatology to the "subjective side" or "subjective realization" of reconciliation, see Welker, *God the Spirit*, 43–44. Neoscholastic Catholic theology has also interpreted the role of the Spirit in more passive, christological terms, relegating the work of the Spirit on the one hand, to the indwelling

of the faithful, as the created grace given through the sacraments that enables them to lives of obedience and virtue, and on the other hand, to the indwelling of the magisterium, as the source and authority of its apostolic teaching so that the faithful are not led astray. See Bradford E. Hinze, "The Spirit in a Trinitarian Ecclesiology," in Bradford E. Hinze and D. Lyle Dabney, eds., *Advents of the Spirit: An Introduction to the Current Study of Pneumatology*, Marquette Studies in Theology, 30 (Milwaukee: Marquette University Press, 2001), 350. The Spirit was at work, Hinze notes, but "only within the restrictive limits established by the institutional and hierarchical concerns that predominated in the late nineteenth and early twentieth centuries" (352).

44. Grey, *Sacred Longings*, 109.

45. Robert W. Jenson, *God after God, The God of the Past and the Future as Seen in the Work of Karl Barth* (New York: Bobbs-Merrill, 1969), 85.

46. Mary C. Grey, "Where Does the Wild Goose Fly To? Seeking a New Theology of the Spirit for Feminist Theology," *New Blackfriars* 72 (1991): 93.

47. Ibid, 95.

48. Nancy M. Victorin-Vangerud, *The Raging Hearth: Spirit in the Household of God* (St. Louis: Chalice, 2000), 189.

49. Ibid., 211.

50. The Large Catechism, BoC, 438, emphasis added.

51. Ibid., 438.

52. Ibid., 439.

53. Marshall, *Joining the Dance*, 148.

CHAPTER TWELVE

1. See, for example, Lamin Sanneh, *Disciples of All Nations: Pillars of World Christianity* (New York: Oxford University Press, 2007), and Philip Jenkins, *The Next Christendom: The Coming of Global Christianity* (New York: Oxford University Press, 2007).

2. See, for example, David H. Jensen, ed., *The Lord and Giver of Life: Perspectives on Constructive Pneumatology* (Louisville: Westminster John Knox, 2008), and Amos Yong, *The Spirit Poured Out on All Flesh: Pentecostalism and the Possibility of Global Theology* (Grand Rapids: Baker Academic, 2005).

3. In addition to the works cited in chapter 11, see Nicola Slee, "The Holy Spirit and Spirituality," in *The Cambridge Companion to Feminist Theology*, ed. Susan Frank Parsons (New York: Cambridge University Press, 2002). See also Andrea Hollingsworth, "Spirit and Voice: Toward a Feminist Pentecostal Pneumatology," *Pneuma* 29 (2007): 189–213; Elizabeth A. Johnson, *Women, Earth, and Creator Spirit* (Mahwah, N.J.: Paulist, 1993); and Emilie M. Townes, *Embracing the Spirit: Womanist Perspectives on Hope, Salvation, and Transformation* (Maryknoll, N.Y.: Orbis, 1997).

4. Dorothee Sölle, *On Earth as in Heaven: A Liberation Spirituality of Sharing*, trans. Marc Batko (Louisville: Westminster John Knox, 1993).

5. See Daphne Hampson, "Luther on the Self: A Feminist Critique," *Word & World* 8, no. 4 (1988) 334-342 and *Theology and Feminism* (Oxford: Basil Blackwell, 1990).

6. See "The Magnificat, 1520," LW 21:299–350.

7. Regin Prenter, *Spiritus Creator: Luther's Concept of the Holy Spirit*, trans. John M. Jensen (Philadelphia: Fortress Press, 1953), 3–26.

8. Ibid., 288–302.

9. Ibid., 13–14.

10. Ibid., 173–204.

11. Ibid., 101–72.

12. Serene Jones, *Feminist Theory and Christian Theology: Cartographies of Grace.* Guides to Theological Inquiry (Minneapolis: Fortress Press, 2000), 61–63.

13. Ibid., 61.

14. On Luce Irigaray's "envelope," see her "Divine Women," in *Sexes and Genealogies,* trans. Gilllian C. Gill (New York: Columbia University Press, 1993), 55–72.

15. Jones, *Feminist Theory and Christian Theology,* 62.

16. See Judith Plaskow, *Sex, Sin, and Grace: Women's Experience and the Theologies of Reinhold Niebuhr and Paul Tillich* (Washington, D.C.: University Press of America, 1994).

17. Jones, *Feminist Theory and Christian Theology,* 62–63.

18. Ibid., 63.

19. "The Magnificat, 1520," LW 21:299. See also Lois Malcolm, "What Mary Has to Say about God's Bare Goodness," in *Blessed One: Protestant Perspectives on Mary,* ed. Beverly Roberts Gaventa and Cynthia Rigby (Louisville: Westminster John Knox, 2002), 131–44.

20. "The Magnificat, 1520," LW 21:331.

21. Ibid., 299.

22. Ibid., 329. As biblical scholars remind us, the "nothing" God creates out of in Genesis 1:2 is not a "void"—as the traditional English translation of the Hebrew word *t bū w b bū* implies when translated as "without form and void"—but something more like "disorder, injustice, subjugation, disease, and death." See Jon Levenson, *Creation and the Persistence of Evil: The Jewish Drama of Divine Omnipotence* (Princeton: Princeton University Press, 1994), xxiv–xxv. When Israel was at her lowest periods of exile and oppression from foreign powers, the prophets spoke about God's creating order out of chaos, justice out of injustice, liberation out of bondage, healing out of disease, and most profoundly, life out of death (see Isaiah 42–44).

23. "The Magnificat, 1520," LW 21:299.

24. Ibid., 306.

25. See, for example, Gerhard O. Forde, *On Being a Theologian of the Cross: Reflections on Luther's Heidelberg Disputation (1518)* (Grand Rapids: Eerdmans, 1997). For feminist interpretations, see Mary M. Solberg, *Compelling Knowledge: A Feminist Proposal for an Epistemology of the Cross* (Albany: State University of New York Press, 1997), and Deanna A. Thompson, *Crossing the Divide: Luther, Feminism, and the Cross* (Minneapolis: Fortress Press, 2004).

26. "The Magnificat, 1520," LW 21:300.

27. The Heidelberg Disputation, 1518, LW 31:39–58.

28. "The Magnificat, 1520," LW 21:302.

29. Ibid.

30. Ibid., 302–306.

31. Ibid., 325.

32. See Michel Corbin's analysis of "redoubling negation" in "Négation et transcendance dans l'oeuvre de Denys," *Revue des sciences philosophiques et théologiques* 69 (1985): 41–76.

33. "The Magnificat, 1520," LW 21:314–15, emphasis added.

34. Ibid., 307–12, emphasis added.

35. Ibid., 332–39.

36. Ibid., 340.

37. Ibid., 332–34.

38. Ibid., 334–35, emphasis added.

39. Jones, *Feminist Theory and Christian Theology,* 61–63.

40. On this, see also my *Holy Spirit: Creative Power in Our Lives* (Minneapolis: Fortress Press, 2008).

41. I am grateful to Andrew Behrendt for pointing out that the same root is used in all three instances.

42. See 1 Cor. 15:21-22; cf. Rom. 5:12-21.

43. For feminist retrievals of the ancient biblical metaphor of the *Spirit's giving birth* to God's new age of justice and mercy, see Beverly Roberts Gaventa, *Our Mother Saint Paul* (Grand Rapids: Eerdmans, 2007), and Mary J. Streufert, "Maternal Sacrifice as a Hermeneutics of the Cross," in *Cross Examinations: Readings in the Meaning of the Cross Today*, ed. Marit Trelstad (Minneapolis: Fortress Press, 2006), 63–65, 283–85.

44. See also Isaiah 42–44; 65:17–25.

45. See, for example, J. Louis Martyn, "Apocalyptic Antinomies in Paul's Letter to the Galatians," *New Testament Studies* 31 (1985); 424.

46. See Alexandra Brown, *The Cross and Human Transformation: Paul's Apocalyptic Word in I Corinthians* (Minneapolis: Fortress Press, 1995).

CHAPTER THIRTEEN

1. Traci C. West, *Disruptive Christian Ethics—When Racism and Women's Lives Matter* (Louisville: Westminster John Knox, 2006), 40.

2. Ibid., 25.

3. Ibid., 38.

4. Reinhard Hütter, "The Twofold Center of Lutheran Ethics: Christian Freedom and God's Commandments" in *The Promise of Lutheran Ethics*, ed. Karen L. Bloomquist and John R. Stumme (Minneapolis: Fortress Press, 1998), 31–54.

5. Karen Baker-Fletcher, "An Irresistible Power Not Ourselves," 1992 Installation Address, *Encounter* 54, no. 3 (Summer 1992): 279–90.

6. Alice Walker, *In Search of Our Mother's Gardens: Womanist Prose* (San Diego: Harvest, 1983), xi–xii.

7. Ibid., xii.

8. See A. Elaine Brown Crawford, *Hope In the Holler: A Womanist Theology* (Louisville: Westminster John Knox, 2002).

9. Jacqueline Grant, *White Women's Christ and Black Women's Jesus: Feminist Christology and Womanist Response* (Atlanta: Scholars Press, 1989), 216.

10. Emilie M. Townes, *In a Blaze of Glory: Womanist Spirituality as Social Witness* (Nashville: Abingdon, 1995), 140.

11. Oswald Bayer, *Freedom in Response: Lutheran Ethics: Sources and Controversies*, trans. Jeff Cayzer (New York: Oxford, 2007), 119.

12. Ibid., 119–20.

13. Ibid., 69–89.

14. Ibid., 16.

15. Baker-Fletcher, "An Irresistible Power Not Ourselves," 288.

16. Ibid., 289.

17. Ibid.

18. Bayer, *Freedom in Response*, 124.

19. Walker, *In Search of Our Mother's Gardens*, xxx.

20. Leif Grane, *The Augsburg Confession—A Commentary* (Minneapolis: Fortress Press, 1987), 81.

21. Martin Luther, *Martin Luther's Basic Theological Writings*, 2nd ed., ed. Timothy F. Lull (Minneapolis: Fortress Press, 2005), 101.

22. Robert Benne, "Lutheran Ethics: Perennial Themes and Contemporary Challenges," in Bloomquist and Stumme, *The Promise of Lutheran Ethics*, 15.

23. Ibid., 29–38.

24. James Childs, *Faith, Formation, and Decision—Ethics in the Community of Promise* (Minneapolis: Fortress Press, 1992), 106.

25. Ibid., 105–18.

26. Stacey Floyd-Thomas, *Mining the Motherlode—Methods in Womanist Ethics* (Cleveland: Pilgrim, 2006), 15.

27. See Delores S. Williams, *Sisters in the Wilderness: The Challenge of Womanist God-Talk* (Maryknoll, N.Y.: Orbis, 1993), and Monica A. Coleman, *Making a Way out of No Way* (Minneapolis: Fortress Press, 2008).

28. Rosetta Ross, *Witnessing & Testifying: Black Women, Religion, and Civil Rights* (Minneapolis: Fortress Press, 2003), 2.

29. Bayer, *Freedom in Response*, 245.

30. Ross, *Witnessing and Testifying*, 228.

31. Ibid., 2–5.

32. West, *Disruptive Christian Ethics*, 1–36.

33. Ibid., 5.

34. See Grant, *White Women's Christ and Black Women's Jesus*.

35. Bloomquist and Stumme, eds., *The Promise of Lutheran Ethics*, 5.

36. Martha Ellen Stortz, "Practicing Christians: Prayer as Formation" in *The Promise of Lutheran Ethics*, 55–73.

37. A sample of convenience is also known as availability sampling. According to Thomas Sullivan, *Methods of Social Research* (New York: Harcourt College Publishers, 2001), sampling of convenience or availability sampling makes it possible to study a phenomenon but with the limitations of generalizability. I chose this sampling method for ease and quickness of obtaining responses for the questions posed. To further develop this construction of a Lutheran womanist ethics, in the future, a more representative sample will be obtained.

38. Floyd-Thomas, *Mining the Motherlode*, 90–98. As one trained as a social scientist, more specifically as a qualitative researcher, I understand the importance of appropriate research methodologies. The research presented here is an initial construction undertaken to open the conversation and is notably limited in scope. Further research is in process.

39. Katie Geneva Cannon, *Black Womanist Ethics* (Atlanta: Scholars Press, 1988).

40. Feistiness has several meanings; similar to some of the descriptions of being a womanist, a woman who is feisty is also bold, courageous, spirited, lively, full of spunk and energy.

41. Katie Geneva Cannon, *Katie's Canon: Womanism and the Soul of the Black Community* (New York: Continuum, 1997), 26.

42. See Richard Perry's description of these African values in "African American Lutheran Ethical Action: The Will to Build," in Bloomquist and Stumme, *The Promise of Lutheran Ethics*, 75–96. These values are taken from the work of Peter Paris, *The Spirituality of African Peoples* (Minneapolis: Fortress Press, 1994).

43. Perry in *The Promise of Lutheran Ethics*, 81.

44. Ibid.

45. For sources of African American Lutheran history, see Albert Pero and Ambrose Moyo, eds., *Theology and the Black Experience: The Lutheran Heritage Interpreted by African and Afri-*

can-American *Theologians* (Minneapolis: Augsburg, 1988), and Jeff Johnson, *Black Christians: The Untold Lutheran Story* (St. Louis: Concordia, 1991).

46. A "lived" experience is the way that a person experiences and understands her world.

47. Marcia Riggs, *Awake, Arise and Act—A Womanist Call for Black Liberation* (Cleveland: Pilgrim, 1994). This line is taken from the title.

48. Ibid., 82–91.

49. Ibid., 100.

50. Ibid., 77.

51. I am creating the term *moderating ethics*, borrowing from the statistical term moderating variables. A moderating variable is one that influences the strength of the relationship between two other variables. They are important because they often enhance or reduce the influence that the variable has on a specific response. In this case a "moderating ethical" process will take into consideration those variables that influence the strength or weakness of African American Lutheran women's ethical responses.

52. Bloomquist and Stumme, eds., *The Promise of Lutheran Ethics*, 4.

53. Dwight Hopkins, *Shoes That Fit Our Feet: Sources for a Constructive Black Theology* (Maryknoll, N.Y.: Orbis, 1993), 59, emphasis added.

54. Moe-Lobeda and Perry in *The Promise of Lutheran Ethics*, 152–53.

55. See Riggs, *Awake, Arise and Act*, x, for a discussion of the ways in which social myths (for example, universal equality and abstract injustice) are internalized by African American people. Also see Hütter's essay in Bloomquist and Stumme, *The Promise of Lutheran Ethics*, 38–40.

56. Daryl Dance, *Honey Hush! An Anthology of African American Women's Humor* (New York, Norton, 1998), back cover.

57. Floyd-Thomas, *Mining the Motherload*, 65–68.

CHAPTER FOURTEEN

1. The term *Earth* herein refers to the planet and its entire ecosystem including its biosphere and all elements and creatures (human included).

2. Caryn Riswold, in this volume, explains this interstructural analysis as a defining feature of "third-wave feminism."

3. "Structural violence" designates the injustice that some groups of people experience as a result of the ways in which power and privilege are structured in a given social context. Structural violence degrades, dehumanizes, damages, and kills people by limiting or preventing their access to the necessities of life with dignity. Racism, classism, sexism, and heterosexism are common forms. "Social structural sin" is a term having various connotations and denotations depending upon the assumed meanings of "sin" and "social structure," and on assumptions regarding the relationship of the individual to the social structural dimensions of life. For purposes here, sin, as an inherent aspect of humanness, is manifest by individuals as well as by "social structures" broadly understood as including humanly constructed institutions, social groups, discourses, and worldviews with their accompanying practices. As used herein, "social structural sin" does not suggest that sin exists outside of human being, given that social structures are fully human structures. Nor does an understanding of sin as social structure reduce human responsibility for sin or human agency in relationship to it; human beings, collectively and individually, are the agents of social structural sin and the agents of resistance to it.

4. Martin Luther, "Two Kinds of Righteousness," in *Martin Luther's Basic Theological Writings*, ed. Timothy F. Lull (Minneapolis: Fortress Press, 1989), 158.

5. Ibid., 157.

6. Ibid., 158.

7. Notable examples of that work include excellent resources of multiple kinds produced by the ELCA's Office of Racial Justice Ministries; "antiracism teams" conducting antiracism training by trained volunteers of the church in thirty synods; the groundbreaking work of the Lutheran Human Relations Association; and steady constant efforts by individuals representing the church.

8. Dietrich Bonhoeffer, *Letters and Papers from Prision*, ed. John W. de Gruchy, trans. Isabel Best, Lisa E. Dahill, Reinhard Krauss, and Nancy Lukens, Dietrich Bonhoeffer Works, vol. 8 (Minneapolis: Fortress Press, 2010), 21.

9. Bernardino Mandlate, Presentation to the United Nations PrepCom for the World Summit on Social Development Plus Ten (New York, February 1999).

10. Oxfam America, *Oxfam Education Report* (London: Oxfam Publishing, 2000).

11. Michael Holman and Quentin Peel, "Debt: Too Much to Bear," *Financial Times*, Saturday, 12 June 1999.

12. In investigating this question, I was delighted to find that—at least in one significant instance—the answer is a resounding yes. Youth at the 2009 ELCA Youth Gathering in New Orleans were led to grapple with racism and economic injustice, and the connections between the two, through Bible studies, "learning stations," documentaries, and service projects.

13. My coming to ask this question and the questions in the following paragraph is due partly to the insight of Traci C. West, *Disruptive Christian Ethics: When Racism and Women's Lives Matter* (Louisville: Westminster John Knox, 2006). See that text for more in-depth treatment of the relationship between worship and white privilege.

14. Tore Johnsen from the Church of Norway in a statement made on the floor of the general assembly.

15. This portion of the chapter draws extensively on Cynthia Moe-Lobeda, "A Theology of the Cross for the 'Un-Creators,'" in *Cross Examinations: Readings on the Meaning of the Cross Today*, ed. Marit Trelstad (Minneapolis: Fortress Press, 2006), 181–95, 297–300.

16. The New Testament word translated into English as "tradition" first appears in the New Testament as a verb meaning "to pass on" as a tradition is passed on. However, that verb also means "to betray." It is, for instance, the verb translated as "betray" when Judas betrayed Jesus into the hands of the Roman soldiers.

17. See Kelly Brown Douglas, *The Black Christ* (Maryknoll, N.Y.: Orbis, 1994).

18. For this insight, I thank Rita Nakashima Brock and Rebecca Anne Parker, Keynote Address, Rauschenbusch Center Annual Dinner, (Seattle, Wash., Nov. 28, 2005). The material is from their book *Saving Paradise: How Christianity Traded Love of This World for Crucifixion and Empire* (Boston: Beacon, 2009).

19. Winston Persaud, "Luther's Theologia Crucis: A Theology of 'Radical Reversal': in response to the Challenge of Marx's *Weltanschauung*," *Dialog* 29:4, no.4 (1990): 265–66.

20. The Heidelberg Disputation, 1518, LW 31:39–58.

21. Douglas John Hall, *Lighten Our Darkness* (Philadelphia: Westminster, 1976), 149. While indebted to Hall for his wisdom here, I must note too that his words here exemplify the ease with which Christian theological discourse identifies "darkness" with negative.

22. Dietrich Bonhoeffer, *Ethics* (New York: Touchstone, 1995), 85.

23. Ibid., 89.

24. Dietrich Bonhoeffer, *Sanctorum Communio*, trans. Ronald Gregor Smith, et al. (New York: Harper & Row, 1963), 56. For the sake of historical accuracy, I retain Bonhoeffer's gendered language for Christ.

25. Conformation with the form of Christ crucified for Bonhoeffer came to mean both standing on behalf of the persecuted, and assuming the guilt of the Western world. In *Ethics*, he develops the concepts of the church's "deputyship," which has these two implications. This convergence of two meanings assumes very personal meaning for Bonhoeffer: he is imprisoned and executed for an assassination plot that was, in significant part, a defense of (standing on behalf of) those persecuted by the Nazi regime. At the same time, in *Letters and Papers from Prison*, he refers often to his role as the guilty, assuming the guilt of Germany and of the Western world. In this sense, Bonhoeffer's understanding of the cross bridges the gap between theologies of the cross that see Christ atoning for human sin and theologies of the cross that see Christ executed by imperial power for his allegiance to the compassionate and justice-making reign of God. The cross for Bonhoeffer was both.

26. He writes: "The relation between the divine love and human love is wrongly understood if we say that the divine love [is] . . . solely for the purpose of setting human love in motion. . . . On the contrary . . . the love with which [humans] love God and neighbor is the love of God and no other. . . . [T]here is no love which is free or independent from the love of God." Dietrich Bonhoeffer, *Ethics*, ed. Eberhard Bethge (New York: Simon & Schuster, 1995), 55–56.

27. This sense of the form of Christ taking form in and among the faithful is expressed most explicitly by Bonhoeffer in elaborating the third approach to ethics, "conformation with the form of Christ," seen in his *Ethics*, chap. 3, esp. 81–89. Throughout Bonhoeffer's work, the process of "conformation with the form of Christ" entails obedience to the will of God and responsibility in the world. In the last year of his life (from the time just before his imprisonment when the last "approach" in *Ethics* was written), the nature of "conformation with the form of Christ" develops from active proclamation to a form of faithfulness in a "season of silence," characterized by silence, waiting, and preparation for the time when once again the redeeming, renewing Word may be proclaimed. For more on the form of Christ, see Anna Mercedes's contribution in this volume.

28. Note that the New Testament Greek generally translated as "faith in Christ," in many instances, also may be translated accurately as faith "of" Christ.

29. "That These Words of Christ," LW 37:57.

30. Ibid., 37:58.

31. WA 23.134. Cited by Heinrich Bornkamm, *Luther's World of Thought*, trans. Martin H. Bertram (St. Louis: Concordia, 1958), 189.

32. Luther, "The Sacrament of the Body and Blood of Christ—Against the Fanatics," in *Martin Luther's Basic Theological Writings*, 321.

33. Luther, "Confession Concerning Christ's Supper," in Ibid., 397.

34. WA 10.143. Cited in H. Paul Santmire, *The Travail of Nature: The Ambiguous Ecological Promise of Christian Theology* (Philadelphia: Fortress Press, 1985), 129.

35. Martin Luther, "Sermon for the Sixteenth Sunday after Trinity," *Sermons of Martin Luther*, ed. John Nicholas Lenker (Grand Rapids: Baker, 1983), 8:275.

CHAPTER FIFTEEN

1. This chapter will address primarily the first two, though the third—flowing from the others—is perhaps the most egregious from a justice perspective. For a disturbingly

insightful discussion of the violent projection of fear onto the (foreign) Other, see Judith Butler, *Precarious Life: The Powers of Mourning and Violence* (New York: Verso, 2004), especially chap. 2, "Violence, Mourning, Politics."

2. Julian of Norwich, *Revelations of Divine Love* (27.92), Christian Classics Ethereal Library, http://www.ccel.org/ccel/julian/revelations.xiv.i.html, accessed May 17, 2010.

3. Sharon V. Betcher, *Spirit and the Politics of Disablement* (Minneapolis: Fortress Press, 2007), 199.

4. While the bounds of this chapter do not allow a full delineation of their respective feminist theologies of the cross, my own proposal is indebted to both. See Deanna A. Thompson, *Crossing the Divide: Luther, Feminism, and the Cross* (Minneapolis: Fortress Press, 2004), and Mary M. Solberg, *Compelling Knowledge: A Feminist Proposal for an Epistemology of the Cross* (Albany: State University of New York Press, 1997). On the matter of Luther and human bodies, see also Samuel Torvend's recent *Luther and the Hungry Poor: Gathered Fragments* (Minneapolis: Fortress Press, 2009), which examines Luther's deep concern for concrete human need.

5. I am especially persuaded by Solberg's conviction that Luther was less concerned about salvation than about "how we live" now. See Mary M. Solberg, "All That Matters: What an Epistemology of the Cross Is Good For," in *Cross Examinations: Readings on the Meaning of the Cross Today*, ed. Marit Trelstad (Minneapolis: Fortress Press, 2006), 139.

6. The Heidelberg Disputation, 1518, LW 31:41.

7. Solberg, *Compelling Knowledge*, 126–31, and "All That Matters," 150–51.

8. Betcher, *Spirit and the Politics of Disablement*, 200. While emerging from the intersection of myriad theological discourses, Betcher's work is deeply informed by both Lutheran and feminist theologies.

9. Ibid.

10. In referring to "privileged groups," I mean those who benefit in a general, consistent way from particular sociocultural structures due to their race, gender, and/or class. Whatever discriminations they may face, white middle-class women in the United States enjoy relative privilege. I have consciously chosen the "abject authorities" of black women and those who are disabled in order to think through a postmodern practice of "naming a thing what it really is." Doing so is not an attempt at co-optation but, rather, an effort to listen to and learn from those whose experiences have informed and formed them—and therefore their theologies—in distinct ways.

11. Betcher, *Spirit and the Politics of Disablement*, 200.

12. See Cynthia Moe-Lobeda's chapter in this book for more on faithful justice.

13. Monica Coleman, *Making a Way Out of No Way: A Womanist Theology* (Minneapolis: Fortress Press, 2008), 12. There is some question as to whether Coleman identifies herself as womanist. In a 2006 essay, Coleman does explore the question "Must I Be a Womanist?," *Journal of Feminist Studies in Religion* 22, no. 1:85–96, citing her discomfort with womanist theology's exclusion of lesbians and non-Christians. The introduction of *Making a Way Out of No Way* narrates her search for "a postmodern womanist theology," which is precisely what she proceeds to offer in the book: a postmodern, third-wave, inclusive womanist theology.

14. Delores S. Williams, *Sisters in the Wilderness: The Challenge of Womanist God-Talk* (Maryknoll, N.Y.: Orbis, 1993), 21. Williams in fact borrows these points from Mexican liberation theologian Elsa Tamez's reading of the Hagar story. See Tamez, "The Woman Who Complicated the History of Salvation," in *New Eyes for Reading: Biblical and Theological Reflections by Women from the Third World*, ed. John S. Pobee and Bärbel Von Wartenberg-Potter (Geneva: World Council of Churches, 1986).

15. Coleman, *Making a Way Out of No Way*, 34. Italics added.

16. Ibid., 33.

17. Betcher, *Spirit and the Politics of Disablement*, 196.

18. Ibid., 194.

19. Ibid., 197.

20. Ibid., 199.

21. On "majesty at the margins," see Mary (Joy) Philip's chapter in this volume.

22. Betcher, *Spirit and the Politics of Disablement*, 199.

23. This positions stands in tension with, though not in opposition to, Deanna Thompson's chapter in this volume. Thompson affirms God's presence "in the flesh" but also insists that feminist theology not sacrifice the future "more" of life beyond death that God promises.

24. Betcher, *Spirit and the Politics of Disablement*, 204.

25. Luther consistently preached that Christians should understand God's work in Christ in personal rather than abstract metaphysical terms: God-in-Christ works *pro nobis*, "for us."

26. Dietrich Bonhoeffer, *Discipleship*, trans. and ed. Martin Kuske and Isle Tödt, Dietrich Bonhoeffer Works, vol. 4 (Minneapolis: Fortress Press, 2003), 176.

27. Our distinctive emphases also arise from what are distinct yet related audiences or purposes. My proposal has a more prophetic impetus, Thompson's a more pastoral one—though ultimately these cannot and should not be sundered, as we both show.

28. Susan Hartman, "The Jump Rope Girls, 20 Years On," *The New York Times*, October 17, 2008, http://www.nytimes.com/2008/10/19/nyregion/thecity, accessed May 17, 2010.

29. I owe this insight to the Rev. Christine Thompson. Upon hearing an earlier version of this essay, she commented that it was not *despite* but *because of* the violence and insecurity these girls faced that they engaged in their daily ritual. Not only is this undoubtedly true, but it more accurately illustrates precisely the clear-eyed and courageous vision I am advocating for this theology of hope.

CHAPTER SIXTEEN

1. My lecture entitled "More than Miracles: Hope in Light of the Cross," given at Augsburg College, Minneapolis, Minn., November 11, 2008, explores the concept of hope in light of my travels in and reading on post-apartheid South Africa.

2. See Serene Jones and Paul Lakeland, eds., *Constructive Theology: A Contemporary Approach to Classic Themes: A Project of the Workgroup on Constructive Christian Theology* (Minneapolis: Fortress Press, 2005).

3. Catherine Keller, "Eschatology," in *Dictionary of Feminist Theologies*, ed. Letty M. Russell and J. Shannon Clarkson (Louisville: Westminster John Knox, 1996), 87. See also Keller's *Apocalypse Now and Then: A Feminist Guide to the End of the World* (Boston: Beacon, 1996).

4. Rosemary Radford Ruether, "Eschatology and Feminism," in *Lift Every Voice: Constructing Christian Theologies from the Underside*, ed. Susan Brooks Thistlethwaite and Mary Potter Engel (San Francisco: HarperSanFrancisco, 1990), 120.

5. Valerie Karras, "Eschatology," in *Cambridge Companion to Feminist Theology*, ed. Susan Frank Parsons (New York: Cambridge University Press, 2002), 243.

6. Ruether, "Eschatology and Feminism," 122. See also Ruether's *Gaia and God: An Ecofeminist Theology of Earth Healing* (New York: HarperCollins, 1992).

7. Sallie McFague, *The Body of God: An Ecological Theology* (Minneapolis: Fortress Press, 1993), 182.

8. Rita Nakashima Brock and Rebecca Ann Parker, *Saving Paradise: How Christianity Traded Love of This World for Crucifixion and Empire* (Boston: Beacon, 2008), 420, emphasis added.

9. Ibid., 330.

10. Ibid., 420.

11. Grace Jantzen, "Luther and the Mystics," *Kings Theological Review* 8, no.2 (Autumn 1985): 49.

12. "Selected Psalms III: Psalm 6," LW 14:142.

13. Kathleen Billman and Daniel Migliore, *Rachel's Cry: Prayer of Lament and Rebirth of Hope* (Cleveland: United Church Press, 1999), 4.

14. Ibid., 12.

15. Ibid., 2.

16. As quoted in ibid., 112.

17. See Jacqueline Bussie, "'A Dream with a Sequel' or 'The Coming Summer'? Martin Luther on Hope for the World" (lecture, Global Luther Conference, Northwestern University, Evanston, Ill., February, 2008).

18. "The Bondage of the Will, 1525," LW 33:139.

19. "Genesis 12:18-19," LW 2:319.

20. "Genesis 21:17," LW 4:57.

21. "Genesis 16:13-14," LW 3:70.

22. "Genesis 21:17," LW 4:57.

23. Krista E. Hughes, "In the Flesh: A Feminist Vision of Hope," 214.

24. Simon Maimela, "The Suffering of Human Divisions and the Cross," in *The Scandal of a Crucified World: Perspectives on the Cross and Suffering*, ed. Yacob Tesfai (Maryknoll, N.Y.: Orbis, 1994), 36.

25. Denise Ackerman, "On Hearing and Lamenting: Faith and Truth-Telling," as quoted in Billman and Migliore, *Rachel's Cry*, 91.

26. See Celia W. Dugger, "Eager Students Fall Prey to Apartheid's Legacy in South Africa," *The New York Times*, 20 September 2009, http://www.nytimes.com/2009/09/20/world/africa/20safrica.html?emc=eta1 accessed May 17, 2010.

27. Jürgen Moltmann, *The Theology of Hope: On the Ground and the Implications of a Christian Eschatology*, trans. James W. Leitch (New York: Harper & Row, 1967), 21.

28. Mary Lowe, "Sin from a Queer, Lutheran Perspective," 79.

29. Mary (Joy) Philip, "The Elusive Lure of the Lotus," esp. 38–41.

30. Moltmann, *The Theology of Hope*, 327.

31. Billman and Migliore, *Rachel's Cry*, 93.

32. Mark Tranvik, translator's introduction to *The Freedom of a Christian* by Martin Luther, ed. and trans. Mark D. Tranvik (Minneapolis: Fortress Press, 2008), 3.

33. Martin Luther, "A Sermon on Preparing to Die," in *Martin Luther's Basic Theological Writings*, ed. Timothy Lull (Minneapolis: Fortress Press, 1989), 739–40.

34. Stanley Hauerwas, "Salvation and Health: Why Medicine Needs the Church," in *From Christ to the World: Introductory Readings in Christian Ethics*, ed. Wayne G. Boulton, Thomas D. Kennedy, and Allen Verhey (Grand Rapids: Eerdmans, 1994), 388.

35. Patricia Lull, "What Kind of Christian?" *Lutheran Woman Today* (May 2009): 24.

36. Wanda Deifelt, "Globalization, Religion and Embodiment: Latin American Feminist Perspectives," in *Shaping a Global Theological Mind*, ed. Darren C. Marks (Burlington, Vt.: Ashgate, 2008), 48.

37. McFague, *The Body of God*, 188.

38. *De libero arbitrio, Luther and Erasmus: Free Will and Salvation*, Library of Christian Classics, ed. E. Gordon Rupp and Philip S. Watson (Philadelphia: Westminster, 1978), 140.

39. Moltmann, *The Theology of Hope*, 63.

40. Carl E. Braaten, *Eschatology and Ethics: Essays on the Theology and Ethics of the Kingdom of God* (Minneapolis: Augsburg, 1974), 82.

41. As quoted in Philip D. W. Krey and Peter D. S. Krey, eds., *Luther's Spirituality* (Mahwah, N.J.: Paulist, 2007), xxiv.

42. McFague, *The Body of God*, 182.

43. As quoted in Hans Schwartz, "Eschatology," in *Christian Dogmatics*, Vol. 2, ed. Carl E. Braaten and Robert W. Jenson (Philadelphia: Fortress Press, 1984), 586.

44. Luther, "A Sermon on Preparing to Die" in *Martin Luther's Basic Theological Writings*, 641.

45. "Lectures on Galatians, 1535," LW 26:280.

46. As recorded by Walter von Lowenich, *Martin Luther: The Man and His Work*, trans. Lawrence Denef (Philadelphia: Fortress Press, 1986), 285.

47. Agnosticism about life after death is appealing, especially when it comes to issues of mind/spirit/body relationships, whether or not there's a soul, and so on.

48. C. S. Lewis, *The Four Loves* (New York: Harcourt, 1960), 139.

49. Ibid., 139.

50. Ruether, *Gaia and God*, 123.

51. "The Large Catechism: The Lord's Prayer," as cited in Krey and Krey, eds., *Luther's Spirituality* 201.

52. Braaten, *Eschatology and Ethics*, 70.

53. Ibid., 111.

54. Krey and Krey, eds., *Luther's Spirituality* 46.

Index